THE DESIRE OF OUR SOUL

To Ronnié

A very Happy Christmas
and a wonderful
2005
All good wishes
from John

Harold Miller

The Desire of Our Soul

A USER'S GUIDE TO THE BOOK OF COMMON PRAYER

the columba press

First published in 2004 by
the columba press
55A Spruce Avenue, Stillorgan Industrial Park,
Blackrock, Co Dublin

Cover designed by Bill Bolger
Cover painting by Kevin Miller
Origination by The Columba Press
Printed in Ireland by ColourBooks Ltd, Dublin

ISBN 1 85607 453 6

Table of Contents

Foreword

The Most Reverend Dr Robin Eames
Archbishop of Armagh, Primate of all-Ireland
And Metropolitan

Armagh
Eastertide 2004

Few events within the life of the Church of Ireland in recent times have so captured the imagination and interest of its people to compare with the launch of the *Book of Common Prayer*, 2004.

As I write this Foreword we look forward to the meeting of the General Synod in Armagh during May 2004 when the new book will be formally received and take its official place in the liturgical literature of our ancient church. I am quite certain that members of the Synod will share a mixture of emotions at that event. There will be relief that the long years of liturgical legislation and debate on revised services has finally produced this book. There will be gratitude for all those whose devoted scholarship and work have brought their church to this point. There will be appreciation for the beauty of this new volume. But I pray there will be above all else gratitude to Almighty God that we possess a prayer book which is rich in content, inclusive in language and expression and provides the basis for worship in public and private worthy of our approach to the God and Father of us all.

Over recent years it has been my privilege to preside at the numerous debates on liturgical reform at General Synod which have led us to this juncture of church history. The parliamentary procedure of Synod where liturgical legislation is concerned, though lengthy and painstaking, has allowed the supreme law-making body of the Church of Ireland to reach consensus on the forms of our worship. The new prayer book is the product of those decisions of General Synod – but the real work has fallen on our Liturgical Advisory Committee to whom we must pay a warm tribute. Inevitably the public face of any committee reporting to Synod involves personalities and in acknowledging the tireless efforts of the many I think in particular of Bishop Edward Darling, Bishop Harold Miller, Canon Ricky Rountree, Canon Brian Mayne and Dean Michael Burrows.

We live in an era when the Anglican tradition is not alone in world Christendom as it engages in a search for identity. Many scholars and theologians have engaged in this search as they have sought to answer the question 'who are we?' In these days of ecclesiastical turmoil in the Anglican Communion and elsewhere one fact is emerging beyond contradiction. As we recognise cultural, national and community autonomy it is *how* we worship which defines most clearly the nature and character of each Christian tradition. That fact transcends controversy, arguments over localised differences in doctrinal interpretations and the emergence of cultural preferences. I can think of no better definition of what the Church of Ireland is than the *Book of Common Prayer*, 2004.

As I read Bishop Miller's *The Desire of our Soul* I am convinced that his purpose in providing us with a guide to this new book encapsulates the priorities of a search for identity through worship together with a most readable, valuable and vital chart to our use of the *Book of Common Prayer* 2004. His words, stemming from a deep knowledge of our liturgy and his personal faith, provide us with an excellent companion to the use of the prayer book. But there is much more in these pages than explanations or guidance alone. He manages to give us genuine encouragement to worship 'in spirit and in truth' in ways which open up the treasures of our services for both clergy and laity. His words point us to the essence of public and private worship – the yearning to know more about God and how we can relate such knowledge to the task of a daily pilgrimage. As the bishop says in the introduction, 'there is nothing more powerful than the coming together of living faith and living liturgy'. How we worship influences the way we live. The expression of our love for God in worship must find its expression in the everyday witness of the believer. The new prayer book contains the liturgical agenda for the lives of those who find their relationship to God in and through membership and worship of the Church of Ireland. As we learn to use it regularly I pray we will find in its pages inspiration, encouragement and spiritual strength to translate vision into reality.

Bishop Miller has provided us with a valuable companion for this process. I am certain *The Desire of our Soul* will be greatly welcomed.

As the Church of Ireland asks 'who are we?' surely we can do none better than find our identity in the *Book of Common Prayer*, 2004. Bishop Miller has provided us in these pages with essential signposts to that discovery.

✠ *Robert Armagh*

Introduction

The publication of a new *Book of Common Prayer* in the Church of Ireland is, by any standards, a momentous event. Since 1662, there have only been two Books of Common Prayer – in 1878 and 1926, so up to now the average is less that one every hundred years!

Of course, all of us have lived through an era of liturgical change which began in the 1960s with the first 'white' Holy Communion booklet.[1] That period of renewal of worship in the Anglican Communion worldwide led, in the context of the Church of Ireland, to two books: the *Alternative Prayer Book* 1984 and *Alternative Occasional Services* 1993. Between those two books, we found ourselves with alternative contemporary services in more or less the areas covered by the 1926 *Book of Common Prayer*.

As questions began to be raised in the General Synod of the Church of Ireland about a further stage of revision, it was concluded in 1997 that, rather than having a new set of alternative services in a separate book, we should aim at integrating our liturgy into a brand new *Book of Common Prayer*, containing both traditional and contemporary services, to be published in 2004.

Much of the initial groundwork for this project was done under Bishop Edward Darling's chairmanship of the Liturgical Advisory Committee and, when he retired, I found myself (at a meeting which I had missed[2]) nominated to be the new chair at

---

1. This was the 1967 experimental form of Holy Communion, which paralleled the Revised Standard Version of the bible, in that people were spoken of in 'you' form, and God in 'thou' form. Its real importance was the beginning of the re-structuring of the eucharistic rite, basically on an English Series 2 model.
2. To be honest, with my permission!

this critical stage. It has been an exciting, busy and creative time
for the committee. Whether members of the General Synod think
the same, after tedious sessions of liturgical business, remains to
be seen. These General Synod sessions were lightened somewhat
by the 'terrible twins', Canon Ricky Rountree and Dean Michael
Burrows,[3] who guided us through the material with both sensitivity and authority. And in the background, but now in the fore-
ground as editor, was Canon Brian Mayne[4] who has given more
hours to this project than anyone could ever imagine.

So we have our new prayer book in our hands, beautifully
published by The Columba Press in Dublin. The first new *Book of
Common Prayer* since 1926. It is radically different. Earlier revis-
ions of the *Book of Common Prayer* were simply 'tweaking' the
1662 book, but this one is quite fresh. It contains both the traditional services (labelled *One*) and thoroughly revised contemporary services (labelled *Two*) alongside each other. The hope is
that churches which have only used one style of worship may
discover something of the riches of the other as well, and that
the traditional and contemporary may be seen as enriching each
other, rather than being in competition. One of the promises the
Liturgical Advisory Committee gave to the General Synod was
that members of the Church of Ireland would still be able to use
traditional services, if they wished, as they had always done.
The only slight change to this, made by the synod itself in 2003,
was the decision to have only one psalter printed, while the 1926
psalter would remain authorised for use. The psalter which has

3. These two people, Canon Ricky Rountree as secretary of the
    Liturgical Advisory Committee, and Michael Burrows, Dean of
    Cork, as a member of the committee, guided the General Synod in a
    masterly way through many sessions of liturgical business. They
    did it with both efficiency and humour, and (I dare to imagine)
    made them at least a little less tedious than they might have been.
    For the introduction of the *Book of Common Prayer*, Ricky Rountree
    was seconded as Central Liturgical Officer for the Church of
    Ireland.
4. Canon Brian Mayne played a key role over many years as secretary
    of the LAC, and latterly as editor of the new *Book of Common Prayer*. I
    thank him also for reading the manuscript for this book, and cor-
    recting what was amiss and supplying what was lacking.

been included is that prepared for the Church of England's *Common Worship*, published in 2000, which keeps so many of the resonances of Coverdale's psalter.[5]

As you read and hopefully pray through the *Book of Common Prayer*, you will discover that it is largely the new services which have been thoroughly revised. For that reason, this *User's Guide* will focus particularly on these. There are numerous commentaries on older versions of the *Book of Common Prayer* which let readers into the thinking behind the traditional services. Of course, if it is desired, I will happily provide a companion volume to the traditional services. In a sense, it is worth noting that it is the modern services which have needed so much revision. I heard someone say recently, speaking of a postmodern world: 'The only thing worse than being 300 years out of date is being 20 years out of date!'

A few years ago, I observed at the General Synod, in introducing the report of the LAC, that there were several reasons why the more recent services would simply have to be revised. These were:

– Inclusive language about people. We no longer speak of people as 'men' or 'brothers' in our ordinary language.
– The fact that the lectionary in the *APB* had passed its 'sell-by date', and the themes[6] were becoming tired and worn.
– The fact that the writing of the 1970s was so often lacking in poetry, and needed to be warmed up.
– The need for more openness and flexibility in our worship, which was straining some of the services at the edge.

To that list, I would now add what I believe to be a major factor in the revision we are encountering: the work of *International*

---

5. The translation of the psalter in the *Book of Common Prayer* from the time of the Reformation has basically been that of Miles Coverdale (1488-1569), a bible translator who served his apprenticeship under William Tyndale. This, of course, makes the translation older than that of the King James (Authorized) Version. The 1926 Irish Psalter was, in fact, a revision made in England in 1915.
6. The lectionary in the *Alternative Prayer Book* was essentially based around themes for each Sunday.

Anglican Liturgical Consultations[7] over the past fifteen years or so, which have given direction to the 'second round' of major revision in the Communion, especially in relation to baptism, eucharist and ministry.

And so we have available the new prayer book of the Church of Ireland, launched at the General Synod 2004, officially *the book* from Trinity Sunday, 6 June 2004. This is now part of our standard of doctrine, the book we will use, 'and none other, except so far as shall be allowed by the lawful authority of the Church'.[8] This is a book which I hope and pray will keep us close to Jesus, vibrant in our worship, and nourished in our personal spirituality. But, in reality, as the 2004 Preface says:

> ... we must always remind ourselves that words, however memorable, beautiful or useful, are never to be confused with worship itself. The words set out on these pages are but the beginning of worship. They need to be appropriated with care and devotion by the People of God so that, with the aid of the Holy Spirit, men and women may bring glory to the Father and grow in the knowledge and likeness of Jesus Christ.

I write this guide convinced that there is nothing more powerful than the coming together of living faith and living liturgy. Powerful in evangelism, powerful in deepening Christian belief, powerful in bringing us into the very presence of our God.

Finding a title for a new book is never easy. My working title was *A User's Guide to the Book of Common Prayer*, which I have retained as the subtitle. In the end of the day, I decided to call the book *The Desire of our Soul*. My reasons are as follows:

– True Worship is always that which comes out of a heartfelt

---

7. These consultations began in 1985 with an informal gathering of Anglican liturgists after the meeting of *Societas Liturgica*, and ecumenical society for the study of liturgy, in Boston. They have met, in different forms, on a biennial basis since then, and have become increasingly representative of the whole communion. I have had the privilege of attending six of the consultations.
8. Part of the second of the declarations made by a new incumbent before or at an institution.

desire to know more of God, and to apply what we know to our day to day lives. The words, 'the desire of our soul', come in that peculiarly Church of Ireland canticle, *Urbs Fortitudinis*, and are completed in Isaiah 26 by the words: '... is to thy name, and to the remembrance of thee.' Worship is always to do with a desire to glorify the name of God, and with the power of memory – remembering what is true about God, how God has acted in the past, and telling and re-telling the story of our salvation. This means that worship is not, in the end of the day, something which we, as humans, invent. It is, rather, a given – something which draws us into the eternal praise and liturgy of heaven.

– True worship is to do with both warm and personal faith *and* corporate, 'common', communal expression. It is the desire of *our* soul. For some of us, we are warmed towards God most easily when we are in the company of other believers; for others we sense God's presence most strongly when quiet and alone. But for all Christians one feeds into the other, and we always pray 'Our Father', even when in solitude.

'The desire of our soul' has a couple of other resonances as well. It is, in a sense, simply one way of describing prayer. This is expressed both beautifully and profoundly by the hymnwriter, James Montgomery:[9]

Prayer is the soul's sincere desire,

unuttered or expressed....

And it is a deeply Celtic way of speaking:

It were my soul's desire

To see the face of God.[10]

That desire of our soul will only fully and finally be realised in heaven. But meanwhile, if God grants that our worship in this world is even a mild foretaste of the eternal worship in God's closer presence, we will be blessed indeed!

9. *Church Hymnal, fifth edition*, Oxford (2000), hymn 625.
10. *op. cit.*, Hymn 633, from the old Irish, versified by Eleanor Hull (1860-1935).

CHAPTER ONE

The Calendar:
The Christian Year

The Christian Church functions on a year by year basis with at least three calendars running alongside each other. The first is the ordinary 'secular' calendar running form 1 January until 31 December. In fact, the Church of England's new *Common Worship*[1] follows the age-old pattern of Anglican prayer books in setting out much of its calendrical framework within the context of the secular year. In our ordinary church life, a great deal of what we do is embraced within that framework. We order our lives in the system of days, weeks, months and years used by everyone around us, even though we know that many of the names we give to these measures of time come from paganism or old Roman or Norse gods.

It is not unusual for churches, too, to order their lives in this way. We do this or that on the 'first Sunday of the month', or 'every Wednesday morning', or whatever. Many churches in the nonconformist tradition plan out their worshipping lives more from the secular calendar than from the 'church' calendar. But this is true also of some parts of Anglican worship. For example, the following services and events (some of which are major occasions in the life of the Church):
- Watchnight services on New Year's Eve
- Covenant Services on the first Sunday of the new year
- The Week of Prayer for Christian Unity (The octave of 18-25 January)
- Harvest Services (whatever Sunday in October – often the law of the Medes and the Persians)
- Remembrance Sunday (Nearest to 11 November).

1. *Common Worship: Services and Prayers for the Church of England* (2000) Church House Publishing.

Specifically Christian Calendars

But alongside, and more important than the secular calendar, are two specifically Christian calendars which tell the story of our salvation. These are sometimes described by the Latin words, the *Temporale* and the *Sanctorale*. The first is the calendar of the Christian Year, running from Advent Sunday through to the Sunday before Advent the next year. The second, which has no real beginning or end, but which is usually laid out according to the secular year, is the list of saints' days and some other holy days which fall on the same date each year. These are two separate calendars, always running concurrently, sometimes bumping into each other and having, accordingly, to be adjusted according to preference and priority. It is these two calendars that we will be focusing on in this chapter.

The *Temporale*

Details of this, the very heart of the Christian Year, can be found on pp. 18-19 in the *Book of Common Prayer*. The first thing we are made aware of is that this particular calendar is the one which is most often experienced in Sunday worship. The first note says:

> All Sundays celebrate the paschal mystery of the death and resurrection of Christ. Nevertheless, they also reflect the character of the seasons in which they are set.

That note is an immediate reminder to all of us that the very heart of the matter for the Christian faith is the 'paschal' mystery.[2] At no point on a Sunday should the centrality of the death and resurrection of Jesus Christ be completely ousted by any other theme or focus. Everything we do in Sunday worship is done in the light of the fact that Sunday, or better – The Lord's Day, is the celebration of the day on which our Lord Jesus rose from the grave.

The most important days

This theme is further emphasised when we see that the 'Principal

---

2. The mystery of our salvation revolving around the Christian Passover at Easter: the death and resurrection of Jesus Christ.

The Calendar

Advent
|
CHRISTMAS DAY 25 Dec
Christmas (to Eve of Epiphany)
|
The Epiphany 6 Jan
Epiphany (Epiphany to Presentation)
The Presentation of Christ 2Feb
|
Sundays before Lent *(Ordinary Time)*
3 Feb until Shrove Tuesday
|
Lent
Ash Wednesday to Easter Eve
Maundy Thursday
Good Friday
|
EASTER DAY
Easter: 50 days until Pentecost
The Ascension Day
Pentecost
|
Trinity Sunday
|
Sundays after Trinity
(All Saints' Day 1Nov)

Holy Days' of the Christian Year, which are noted first in the list on p. 18, are:
– Christmas Day 25 December
– Easter Day
– The Day of Pentecost (Whitsunday).

However, even within these three days there is a distinctive 'order of priority'. The most important of all is Easter Day, prepared for by the forty days of Lent, and continuing to be the focus during the fifty days of Easter. The second most important is Christmas Day, prepared for by the four weeks of Advent, and continuing to be celebrated in the twelve days of Christmas, up to the Epiphany. The third most important in the new calendar is Pentecost, which is now seen not as an event in its own right, or even as ushering in days or a season after it, but as the climax of the story of the risen Christ, as he pours out his Spirit on his Church. The *Revised Common Lectionary*, which will be discussed in detail in the next chapter, is focused around the first two of these events, Christmas and Easter, leading into and out of them. This is, of course, a right and biblical balance, because the faith we proclaim, and the story we re-tell year by year is centred around the events of the incarnation and the atonement, and has no deep meaning without these centralities in place.

Other Principal Holy Days

The Church of Ireland calendar lists seven of these, and we will look at them one by one:

The Epiphany (6 January)

The old title given to this day was, of course, 'The Manifestation of Christ to the Gentiles.' You may well notice that Epiphany is unlike the other days in these seven, in that it is both the title of a day and of a season. The day is, in a sense, the conclusion of the Christmas story, with the coming of the Magi. It is the day on which we take our Christmas trees down. The Calendar is faced, however, with an issue here: How many people are to be seen in church on this feast? Indeed, how many churches have a service on 6 January? So, philosophically, rather than lose the celebration altogether, the rubric is added:

> In any year where there is a Second Sunday of Christmas The Epiphany may be observed on that Sunday.

According to my calculations, that would allow the Feast of the Epiphany to be celebrated on a Sunday in five out of every seven years, and therefore it would not be lost to our worshippers.

The Presentation of Christ (2 February)

In the Church of England's way of doing things, the feast of the Presentation (also called Candlemas or The Purification of St Mary the Virgin) has become a 'hinge' in its understanding of the church year. Some have even suggested that the crib should

remain in church until 2 February. Undoubtedly this feast does
have a wonderful way both of pointing back to Christmas (It is
forty days after Christmas Day and the point at which the baby
Jesus is presented in the Temple); and of pointing forward to the
Paschal mystery (The Gospel of the Day includes those wonderful 'hinge' words said by Simeon to Mary: 'This child is destined
for the falling and the rising of many in Israel, and a sign that
will be opposed so that the inner thoughts of many will be revealed – and a sword will pierce your own soul too'). Because
the Presentation has been given this new status in the calendar,
the note is added here:

> The Presentation of Christ may be observed on the Sunday
> falling between 28 January and 3 February.

This, again, is to ensure that such a pivotal day is not missed by
being tucked away where no one will notice.

Maundy Thursday/Good Friday

These two Principal Holy Days are separated out in the list because of the rubric at the end of the first six:

> On these days it is fitting that Holy Communion be celebrated
> in every cathedral and in each parish church ...

Good Friday is left to the end, because some traditions believe it
not to be fitting to celebrate Holy Communion on that day or on
Easter Eve.

In actual fact the regulations of the Church of Ireland[3] only
require Holy Communion to be celebrated on the days for which
proper prefaces are provided in the Book of Common Prayer (at
the time when the canons were written these were clearly:
Christmas Day, Easter Day, Ascension Day, Whitsunday and
Trinity Sunday. How they are to be interpreted now, when our
new book has more proper prefaces, is another matter...).

---

3. *The Book of Common Prayer* directs in Canon 13 (1) that Holy
    Communion shall be celebrated on these days, but also says that on
    other holy days it is fitting that Holy Communion be celebrated.
    Also Canon 13 (1) states: 'In every church or chapel where the sacra-
    ments are to be administered, the Holy Communion shall be minis-
    tered at least once a month, unless the Ordinary shall otherwise
    order.' Perhaps the time has come for this canon to be re-written.

Maundy Thursday (so called because of the 'mandatum' or mandate given by Christ to 'love one another'). It might be noted here that these two days are part of what is called, in some traditions, the Easter Triduum – in other words the three day period from Maundy Thursday to Easter morning, covering the liturgy of Maundy Thursday evening (focusing on the washing of feet, prayer for unity, the institution of the Lord's Supper, the stripping of the church and the watch[4]) through to the end of the Easter Vigil (for which readings are given on p. 40).[5] The reason for Maundy Thursday and Good Friday being Principal Holy Days is clear, and indeed some of the earliest liturgies known in the Church outside the eucharist are Holy Week liturgies.

In the Roman Catholic tradition, Maundy Thursday is usually called Holy Thursday, and Easter Eve is usually called Holy Saturday.

The Ascension Day

The Ascension Day is celebrated on the Thursday forty days after Easter Day. This is another feast which needs to be rescued from small congregations, and marginalisation. In our former prayer books, the Ascension Day was seen as the climax of Easter. Now it is seen, not as the finale to the great forty days, but as a major event in the great fifty days, which has as its finale, the outpouring of the Holy Spirit on the church on the Day of Pentecost. This means that the small season in the old calendars which covered the novena[6] of prayer between Ascension and

---

4. Coming from Jesus asking his disciples in the Garden of Gethsemane to 'watch and pray', a tradition developed in many churches where the people remained in quiet prayer (often before the blessed sacrament) on the evening, and sometimes throughout the night of Maundy Thursday.

5. Our present *Book of Common Prayer* is the first to give readings specifically for the Easter Vigil, which may be observed late on Easter Eve, or better in the darkness before dawn on Easter Day.

6. The word 'novena', from the Latin *novem*, meaning 'nine', is a time of focused prayer and devotion with its roots in the nine days of waiting, prayer and preparation between the ascension and Pentecost. It is not a word in common use in protestantism, because of particular associations with indulgences and Mary; but perhaps

Pentecost does not have a Sunday any longer called 'The
Sunday after the Ascension Day'. Instead, this Sunday is now
the seventh Sunday of Easter and the other name is a sub-title.

Trinity Sunday

Trinity Sunday is a feast which is quite different to all the others.
The others, in some way or other (even Pentecost) revolve
around the story of Jesus in the New Testament. Trinity Sunday
is, in a sense, a theological feast, summing up the nature of the
Triune God who is central to our entire faith. This holy day
emerged in the tenth century from observance in the British
Isles, and became a universal observance under Pope John XXII
in 1334. The numbering of Sundays as 'after Trinity' (which has
been reverted to in the *Book of Common Prayer*) was begun in the
medieval Sarum calendar. It might be noted at this point that
one of the traditions in the 1662 *Book of Common Prayer*, which
has not been required for many years in the Church of Ireland,[7]
was the singing of the *Quicunque Vult* [The Creed (Commonly
called) of Athanasius] which is one of the three creeds which, according to *Article 8* (p. 780):

'ought thoroughly to be received and believed: for they may
be proved by the most certain warrants of Holy Scripture.'

Perhaps at least the saying of part of this creed might be revived
on Trinity Sunday? The Athanasian Creed can, of course, be
found in the *Book of Common Prayer* at the back of the book on p.
771.

All Saints' Day 1 November

Because of the importance of All Saints' Day as another of the
'hinge' days in the Christian Year, churches are given encouragement to consider observing it on the nearest Sunday with the
rubric:

All Saints' Day may be observed on the Sunday falling between 30 October and 5 November.

---

the idea of a novena as a nine day period given to prayer is not such
a bad one after all!

7. The obligation to use it on principal holy days was removed in the
    1878 revision of the Irish *BCP*.

A great deal of thought and discussion has gone into the question of what should be done liturgically with the Sundays in November. In the Church of England, they have become a kind of 'Kingdom Season', ushered in by All Saints' Day. In the Church of Ireland, these are Sundays before Advent. Their purpose is described in the *Seasonal Notes to Daily Prayer: Preliminary Edition:*

> ... the period between all Saints' Day and the First Sunday of Advent is observed as a time of celebration and reflection on the reign of Christ in earth and in heaven.

The issue is this: Given that the first Sunday in November will often be focused on All Saints, the second on Remembrance Sunday, and the penultimate or last on Christ the King, is there any point in trying to sustain a semi-continuous reading of scripture at this time? Overall, the Church of Ireland has decided to stick with the *Revised Common Lectionary* firmly at this point. However, it is vital that we reckon on the importance of this time of the year for so many people. There is something very creative about using the time when the year is dying as a time for memorial and, although we in the Church of Ireland do not celebrate All Souls' Day on 2 November, the celebration of All Saints through to Remembrance Sunday is surely the natural, God-given time to do this.

The Seasons

Just as there are seasons of the natural year (spring, summer, autumn, winter), so there are seasons in the 'supernatural' year as well. Five of these are mentioned on p. 19. In these seasons, particular theological themes are explored, particular parts of the Christian story read and meditated on, and particular aspects of personal and corporate spirituality focused on. Each of these seasons has also a particular 'mood' and atmosphere; and in following them through faithfully, it is the conviction of the Church that we find a fully-rounded expression of the gospel of Jesus Christ.

Liturgical Colours

Sundays of Advent Violet

Christmas Day until The Presentation of Christ (2 Feb)
White (or Gold in Christmastide)

Ordinary Time, between 2 Feb and Shrove Tuesday *Green*

Ash Wednesday until the Saturday before Palm Sunday *Violet*

Palm Sunday and Monday in Holy Week until Maundy Thursday
Red or Violet

(except for Maundy Thursday Communion of the Last Supper *White*)

Good Friday and Easter Eve *no colour*

Easter Day until the Eve of Pentecost
White (or Gold on Easter Day and Ascension Day)

The Day of Pentecost *Red*

Ordinary Time, between the Monday after Pentecost and the day
before the First Sunday of Advent *Green*

Saints' Days *White*
Commemorations of Martyrs *Red*
Confirmations *normally Red or White, at the discretion of the bishop*
Ordinations *normally Red or White, at the discretion of the bishop*

Advent

The First Sunday of Advent is, again, the beginning of the Christian Year. 'Again', because the Joint Liturgical Group calendar adopted by the *APB* and the English *ASB* created an unnatural new start to the year on the 'Ninth Sunday before Christmas'.[8] The Sundays before Advent in the *BCP* are not intended to replicate this mistake. The clear beginning of the church year is now the First Sunday of Advent.

---

8. This strange system was evolved to service a 'trinitarian' calendar where the Sundays before Christmas were focused on the first Person of the Trinity, with Old Testament readings being focal; the Sundays between Christmas and Easter were focused on Jesus Christ, with the Gospel Readings focal; and Pentecost and the Sundays following of the life and work of the Holy Spirit with the Acts and Epistles focal.

The season of Advent is, of course, one with two foci. The first focus is preparation for the second coming of our Lord; and the second focus is preparation for the coming of Christ at Christmas. This can make the season either confusing or creative. In holding together both features, Advent can rescue us from the sentimentality of simply being Christmas-orientated, but we also need to realise that the four weeks of Advent are the one time in the year when thousands of people who do not normally come to church are prepared to come to carol services, christingle services and nativity plays. For many churches this means living a double-life in those weeks. On the one level, violet (the colour of Advent) is still the colour of the hangings,[9] and being faithfully celebrated on Sundays; while on the other, on the weekdays 'O come all ye faithful' is the order of the day, and the Christmas tree may well be ablaze with lights.

Liturgically speaking, Advent progresses through different stages. The first Sunday is usually well and truly focused on the Second Coming, and then it begins to focus around the ministry of John the Baptist and the Blessed Virgin Mary, in preparation for the coming Saviour. Thankfully, 'Bible Sunday' has been moved to late October, from the Second Sunday of Advent, where it had traditionally been because of the beautiful collect:

Blessed Lord,

who hast caused all holy scriptures

to be written for our learning …

Now the collect and the Sunday have been moved, and left the way clearer to focus on Advent themes, not forgetting the traditional ones of death, judgement, heaven and hell, which are often forgotten in our age.

The Sundays in this period are now called 'Sundays of Advent', and the first of these is 'The First Sunday of Advent' rather than 'Advent Sunday'. These four Sundays are often represented by the lighting of purple candles on an Advent Wreath,

---

9. The 'hangings' in the church refer usually to the frontal on the communion table, the pulpit fall, and the markers in the bible on the lectern, and may be extended to refer to vestments/stoles etc.

Names of Sundays

Sundays *of* Advent

Sundays *of* Christmas

Sundays *after* The Epiphany

Sundays *before* Lent

Sundays *in* Lent

Days *in* Holy Week

Sundays *of* Easter
*(NB Easter Day is 'The First Sunday of Easter',
and Low Sunday is 'The Second Sunday of Easter';
The Sunday after Ascension Day is 'The Seventh Sunday of Easter)*

Sundays *after* Trinity

Sundays *before* Advent

with a large white candle for Christmas Day, representing the coming of Christ as the light of the world.

Just to complete the picture, the last days leading up to Christmas Day are sometimes described by the 'O' antiphons which were traditionally recited on those days. These 'O' antiphons are the subject matter for the most famous of Advent hymns, 'O come, O come Emmanuel'. You will find the seven of them in the right order, as they would be used for meditation one each day between 17 and 23 December, at Hymn 135 *(Church Hymnal – fifth edition)*.

The season of Advent is not interrupted by any saints' days (unless it begins before 30 November which is St Andrew's Day). The last remaining saint's day was St Thomas on 21 December, which has now been moved to 3 July.

Christmas

The Christmas season begins officially with the First Communion of Christmas. Up to that point, it is Christmas Eve. There is, therefore, no such thing as the First Evensong of Christmas (The same is true of Easter). Both these key Great Feasts begin with the eucharist. The season of Christmas continues, of course, for the famous 'twelve days'. The colour is white (or gold on Christmas Day), and everything which decorates the church and makes it glorious should remain until 6 January.

In my own upbringing, the tradition was to sing Christmas Carols only in Christmastide itself. In one sense, it was wonderful to wait, but nowadays it is no longer sustainable. We need to recognise that non-churchgoing people will come to church up to Christmas Eve (and sometimes on Christmas Day), but rarely will they come after that. At that point for many people, Christmas focuses down into the home and family.

The season of Christmas included several 'red letter days'. Some of these, such as Holy Innocents on 28 December and The Naming and Circumcision of Jesus on 1 January, are very much part of the Christmas story, and naturally 'fit', even if they are in slightly the wrong order! Others (and we will look at these in the *Sanctorale*) may not appear to 'fit' naturally, but have a strong traditional attachment to this part of the year.

The Sunday(s) in the season of Christmas are entitled 'Sundays of Christmas'.

Epiphany

Epiphany, as I have mentioned, is both a day and a season. However, it is not as strongly a season as is the case with Christmas or Advent. For most people the Feast of the Epiphany is co-terminus with the visit of the wise men to the Christ-child. When we think of the Epiphany, we think of gold, frankincense and myrrh and hymns like 'As with gladness men of old', 'We three kings' or 'Brightest and best'. But traditionally, Epiphany was much more than that. It included, as we were reminded of in the Church of England publication *Promise of His Glory*,[10] not only the making known of Christ to the Gentiles symbolised by the Magi, but also the revealing of the nature and purpose of the Christ in his baptism and in his first miracle of turning water into wine at Cana of Galilee. These, too, are key manifestations

10. *The Promise of his Glory: Services and Prayers for the season from All Saints to Candlemas* (1991) Church House Publishing/ Mowbray.

of the Christ, and so they become part of the proclamation of the word during this season. Indeed, the revelation of the Christ-child to elderly Simeon, who sings his *Nunc Dimittis* at the Presentation of Christ in the Temple, is in a sense the summation of this period of manifestation:

My own eyes have seen the salvation

which you have prepared in the sight of every people.

A light to reveal you to the nations

and the glory of your people Israel.

The liturgical colour for this season is now white, continuing right through the forty days up to 'Candlemas', and ending appropriately with the revelation of the light on that day, which is how it got its popular name.

The Sundays in this season are called 'Sundays *after* the Epiphany'. In the Church of England they are 'Sundays *of* Epiphany'. Neither word is quite right. The season is not as strong as Easter, Advent or Christmas, but neither is it as weak as the Sundays after Trinity.

Lent

Lent is perhaps the time which is most recognisable of all as a season. It is used by all sorts of groups to encourage people to lose weight, give up smoking, or support developing world agencies. It might also be true to say that it is a season which many Christians dread, not only because it smacks of discipline and coming face to face with ourselves, but also because of its association in some places with dull, dreary and dirge-like music and liturgy. Because Lent begins, after the excesses of *Mardi Gras* or Shrove Tuesday, with ashes, fasting and sackcloth, it is often assumed that the forty days of its existence are intended to be a reminder of the forty days spent by Jesus in the wilderness. Perhaps the reading of the wilderness story on the First Sunday in Lent gives even greater weight to this perception. But Lent, in its original roots and intention, was really a period of preparation for catechumens[11] who were preparing for baptism at Easter.

11. Newly converted people undergoing an intense period of teaching and spiritual preparation called the catechumenate.

There may be one or two aspects of Lent which you have not noticed:

a) From Ash Wednesday to Easter Eve is actually forty-six days, not forty. However, the period of discipline and abstinence is forty days, as Sundays are always feast-days. So, no fasting is intended on Sundays. In Ireland, we also traditionally add our national patron saint's day[12] as a day of celebration, which brings us down to thirty-nine! It is because the Sundays are 'in' Lent, but not 'of' Lent that our new prayer book continues to follow the convention of Sundays 'in Lent'.

b) There is a change of tenor in the last week (and in some cases two weeks) of Lent. Although the Fifth Sunday in Lent is not called 'Passion Sunday' any longer, there is a strong convention of re-focusing our attention toward Calvary at that stage (after the natural 'break' of Mothering Sunday). The reason that we do not call this Sunday 'Passion Sunday' is that, if any Sunday is the Sunday of the Passion it is the Sunday before Easter. Nevertheless, the Calendar notes on p. 19 that

> Within Lent the last two weeks are commonly called Passiontide.

The change of mood is seen more clearly in the provisions for Palm Sunday when the liturgical colour may change from Violet to Red for the first part of Holy Week, reminding us of the blood of Christ.

Easter

Easter has become more of a season than ever in the new prayer book. In a sense there was always a realisation that you could not fast for forty days and then only celebrate for one. So, in the 1926 *Book of Common Prayer*, the days in Easter Week were given special readings and collects. Now, the feasting is intended to go on for 50 days, expounding the glories of the resurrection, and praising the living Christ. In truth, people in the Church of Ireland often find it easier to lament than to celebrate, and this season of Eastertide needs worked on and worked out. For

---

12. St Patrick's Day, 17 March.

example, we should be singing Easter hymns and songs and canticles right through.[13] The church should be ablaze with flowers, banners and decoration right through, and the Easter garden should remain right through. The colour of the hangings is white or gold on Easter Day and white for the rest of the season. The liturgical colour for Pentecost is, of course, red, symbolising the coming of the Holy Spirit.

These Sundays are described as Sundays *of* Easter, and Easter Day itself is now given the title: 'The First Sunday of Easter: Easter Day'. Here is one of the possible confusions of the new calendar, because we are used to calling 'Low'[14] Sunday the First Sunday after Easter. We need to get this change into our heads or there will be abiding difficulties.

The Sanctorale
Over the past years, the pope has been very busy creating new saints, and the Roman Catholic Church has a particular process by which 'saints' are recognised.

In the Church of Ireland there is a much more ambivalent attitude to sainthood. There is, first of all, a strong recognition that when 'St' Paul writes his letters to 'the saints' of one place or another, he simply means 'to the church' or 'to the Christians' in that particular place. And yet, in the Anglican tradition most of our churches are dedicated in the name of a particular saint – some of whom are well-known from the scriptures, others of whom have had a particular place in the worldwide history of the church, and still others who have a particularly Irish flavour, some of whom are known only in a particular locality. What this

13. There is a small inconsistency in the *BCP* in relation to this. The rubric introducing the Easter Greeting in *Holy Communion Two* says: 'from Easter Day until Pentecost', whereas, in *Morning Prayer Two* it says 'on Easter Day', even though the Easter Anthems are to be sung 'in Eastertide'. My personal suggestion is that the Easter Greeting is used throughout Eastertide, but I understand the point of view that wants to maintain it for Easter Day alone.
14. 'Low' Sunday is simply a nickname given to the Sunday which follows Easter Day, probably so designated because of the 'high' experience of Easter Day itself and the celebration of 'low' mass that day.

means is that, although we become 'saints' in the true sense of the word only by the grace of God through the imputed right-eousness of Jesus Christ, nevertheless, there are certain people in whom the holiness of God has shone particularly clearly, and these are examples to us for our Christian living.

At the Reformation, the issue of saints' days was a hot potato. The 1549 *Book of Common Prayer* reduced the number of saints' days dramatically to simply those of the New Testament 'saints' (These are the ones which became known as 'red letter days[15]). However, in the 1552 prayer book (which many consider more 'Protestant' than its predecessor[16]), some of the older saints' days were returned to the calendar. This, however, is most likely because they were important days in the secular calendar, mark-ing out different points in the year. The collects, epistles and gospels continue to be provided only for the biblical saints.

In the Church of Ireland, these have been added to in only a minimal way over the years with the addition of St Patrick (17 March), St Brigid (1 February – seen in the Republic as 'the first day of spring'[17]) and St Columba (9 June). We have also added The Transfiguration (6 August), The Visitation of the BVM[18] (31 May), the Birth of the BVM (8 September), The Baptism of Our Lord (First Sunday after the Epiphany) and The Kingship of Christ (Sunday before Advent). Also, in the most recent revision, three new New Testament saints have been added. These are:
- St Joseph of Nazareth 19 March
- St Philip the Deacon 11 October
- St James, the Brother of our Lord 23 October.

---

15. They were, of course, printed in red in some editions of the *Book of Common Prayer*.
16. This rather simplistic idea, though material can be rallied to com-mend it, is only really a half-truth, if it is realised that Cramner was engaged in progressive reforming of the liturgy during this period. And, of course, 1552 was itself never used in Ireland.
17. I never cease to be amazed at TV commentators being surprised that the beginning of February is the beginning of spring. It has to be, if Midsummer's Day is 21 June!
18. Abbreviation for the 'Blessed Virgin Mary', properly called by this entire title, because 'all generations shall call me blessed'.

One of the hymns in the *Church Hymnal fifth edition* (Hymn 460) has been adapted to provide an opening and closing verse for each saint's day in the year:

For all your saints in glory, for all your saints art rest,
to you, our Lord and Saviour, all praises be addressed;
apostles, martyrs, prophets, who served you in their day,
have left us their example of following your way.
... ...
All praise to God the Father, all praise to God the Son,
and God the Holy Spirit, eternal Three in One;
till all the ransomed number fall down before the throne,
and honour, power and glory ascribe to God alone.

This hymn is based on a similar hymn by Horatio Bolton Nelson (1823-1913) found in the Sarum Hymnal (1868), and has been adapted for modern usage by Bishop Edward Darling. It offers a middle verse for every 'red letter' saint's day in the year, and its author has now written three extra verses for the three 'new' saints' days, which will be published in his new *Companion to the Church Hymnal fifth edition*, being co-authored with Dr Donald Davison.[19]

The Church of Ireland deals with saints' days in different ways in different places. In some parts of the church, they are more or less ignored. In others, they are celebrated with rigour on the set day. In still others, they are transferred to a midweek communion, or only observed when they fall on a day on which a service is already provided. On those occasions, they often provide a personal focus for devotion, and a reminder of wonderfully exemplary Christian lives.

The liturgical colour for saints days is white unless the saint is a martyr, when it is red.

Rules for 'Festivals'
The *Book of Common Prayer* provides us with a set of rules about the observance of these 'Festivals'. The specific rules look complicated but the basics are:
–   When one of these days falls on a Sunday, it may be trans-

---

19. See Appendix 3.

ferred to a Monday or other weekday. This is, generally, in
my view, preferable, as such a celebration on a Sunday can
break the 'flow' especially at times of the year where there is
semi-continuous reading of the scriptures. However, if the
particular saint's day has a special place in the hearts of the
congregation, it may be desired to hold it on the Sunday, or
perhaps to focus on it at Evening Prayer.

- St Patrick's Day is theoretically transferable, and should be
  transferred if it clashes with something more important in
  the *Temporale*. In other words, it should not replace Palm
  Sunday or the Monday or Tuesday of Holy Week, but should
  in that case be transferred to the previous Saturday. If it falls
  on a Sunday in Lent, it may be observed on the Saturday before or the Monday after. All I can say is, 'Try it!' Sometimes
  with these kinds of celebrations it is very difficult to be out of
  line with what the world is doing.
- No celebration of a festival takes place during Holy Week.
  This rule could easily be missed as it is found under 'Days of
  Special Observance' on p. 20, and is very important indeed

Commemorations

A list of 'Commemorations' is given on p. 22. Most of these are
Irish Saints, connected with a particular diocese or part of the
country. George Simms (not long before he died) worked with
Brian Mayne on producing a beautiful little 'Irish Cloud of
Witnesses' Book[20] which gives some material about each of
these people, and is very useful for private or public prayer.
Although many of these names will be unknown to most members of the Church of Ireland, they are generally not forgotten in
the parts of the country associated with them, and are a reminder of the inheritance of faith in which we stand in this 'land
of saints and scholars'.

Other Days

There are other important reminders in these pages.

---

20. *Commemorating Saints and Others of the Irish Church* (1999) George
    Otto Simms and Brian Mayne, The Columba Press.

First of all, the reminder that there are certain times of the year designated for particular prayer.

Rogation Days (from the Latin for 'asking') are days of prayers for 'God's blessing on the fruits of the earth and human labour'. These are the three weekdays before the Ascension Day, and emphasise the work of the Creator and our dependence on God to sustain us.

Ember Days are days of particular prayer for those who are preparing for ordination, and indeed for vocations to the ordained ministry (Not an unimportant theme in our day). They can easily be forgotten, but are normally to be observed on the Wednesday, Friday and Saturday after:

– The First Sunday in Lent
– The Day of Pentecost
– 14 September
– 13 December.

They are, therefore quarterly focused periods of prayer for the ministry.

Days of Special Observance

These begin with Ash Wednesday. Interestingly, this is the only special day for which a particular service is provided in the *Book of Common Prayer*. The service provided is to be found on p. 338, and replaces the old Penitential Service in the book, though the use of the older service is still allowed, and in my own view, still valuable.

They also include the Monday, Tuesday and Wednesday of Holy Week and Easter Eve. The vigil readings which may be used on Easter Eve at the Easter Vigil are to be found on p. 40.

Days of Discipline and Self-Denial

This is the one that we least like! Basically, this little paragraph is a reminder to all of us that fasting and abstinence are part of the Christian life, not only in Lent (but at least that) but also on a regular basis. In our day, it is often the 'new' churches which remind us of this part of our heritage. On one level, there might háve been a temptation to weaken this particular 'rule'. After all, how many Anglicans whom we know abstain from anything on

Fridays (the weekly celebration of our Lord's atoning sacrifice)? But this paragraph holds out a reminder and a standard for all of us to aspire to again – not just for the sake of keeping a 'law' but to bring us closer to the Lord in prayer and fasting, and to enable us to discipline our own bodies. Surely too, an age in which our governments in the western world are concerned about serious problems of obesity is one in which we need to be reminded about controlling our eating!

But the good news at the end is that the major celebratory feast days are not to be days of fasting!

Dates of Easter and other Variable Dates
Many of us remember the days when, if the sermon was boring, there were always the 'Golden Numbers'.[21] If you don't know what they are, go back to the 1926 *Book of Common Prayer* and explore! Meanwhile, the new prayer book has made it easy, and provides, on p. 74, a list of variable dates in the church calendar (all but Advent 1 based around the date of Easter). These run out in 2030, which is not necessarily a prophetic word to suggest that the 2004 book will have run its course by then …!

Liturgical Colours
As we have moved through the different times and seasons, we have noted the appropriate liturgical colour for each (see the chart on page 22). Of course, this is not something fixed in an absolute way, but colour can help to highlight the mood of the different seasons and days of the Christian Year. Details of colours which are appropriate can be found with the lectionary provision in the *Book of Common Prayer*. Generally it is white for major times of celebration (with gold as an option for the very high days); violet for times of penitence and preparation; red for the Holy Spirit, Holy Week and martyrs; and green (the basic colour of nature) for 'ordinary time'.

---

21. The chart by which the date of Easter could be worked out.

Questions for Reflection and Discussion

1. In what ways is it valuable to have a 'Christian' calendar as well as a secular one?

2. In what ways are the symbolic 'colours' of the Church Year of help to you in worship? What do the different colours mean to you?

3. How can we best help one another to 'feel' the impact of the Christian story as it is told and re-told year after year? Are there parts of the story you find it hard to engage with?

4. Using Holy Week as an example, what has most helped the story of that week to come to life for you? Have you ideas of other ways of bringing the story of this week to life in worship?

5. Many people find lamentation easier than celebration. What would help you to celebrate Easter for its full fifty days?

CHAPTER TWO

The Table of Readings

Two 'lectionaries' are provided. The first, and by far the more important and thorough, is a version of *The Revised Common Lectionary*[1] (beginning on p. 27). The second, provided to complete the provision for using the traditional services, is *A Table of Epistles and Gospels, drawn from those appointed in the Book of Common Prayer 1926, which may be used at Holy Communion with Collects One* (beginning on p. 71). The readings for neither lectionary are printed in full, as there are so many of them, but there are various versions of *The Revised Common Lectionary* available for those who would like to have the readings in front of them in the order in which they are read. The most suitable of these is the Church of Ireland edition of *The Word of the Lord*.[2] Of course, a Bible may be a better option, especially in an age in which people need to learn again how to find their way around what is, after all, the core book of our faith!

This chapter will focus on explaining the background, rationale, and use of *The Revised Common Lectionary*, which is bound to be at the heart of our lectionary provision for many years to come.

What is a Lectionary?
In essence, 'lectionary' (from the same root as 'lectern') is a latinised title for a 'table of readings' or for a set of readings written or printed out by ecclesiastical authority. One of the issues we all

---

1. For full details see *The Revised Common Lectionary* (1992), The Consultation on English Texts, Canterbury Press, Norwich.
2. *The Word of the Lord: Readings for Principal Services on Sundays, Principal Holy Days and Festivals, authorized for use with The Book of Common Prayer in the Church of Ireland* (2003) Canterbury Press, Norwich. Brian Mayne did much of the work to make this publication possible.

have to face in our Christian lives is how we might go about reading and engaging with the scriptures most effectively. Some simply begin with Genesis and go through to Revelation, though the question of whether that is the wisest way is often raised. Sometimes stories are told of seekers or new Christians beginning in that most obvious of ways, and getting rather stuck at the Book of *Leviticus!* So, we find other and perhaps more productive methods, intertwining the Old and New Testament scriptures, or providing sets of bible reading notes which select certain books or linked passages of scripture, and in the process bring the bible to life.

Anglican Roots

Thomas Cranmer was faced with exactly this question in a era in which the scriptures were not well known, and in which few bibles were available. His essential answer was to provide a more-or-less continuous reading of the scriptures at Matins and Evensong every day. The idea was that the clergyman would ring the bell, calling the people to worship twice daily, and there they would hear the whole counsel of God (or the vast majority of it) read to them.

In the 1549 *Book of Common Prayer*, he provided, therefore *The Ordre howe the reste of Holy Scripture (beside the Psalter) is appointed to bee redde,* in which the principle is clearly laid out:

The olde Testament

The Olde Testament is appointed for the first Lessons, at Matins and Euensong, and shall bee redde through euery yere once, except certain Bokes and Chapiters, which bee least edifying, and might be spared, And therefore are left unred.

The newe Testament

The newe Testament is appointed for the second Lessons, at Matins and Euensong, and shalbe red ouer orderly euery yere thrise, beside the Epistles and Gospelles: except the Apocalips[3], out of the which there be Only certain Lessons appointed upon diuerse proper feastes.

---

3. The Apocalypse is, of course, the Book of *Revelation*.

These principles held for Morning and Evening Prayer on a seven-day-a-week daily basis (including Sundays). The congregation on Sundays, therefore, would simply find the readings (apart from the epistles and gospels provided for each Sunday) carrying on from Saturday, and being continued on Monday.

Out of these principles developed by Cranmer, and to some degree deeply etched in the sub-consciousness of Anglicans, we can find some which continue to be of great importance, and to which *The Revised Common Lectionary* has returned for its Sunday readings:

i) It is important to read the Old and New Testaments along-side each other as our normal diet of worship. One without the other is inadequate. This might well be affirmed in situations where churches find it easier simply to have one reading and preach on it. That pattern was followed by some of the other reformers, but not accepted by Cranmer.

ii) There is great power in the continuous (or at least semi-continuous) reading of the scriptures. For example, Cranmer's lectionary simply reads Genesis chapter by chapter for most of January, going in order from Morning to Evening Prayer each day, assuming that people would attend both.

iii) Some passages might reasonably be omitted, which does not denigrate them as the Word of God, but simply means that they might not be particularly edifying in public worship.

iv) However, Cranmer is a reminder to us that every compiler of a lectionary, or even every preacher without a lectionary choosing their own readings, has blind spots. For Cranmer, the book omitted was the Apocalypse, or Book of *Revelation*, just as Luther omitted the Epistle of James. Compilers of lectionaries need to be aware of these blind spots, and a few may be seen in *The Revised Common Lectionary*.

Roots of The Revised Common Lectionary

The starting point for *The Revised Common Lectionary* is really the Second Vatican Council in the Roman Catholic Church. One of the fruits of this council was to provide for a much fuller reading of the scriptures, especially in the Sunday eucharist. This led to

the new *Lectionary for Mass* in 1969, which provides the starting
point for *The Revised Common Lectionary*.[4] The next stage was the
Common Lectionary of 1983, which is an amended form of the
Roman lectionary, adapted for ecumenical purposes. This be-
came the lectionary which was adopted by a number of
Anglican provinces, including Canada and the USA.

Meanwhile, back at the ranch, the Church of Ireland along
with the Church of England, and several other churches (including the British Methodist and Baptist churches), were going
along a totally different route, one which would prove to have a
more limited lifetime. This was the two-year lectionary which
was designed in 1967 by the Joint Liturgical Group[5] and incor-
porated into the *Alternative Prayer Book* 1984. Although it had
some similarities to *The Revised Common Lectionary*, in that it was
based on three readings and a psalm, and was over a more-than-
one year period, it had worn thin, especially in terms of its
'themes', by the 1990s. In the *APB*, the themes were given too
much prominence, as they were placed as headings for each
Sunday of the year (whereas in the Church of England's *ASB
1980* they were placed in very small print at the back of the
book), and began to over-determine our understanding of the
scriptures, and rather over-limit our diet of the bible. Apart from
this, the 'thematic' approach to education had become rather
less dominant during this period, with a resurgence of the story-
telling approach, and it had become clear by the time the *JLG*
proposed a new four-year lectionary, that the future ecumenically lay with the *RCL*.

4. Following the adoption and ready acceptance by the Presbyterian
    Church of the USA and other Protestant denominations in North
    America, an amended form of the Roman lectionary was produced
    for trial use in their churches in 1983 as the *Common Lectionary*.
5. The Joint Liturgical Group was a group made up of representatives
    from the Protestant churches in England and Scotland, which inter-
    estingly included The Baptist Union of Great Britain and Ireland. It
    did some very significant liturgical work, especially in the late six-
    ties and seventies, and was responsible for a greater acceptance of
    liturgy in nonconformist churches. It also is the root of the *Weekday
    Intercessions and Thanksgivings* in the present prayer book.

Tables of Readings

There are three Tables of Readings which relate to the regular worship of the Church of Ireland

- *The Revised Common Lectionary* (p. 27ff). This gives three readings and a psalm for each Sunday and for Principal Holy Days, on a three-year cycle, and also a set of readings for a second and third service. This is the main lectionary of the church, and is used ecumenically in many parts of the world. The table for festivals was developed in the Church of Ireland.

- **The 1926 Prayer Book Epistles and Gospels** (pp.71-73), which may be used with Holy Communion One.

- **The Weekday Lectionary** for use at Morning and Evening Prayer and at Weekday Holy Communion Services (apart from Saints' Days and Holy Days). As this is still in a transitional state at the time of publication, it may be found each year in *The Church of Ireland Directory*.

- The Prayer Book also allows for the minister to 'occasionally depart from the lectionary provision' in periods of ordinary time (See note p. 26).

It should, perhaps, be mentioned at this point that *The Revised Common Lectionary* differs in certain aspects from that used in the Roman Catholic Church, and that the changes have not yet proved acceptable to Rome, so that there are still some differences in approach and usage, though in most ways the two lectionaries are the same. One of the major ecumenical concerns with the Roman lectionary was the lack of continuous reading of the Old Testament in its own right. So, a new strand of semi-continuous reading of the Old Testament was added in ordinary time[6] after Trinity, which has become the basic usage in many parts of the worldwide church. It might also be noted that each part of the Church had adapted the *RCL* in different ways to meet the needs of its own approach to the Calendar. So, not every version is the same. People need to be aware of that if they

---

6. 'Ordinary time' is essentially the time when the hangings are green, and there is no particular focus to the Sunday or the day. About half the year is in this category.

are following *RCL* readings in lectionaries, lectionary books, and internet sites which may not be fully compatible with the Church of Ireland *Book of Common Prayer*.

Basic Principles of The Revised Common Lectionary

The basic principle of the *RCL* is that reading of the scriptures is to be approached in different ways at different times of the year. In simple terms, the high points of the christological celebration (Advent and Christmas; Lent and Easter) are treated differently to 'ordinary time'.

At the high points, although there may be a semi-continuous nature to some of the strands, the readings are essentially focused around, and back up, the gospel proclamation. That is understandable and right, because these focal points, around Christmas and Easter, are about the story of Jesus.

In 'ordinary time', the way the readings are done is quite different, and can best be explained as follows:

i) The readings are what we would call, in television terms, 'stripped' across the weeks. In other words, *Neighbours* tells its story at 5.35, *Emmerdale* at 7 and *Coronation Street* at 7.30, and the story carries over from night to night, episode to episode. So, in the readings (when using the continuous Old Testament strand), the Old Testament tells its story, the New Testament its story and the gospel its story, and all are 'to be continued' same time, same place, next week! This is the very opposite to thematic readings, which are grouped according to a predetermined theme.

ii) Each year is a year of one particular gospel. Year A is the Year of Matthew, Year B the Year of Mark, and Year C the Year of Luke. John is essentially read during high points of the different years, and to 'fill the gap' of a shorter gospel in the Year of Mark. Each year of readings begins on the First Sunday of Advent and follows through to the feast of Christ the King, which can make it difficult for a congregation to know 'emotionally' which year they are in, as the gospel of that year is not always followed through at the high points and may not therefore be apparent.

iii) Although the three readings are not connected (unless the alternative Old Testament strand is being used, in which case the Old Testament lections prefigure the gospel), the psalm is a reflection on the Old Testament reading in each case. The psalm, therefore, should normally follow the Old Testament reading as a reflection on it.

iv) The result of this is that any themes which emerge connecting the readings in ordinary time, are purely serendipitous; but, in my own experience, it is amazing how the scriptures, read in this way, draw out different themes at different times and in different situations. There are many commentaries and aids for sermons which connect together the three readings and psalm of a particular Sunday. These can be either creative or limiting depending on how they are approached and used.[7]

Another basic starting point of the *RCL* is that it is a Sunday and holy day lectionary based on three readings and a psalm. In the Roman Catholic tradition and in parts of the Anglican Communion, this means that it is in essence a eucharistic lectionary, but in the case of the Church of Ireland and indeed the Church of England, it is intended as the lectionary for the principal service on a Sunday. This means that Sunday principal services (no matter whether eucharistic or not) should normally have three readings and a psalm, which is quite a change for many churches in their worship pattern. It means a much greater diet of scripture.

There are a few 'quirks' of the new lectionary which might also be noted at this point:

i) Although not thematic, there are three or four Sundays in which particular 'themes' emerge as controlling the readings. These are outside the main christological period, and can be

---

7. I will not attempt to list the different series of preaching aids here. Simply to say that preachers need to be careful of aids which, in ordinary time, try to find themes holding the readings of a particular Sunday together. These could, in the end, restrict the free impact of the scriptures themselves, if we only viewed them in the light of the connections made by a particular author.

confusing if the new lectionary has been introduced as not being thematic. These are:

–*The Second Sunday before Lent*, when a creation 'theme' is given an alternative set of readings, reminiscent of the old Septuagesima theme.

–*The Sunday before Lent*, which has a transfiguration theme, not as an alternative, but as the only set of readings.

–*The Sunday between 23-29 October*, which is the new 'Bible Sunday', replacing the Second Sunday of Advent. This Sunday, in the Church of Ireland Calendar, is called 'The Fifth Sunday before Advent', but in the Church of England calendar it is called 'The Last Sunday after Trinity'.

–*The Sunday between 20-26 November*, which is a 'festival' of the Kingship of Christ.

ii) The First Reading (first option) during Eastertide is from the *Acts of the Apostles*. The reason for this is that the book of *Acts* is such a suitable exposition of the life of the risen Christ in the early church. An Old Testament alternative is also provided, but it is worth worship leaders trying out the '*Acts*' option which gives a particularly distinctive feel to Eastertide.

iii) When it comes to the major festival of Christmas, the readings are not arranged in a Year A, B, C cycle, but in Sets I, II, and III. This is presumably because of the number of eucharists celebrated in most churches on Christmas Eve and Christmas Day.

Other Lectionary issues

The notes provided at the beginning of the Table of Readings (pp. 24-26) are very helpful indeed. These give a more detailed explanation of:

– A Lectionary for a Second Service
– A Lectionary for a Third Service
– Festivals and Other Occasions
– Readings from the Books called 'Apocrypha'.

Bible Versions

The notes continue by looking at the issue of bible versions. The *Alternative Prayer Book* 1984 used the *New International Version* as its normative text, whereas the Church of England *Alternative Service Book* 1980 used a whole variety of versions, choosing the one which the compilers felt best conveyed the meaning of the particular passage. In this note (p. 26), there is a mild suggestion that the *New Revised Standard Version* might be the normative text. It is certainly a version which reads well, with a sensitivity to resonant words stored in the memory, with excellent scholarship and with a mild use of inclusive language in relation to people. However, it should not be presumed that the bible verses printed in full in the liturgy itself are of necessity from the *NRSV*. In these cases the Liturgical Advisory Committee chose what they considered was the best translation for the particular purpose.

As no full texts for readings are produced in the 2004 prayer book, each church will have the opportunity to review which version or versions of the scriptures are used. The House of Bishops from time to time produce a list of 'approved' versions of the Bible, and you will find the present list as Appendix 1 (p. 244).

Readings at Holy Communion Services

Apart from the old *BCP 1926* epistles and gospels, the readings at Holy Communion services will be the same as if the service were Morning or Evening Prayer, except for the fact that there will always be a gospel reading at Holy Communion. In other words, a particular lectionary strand should be followed through at the same time each Sunday, no matter what the service may be. Otherwise, there is a total confusion in relation to the continuity of readings. For many Anglicans this is a new way of thinking.

Weekday Readings

The new *Book of Common Prayer* does not include daily readings. This is for a variety of reasons:

a) We are at a point in our history where there is no agreed weekday lectionary.

b) It is likely that, within the lifetime of this prayer book, there may be a series of different weekday lectionaries.

c) It is probably better to produce a 'dated' lectionary each year. This is simpler and easy to follow. In the case of the Church of Ireland, at the moment this lectionary is available in the *Desk Diary and Lectionary*.[8]

How the Revised Common Lectionary and Calendar 'fit' in Ordinary time

On one level, the lectionary and the calendar are completely separate. The readings in ordinary time are not linked (as has been the case in the past) with the particular Sunday of the year. In other words, for example, on the Sixth Sunday after Trinity, there are no set readings appointed for that liturgical Sunday of the year. The collect and post-communion prayer are appointed by the 'liturgical' Sunday, but the readings are appointed according to the date in the ordinary calendar. So, the reading may, for example, be that for 'The Sunday between 17 and 23 July' or 'The Sunday between 24 and 30 July' depending on the date on which the Sixth Sunday after Trinity falls. This may sound complex, but is really quite easy. The readings in ordinary time are designated from 'Proper 0' to 'Proper 29'.

Readings from the Apocrypha

Note 5 on p. 25 deals with readings from the Apocrypha, and there are certain keys things which we should note:

a) There is nothing un-Anglican about reading from the Apocrypha. Some of the readings are very helpful and suitable. Try them from time to time.

b) The Apocryphal books are not treated in the same way as the canonical books. The phrase used here is that they are 'non-canonical', but sometimes they are described as 'deutero-

---

8. *Church of Ireland Directory, including Desk Diary and Lectionary Styletype*, Belfast and Press-Tige Publications, Dublin; published annually, available from The Good Book Shop, Belfast and other outlets.

canonical'. Readings from these books do not end with the phrase 'This is the word of the Lord', but with 'Here ends the reading'.

c) There is always a canonical alternative given to any reading from the Apocrypha.

d) We might note that we have always used in our liturgy some canticles from the Apocrypha.

Freedom to use other readings

One of the benefits of the new prayer book is that it is less restrictive than things have been in the past. That is seen in the note on 'Extensions and Options' on p. 26, where it says:

> On Sundays between Epiphany and Ash Wednesday and between Trinity Sunday and Advent Sunday, while the authorised lectionary remains the norm, the minister may occasionally depart from the lectionary provision for sufficient pastoral reasons or for preaching and teaching purposes.

There are some points to be noted about this:

a) This note is essentially about the 'ordinary Sundays', so 'Epiphany' up to 2 February is, in my view, best considered as the season rather than the day, as it is not ordinary time.

b) The departure from the lectionary should be occasional – perhaps a special series, or a special service.

c) The danger of doing this too often is to lose the flow of the scriptures being read in order. Careful thought should be given by worship leaders before using this provision.

Questions for reflection or discussion

1. What can we do in our Sunday worship to help the readings from the bible to have more impact on the congregation?

2. What are the benefits in having a lectionary with set readings? What are the drawbacks?

3. What ways have you found in your own personal devotions to help the bible to come alive?

4. How do you think local churches could best recognise and equip people to read the scriptures publicly?

5. Which versions of the bible do you find particularly helpful, and why?

6. How can members of the congregation be enabled to follow the readings? Is it more helpful to have them printed out, or simply to listen?

CHAPTER THREE

Morning and Evening Prayer

The material which is needed for Morning and Evening Prayer is found in the prayer book between page 78 and page 153.

First of all, you will notice that there are two different 'orders' for these services. The first (beginning on p. 84) has the title '*The* Order for Morning and Evening Prayer', while the second has the title '*An* Order for Morning and Evening Prayer'. The reason for that is that the old 1662 title has been retained for the first, though interestingly, the title of the second service goes right back to Cranmer's Prayer Book of 1552. In simple terms, as you can see at the bottom of the page, these can be described as *Morning and Evening Prayer One* and *Morning and Evening Prayer Two*, 'One' describing the traditional language form, and 'two' describing the contemporary language form.

One of the things you will observe is that both forms integrate material for both morning and evening. In former Books of Common Prayer, this was not so: there was a separate order for morning and one for evening. However, in the *Alternative Prayer Book* 1984, the two were integrated, and (apart from the canticles not being printed in the service itself) this way of doing things seemed to work. This time round, the basic canticles are printed and, after the preliminary part of the service, the congregation is invited to 'turn to page 93' (in *Morning and Evening Prayer One*) or 'turn to page 109' (in *Morning and Evening Prayer Two*) if it is a service of Evening Prayer, for the evening strand. In reality, apart from canticles and collects, the two services are precisely the same, and there is no point in printing them out twice.

You might also observe that there are other names which, from time to time, are used to designate these services: Mattins (sometimes spelt 'Matins') and Evensong. These are very ancient titles, going back to monastic offices, which were used for the two services in the 1549 prayer book. Cranmer changed these to Morning Prayer and Evening Prayer in the 1552 prayer book. The former are perfectly good titles, and are often used today to designate sung services rather than said services: Indeed, Choral Evensong is widely considered to be one of the most balanced and beautiful services in the Christian Church and almost a work of art in its own right. It is the longest running programme on BBC Radio, and continues weekly on Wednesdays at 4pm on BBC Radio Three.

Another point arising from the title itself is why we would call a service which includes a wide range of elements by only one of them (ie prayer). It could, in fact, be said that these services are much more centred around the reading of the scriptures and the praise of God in the psalms and canticles, than they are around prayer, and that would be true. However, we soon realise that no word is perfect in describing the totality of what we do in these liturgies. We can describe it as 'worship', but that too is imperfect, and even the word 'service' which we so frequently use to describe what we do when we meet in church (presumably coming from the root meaning of 'liturgy', which is our work or service), is slightly more strange the more we think about it.

And lastly, with regard to the title, we note that each of the two orders is described as 'Daily throughout the year'. That is a reminder that these are, in their essence, daily services. They come from a conflation of the various monastic offices with which the monks marked the different stages of the day: Matins, Lauds, Prime, Terce, None, Vespers, Compline, which in turn have their roots in the injunctions of St Paul to 'pray continually' (1 Thessalonians 5:17; Romans 12:12), and indeed, the marking out of the day so often found in the faith of the Old Testament (Deuteronomy 6:7; 11:19; Psalm 119:164; Daniel 6:10). The key theme of these verses is that regular times of prayer lead to a life where prayer is a constant part of our relationship with God.

Thomas Cranmer's stroke of genius was to create out of a

very complicated structure for daily prayer, a simple one; and his desire, of course was to enable the whole people of God to hear the scriptures read on a twice-daily basis, so that they would be instructed in God's word, and so he writes, in the Preface to the 1552 *Book of Common Prayer:*[1]

> And all priests and deacons shall be bound to say daily the Morning and Evening prayer, either privately or openly, except they be letted by preaching, studying of divinity or by some other urgent cause. And the curate[2] that ministereth in every Parish Church or Chapel where he ministereth, shall toll a bell thereto, a convenient time before he begin, that such as be disposed may come to hear God's word and to pray with him.

Although the recognition is there right from the start that these are in their very essence daily services, there is also a sense that, especially with *Morning and Evening Prayer Two*, we have them here in a form which will be used as regular Sunday worship, while the more abbreviated forms which will be found most useful for weekday worship are found on pp. 136-138, with the hope of encouraging more regular daily use in churches and at home.

THE DIFFERENT PARTS OF MORNING AND EVENING PRAYER

The Gathering of God's People

In *One* there are no 'section headings' in the service, while in *Two* the heading taken from the contemporary Holy Communion Service is used: *The Gathering of God's People* (The meaning of the different headings is dealt with in full when discussing the communion services). In both cases, the elements are similar:

---

1. The 1552 *Book of Common Prayer* was never actually authorized for use in Ireland. See Michael Kennedy's essay on 'The First Prayer Books 1551-1666' in *The Prayer Books of The Church of Ireland,* ed. Brian Mayne, Columba Press, 2004
2. The word 'curate' here, as in the Prayer for the Church Militant in *Holy Communion One,* does not of course have our modern colloquial meaning of 'curate-assistant', but means the person with the cure of souls in the parish.

Morning and Evening Prayer Two

THE GATHERING OF GOD'S PEOPLE
Greeting
(Sentence of Scripture)
(Hymn)
(Introduction)
|
Confession
Absolution

PROCLAIMING AND RECEIVING THE WORD
Versicles and Responses
|
First Canticle

MP Venite, Jubilate or Easter Anthems   *EP A Song of the Light, Deus*
Misereatur or Ecce Nunc

(Reading *May be omitted at MP. Omitted at EP.*)
MP First Reading

Psalm
Reading

MP Second Reading   *EP First Reading*

Second Canticle

MP Te Deum or other canticle   *EP Magnificat or other*
*   except Benedictus*   *NT canticle*

Reading

MP Third(Gospel) Reading   *EP Second Reading*

Third Canticle

MP Benedictus or any NT canticle   *EP Nunc Dimittis or any NT canticle*
|
(Sermon)
|
Apostles' Creed

THE PRAYERS OF THE PEOPLE
Lesser Litany
Lord's Prayer
(Versicles and Responses)
Collect of the Day
One or more other collect
(Hymn or anthem)
(Prayers, thanksgivings or a litany)
(Hymn)

GOING OUT AS GOD'S PEOPLE
(Concluding Prayer, ascription, The Grace or Blessing)

a) Sentences of Scripture: It could be said that Morning and Evening Prayer always begin with the scriptures. Indeed, if you were to go through the whole service you would discover that almost everything which is said comes directly from the scriptures. Anglican services are fully biblical: they are called into being by the scriptures, soaked in the scriptures, and even our response to God's word is usually formulated in the words of the scriptures.

The sentences themselves are found on pp. 78-83, and again at the beginning of *Morning and Evening Prayer One*. They can be grouped in the following way:

– General sentences focusing on the nature of worship
– Seasonal sentences, suitable for beginning services at particular times.
– Penitential sentences, leading into the confession of our sins.

The value of a limited number of sentences of scripture being printed is that we can actually get to know them. One of the great values of liturgy in the Anglican tradition, with limited variations, has been the storing of our memories with words which will be of value to us in our own personal lives.

The placing of the scriptures right at the beginning of worship also has the effect of reminding us that all we are, and all we do, and all we offer to God is called into being by his word, and responsive to what he has already done in revealing his truth to us, especially in the living word, Jesus Christ. So, the bible is used here in a simple way to tell us why we worship, why we celebrate certain seasons, and why we confess our sins to God.

b) Greeting. This is more immediately evident in order *Two*, with the opening words, which are again from the scriptures *(Ruth 2:4)*, 'The Lord be with you.'

c) Opening Hymn. In reality, most services of Morning or Evening Prayer on a Sunday begin with a hymn. It may be a processional hymn, during which the choir and worship leaders go to their places, or it may simply be a hymn which is announced when the minister is in his place. The place suggested for such a hymn in order *Two* is after the opening greeting and any sentence of scripture which may be used. A hymn at this point may be used to focus our minds on the greatness or holiness of God, to set the focus for the theme of the worship of that day, or simply to give thanks to God for his mercies which are new every morning.

d) Introduction or Exhortation. The two versions of Morning and Evening Prayer both have a 'teaching' passage which may be read by the minister at this point, but the two are quite different. In *Morning Prayer Two*, the Introduction maps out the agenda for Christian worship. We come together:

... to offer to Almighty God

our worship and praise and thanksgiving,

to confess our sins and to receive God's forgiveness,

to hear his holy word proclaimed,

to bring before him our needs and the needs of the world,

and to pray that in the power of this Spirit

we may serve him and know the greatness of his love.

The service also gives freedom for the minister to introduce the service in a more informal way when he or she sees fit.

In *Morning Prayer One*, the 'exhortation' is, like most of the sentences of scripture, not so much focused on laying out the contents of the worship as on preparing us to make our confession of sins. However, it does include within that context the fact that the most important time for us to make our confession of our sins is:

... when we assemble and meet together to render thanks for the great benefits that we have received at his hands, to set forth his most worthy praise, to hear his most holy Word, and to ask those things which are requisite and necessary as well for the body as the soul.

e) Confession. The simpler way of beginning the traditional language service is with the words introduced in the 1926 *Book of Common Prayer*:

Let us humbly confess our sins to Almighty God.

And in the contemporary version:

Let us confess our sins to God our Father.

Interestingly, in the earliest of the prayer books, 1549, there was no confession of sins at the beginning of Morning and Evening Prayer. The service began simply (after the Lord's Prayer) in the way in which many cathedral evensongs begin, with the words: 'O Lord, open thou our lips'. But when he revised his prayer book in 1552, Thomas Cranmer added the most wonderful and memorable General Confession, which has resonances of *Romans 7:8-25* and the Parable of the Lost Sheep in *Luke 15*. This confession is probably the work of Cranmer himself, based on a confession in the Strasbourg Liturgy. At this point, Reformers all over Europe were learning and indeed stealing ideas from one another.

Order *Two* also provides a time of silence to reflect on and make personal our confession, and a simpler form of penitence. What is true of both orders is that these are 'general' confessions. That is, they are different from personal confessions. They provide a recognition in a general way of what is true of all humanity at any point in our lives. They are a reminder that sin, as an 'infection of nature' (*Article 9*, p. 780) is something which we have as part of our human condition, even when we are put right with God through Christ; and therefore, that repentance is not only the beginning of the Christian life, but its continuance as well.

d) Absolution. The absolution or remission of sins follows. It is vitally important not only that we confess our sins in worship, but also that we receive the full and free forgiveness which comes to us through Jesus Christ. The absolution in the older form of service is much stronger than the simple and direct absolution in the contemporary form. Indeed, it is a very powerful exposition of the heart of the gospel itself, and of the wonderful freedom which is provided by Christ for those who turn from sin. Not only does God pardon and absolve us, but he also gives us a penitent heart, the power of the Holy Spirit, and the grace to live holy lives.

The absolution is a kind of 'declaratory prayer' with, some believe, its roots in Calvin's liturgical work. It is pronounced by the priest as an ambassador of the grace of God, directly in 'you' form, but it is quite clear that God alone does the pardoning and absolving of sins, and that the task of the minister is to pronounce it. Hearing the absolution is intended to give us the assurance that God has cleansed us and totally forgiven us.

e) The Lord's Prayer. In *Morning Prayer One*, the absolution is followed by The Lord's Prayer. In fact, as I have already mentioned, this is where the service originally began. In much of the liturgy of Cranmer's Books of Common Prayer, the Lord's Prayer is used as the model and starting point of all worship and prayer. It is important to remember that, in a service of Morning Prayer, Litany and Holy Communion, there could have been up to five uses of The Lord's Prayer, so that the two which are found in the traditional form are modest! It should also be noted that, at times where the Lord's Prayer is an introduction to praise, Cranmer adds the doxology ('For thine is the kingdom ...'), whereas, when the Lord's Prayer is used as an introduction to prayer or penitence, the doxology is omitted.

f) Versicles and Responses. In other words, the short dialogue which moves the service into praise: These responses, apart from the *Gloria Patri* (Glory to the Father ...) are found in daily offices from the sixth century, and come from the scriptures ('O Lord, open our lips', for example, being from *Psalm 51:15*). The *Gloria Patri*, needless to say, in its substance, goes right back to the fourth century, when the doctrine of the Trinity was being defined, with the second half being added in the sixth century.

Proclaiming and Receiving the Word
a) Opening or Invitatory Canticles. In the 'Canticles' chapter later in the book, I will look at each of the canticles used in the *BCP* in its own right, helping us to understand its background and meaning. Suffice it here to understand why we use canticles in liturgy and why we have placed certain ones at particular points in the services of Morning and Evening Prayer. Essentially (although not all

canticles are straight from the scriptures – some are Christian 'hymns'), canticles in this section of the Ministry of the Word are used as a preparation to hear the Word of God, a response to it, and a device by which we use the actual revealed words of scripture for the praise of God, and store them in our memory.

The word 'canticle' itself simply comes from the Latin word for 'song', and most of the canticles are described simply by their first words in the Latin version (eg *Venite, Benedictus, Magnificat* etc.). In Morning and Evening Prayer Two, they are also given simple English titles (*Psalm 95, The Song of Zechariah, The Song of Mary,* to use the same examples as we have used in Latin). In our services they are pointed[3] for use with Anglican chant, though it is possible to sing canticles in a whole variety of ways, not least as pointed out on p. 105 in the rubric:

These and other canticles may be used in other versions and forms e.g. from the *Church Hymnal.*[4]

The Opening or Invitatory Canticles which are used are as follows:

At Morning Prayer: *Venite* Psalm 95 (*One* and *Two*)
                      Easter Anthems (*One:* on Easter Day and
                      the seven days after; *Two:* in Eastertide)
                      Jubliate Psalm 100 (*Two*)
At Evening Prayer: A Song of the Light (*Two*)
                      Deus Misereatur Psalm 67 (*Two*)
                      Ecce Nunc Psalm 134 (*Two*)
                      Easter Anthems (*Two,* in Eastertide)

---

3. The whole question of whether or not to include 'pointing' (ie the marks in red which show us when to change the note in Anglican chant) is controversial. Some editions of the 1926 *Book of Common Prayer* included pointing, some did not. The pointing makes the text less 'clean', and may discourage other appropriate ways of singing it. However, chanting without pointing is a difficult exercise. It is hoped that the pointing in the *Book of Common Prayer* is printed in such a way as not to overly distract from the words themselves.
4. The last section of the *Church Hymnal fifth edition* is full of versions of canticles which may be used in place of the ones in the *BCP*. There are of course, numerous other versions available as well.

Overall, these canticles 'set the scene', and draw us into worship. They (or when they are omitted), the psalm, are our first response to the prayer 'O Lord, open our lips', and need to be said or sung with conviction, lest it appear that our prayer has not been answered!

The *Venite* was a very clever choice for this position in the service, as it both holds together the praise of God and our preparation to hear and receive his word:

Today, if only you would hear his voice,

do not harden your hearts as you did in the wilderness.

It often strikes me as important to note that an opening canticle like the *Venite* is not addressed to God as such but, like many hymns, is addressed to each other. Here we are inciting one another to worship God, and in the *Jubilate*, we go even further and incite the whole world to worship:

O shout to the Lord in triumph all the earth …

The use of this type of opening or invitatory canticle at Evening Prayer is relatively new, though the first canticle in *Evening Prayer Two* is in fact a very old one (from the third century). In Greek, it is called the *Phos Hilaron*, and it takes up the theme of lighting the evening lamps when darkness falls. In some parts of the church a candle or candles are lit as this song is sung. The version we have in the prayer book is 'Hail, gladdening light'. The *Ecce Nunc* is a psalm many of us have become used to through its use in the *Late Evening Office*.[5]

b) The First Reading (Morning Prayer only). This is one of the few changes which have been made in the traditional language service, and which follows through also to the contemporary language version. In the 1926 Prayer Book, we had the opening canticle followed immediately by the psalm, or, in the old days, perhaps several psalms. Now, the psalm comes after the first reading in both versions of Morning Prayer. The reason for this is that the new lectionary (chapter two explores this in more detail) uses the psalm as a response to the first (normally Old Testament) reading, so it is important that it follow the reading

5. See *Book of Common Prayer* p. 162.

to which it responds. In the lectionary used for a second or third service, this is not the case, and there are only two readings, rather then the three here. Some may feel that three readings are too many for a morning service (and of course there are other forms like the *Service of the Word* which do not have as many), but, if we are to take seriously the public reading of the whole counsel of God in the scriptures, then it is important not to reduce this, but rather to do it well, with readers carefully chosen and trained to convey the meaning of the passage.

c) *The Psalms*. Another small change which should be noticed, especially by those who are used to the 1926 *Book of Common Prayer*, is that there are no longer 'day' numbers given in the psalter. These, of course, conveyed which particular psalms should be sung on which days. I even remember one or two old hymn boards which had at the top of them 'Day 24' or whatever. From that information, the congregation could look up the psalms. In Cranmer's pattern, the whole psalter was gone through every month. The singing of a large number of psalms was a very important part of the monastic liturgical tradition. Many monastic communities went through the whole psalter each week. St Benedict had strong views on the matter:

> For monks give a very feeble proof of their devotedness in the service of God, if they chant less than the Psalter with its customary canticles in the course of a week, whenwe read how our holy fathers strenuously accomplished in one day what I hope the lukewarm monks manage to achieve in a whole week' *Rule of St Benedict*, Chapter 18.

That way of using the psalms as the heart of daily worship was seen by some as being like chewing the cud. The more we read them, the more we get from them and they become part of our very sustenance. Some will miss the fuller provision for the use of the psalms, and may well feel that the diet in our new worship services is less adequate. The Sunday psalms are no longer used in a *lectio continua*[6] kind of way, but are chosen to relate to

---

6. Essentially, where one reading or psalm follows on in order from the last one, so continuously reading the scriptures. This is the basic lectionary tradition of Anglicanism.

the readings. However, you will find that, in the daily lectionary[7] there is a good deal of use of the psalms in order.

d) Readings after the Psalm. At Morning Prayer this will be reading two and the gospel reading. In the evening both readings
will come into this category. Order *Two* suggests in the simplest
possible way how readings might best be introduced:

'A reading from ... chapter ... beginning at verse ...',

and the same suggestion is made in general terms in note 5, p.
75. This is quite adequate. There is no need for complicated introductions but, equally, it is good to give chapter and verse for
anyone who may wish to follow the reading.

No particular instruction is given as to how a reading might
best be ended, other than the simple rubric: 'After the reading
silence may be kept.'

On the question of versions of the bible, note 4 on p. 75 allows
any translation of the scriptures to be used which is 'sanctioned
by the House of Bishops for use in public worship'. (Appendix
1, p. 244)

e) The Second and Third Canticles. At Morning Prayer these are as
follows:

Second Canticle: *Te Deum* (*One,Two* printed in services)
                        Benedicite (*One,* not printed in service)
                        Urbs Fortitudinis (*One,* printed in service)
                        Laudate Dominum (*One,* not printed)
                        Any canticle on pp. 117-135 except
                        Benedictus (*Two*)

Third Canticle: *Benedictus* (*One, Two* printed in services)
                        Jubilate (*One,* printed in service)
                        Any New Testament Canticle on pp. 117-
                        135 (*Two*)

At Evening Prayer these are as follows:

Second Canticle: *Magnificat* (*One, Two* printed in services)

---

7. The daily lectionary in use at the time of writing is one used by the
    Church in Wales and the Scottish Episcopal Church as well as the
    Church of Ireland. The arrangement of psalms is unique to the
    Church of Ireland.

	Cantate Domino (*One*, not printed)
	Any New Testament Canticle on pp. 117-135
Third Canticle	*Nunc Dimittis* (*One, Two* printed in services)
	Deus Misereatur (*One*, not printed)
	Any New Testament Canticle on pp. 117-135

How the canticles came to be in particular positions in the services is clouded in history, but you will find some rationale which comes through:

–   First of all, the major canticles are the three gospel canticles, found in the gospel of Luke. These are The Song of Zechariah (*Benedictus*), The Song of Mary (*Magnificat*), and The Song of Simeon (*Nunc Dimittis*). There is an exposition of each of these in the chapter on canticles. Suffice it for now to note that they all stand at the very hinge of our salvation, both looking back to the revelation of God in the Old Testament, and rejoicing in the fullness of his revelation in Jesus Christ. They are, of course, all intensely personal songs, but that imbues them with a particular power and warmth.

–   There is also a possible use of the 'canticle' slots in Morning Prayer which allows a development of revelation, from the Old Testament first canticle, through the psalm, leading to a New Testament second canticle, summed up in the gospel canticle at the end.

–   Canticles can also be used 'thematically', not least to relate to the time of the Christian Year. For example, the *Benedicite* has often been used at Rogation and Harvest, Saviour of the World in Lent, and The Song of Christ's Glory around Ascension. It can be good to sing canticles, like the Easter Anthems for a 'season'.

My plea would be that we discover the riches which are in the canticles, that we find ways of saying and singing them which bring them to life, and that, through them, the Word of God would be etched in our hearts and on our minds.

f) The Sermon. Because Morning and Evening Prayer were, in their essence, daily services, they had no mention of a sermon in them. The sermon slot was found essentially in the Holy Communion service. Of course, as these offices came to be used as the main Sunday service, we developed the tradition of 'Morning Prayer and Sermon' or 'Evening Prayer and Sermon', where the office ended completely (in some cases the snuffing of the candles on the altar was a sign of how completely it had ended!), the hymn before the sermon was sung, the sermon preached (often with no reference to what had gone before), a hymn after the sermon sung, and a blessing put in to end what had already been ended once with 'The Grace'. Interestingly, this pattern had a profound effect on nonconformist churches, which also in many cases took over the idea that the sermon should always be preached at the end of the service. Order *One* retains this traditional position and, in fact, writes it in to the service, recognising the reality in many churches (and also distinguishing this service from the order in *A Service of the Word* and in the Holy Communion service). However, it allows the sermon to take place whether before or after the occasional prayers. In Order Two, the sermon first appears in the section, 'Proclaiming and Receiving the Word' after the third canticle, and before the Apostles' Creed, giving it a position similar to that in *Holy Communion One.*

The sermon is, of course, a vital part of regular Sunday worship. It is the time for the Word of God to be broken open, and related to the lives of the people. It is important for worshippers not to denigrate preaching, which is after all a key part of God's communication ('How shall they hear without a preacher?'), and it is vital for preachers to give the time for prayer and study which sermons need and to be convinced themselves that God can use preaching to change people's lives.

g) The Apostles' Creed. This is an integral part of Sunday offices in the Anglican tradition. When it comes to daily offices, the creed is given a less prominent position – it may be said in the morning in order *Two* and is not used in the evening. In reality, the

Apostles' Creed was not part of any of the offices of the church until the time of the Reformation. At that stage in history, the teaching of people, who in many cases were biblically untaught, was very high on the agenda in the writing of the *Book of Common Prayer* and in its use. The Apostles' Creed was not, of course, written by the apostles themselves, as some imagine, but is intended, in the simplest possible form, to embody the basic teaching of the Christian faith, as required for baptism. It is essentially a personal 'I' form creed because of its baptismal use and connections. This creed was generally adopted in the Western church around the year 1000.

There are several traditions in relation to the Apostles' Creed which have grown up in some churches:
- The habit of saying it by memory standing upright (hands by your side!) This is, I suppose, intended to point to the firmness with which we believe these essential teachings of the faith.
- The habit of bowing one's head at the name of Jesus. The 18th canon of 1604 gives direction for 'due and lowly reverence' whenever the name of Jesus is uttered, and the canon of 1878 printed in the 1926 *Book of Common Prayer*. The symbol can be a very good one, and possibly arises because of the controversies in the early history of the Church over the nature of Jesus. It can be a simple sign of commitment to him.
- The habit of turning eastwards to say the creed. This is a habit which developed during the heyday of Victorian anglo-catholicism. It uses the symbolic 'frame' of the Victorian church, with the east window and the altar at the east end, symbolising the presence of God, and the west end of the church symbolising the darkness which we are rescued from, as we enter the church through baptism.

The Prayers of the People
After the initial greeting, the prayers are divided up into several different types of prayer:

a) The Lesser Litany or the Kyries:

> Lord, have mercy (upon us)
>
> Christ, have mercy (upon us)
>
> Lord, have mercy (upon us)

In a sense, this is where all prayer starts. It uses the biblical words found in so many places (eg *Psalm 123:3*), and at the heart of the prayer of the publican, as opposed to the prayer of the Pharisee *(Luke 18:9-14)*. In this form it is used in a trinitarian way, the 'Lord' in the first line referring to the Father, the 'Christ' in the second line referring to the Son, and the 'Lord' in the third line referring to the Spirit.

b)The Lord's Prayer. In order *One*, without the doxology; in order *Two*, with the doxology, as it is the only place the Lord's Prayer occurs in the order. This, of course, is the model for all prayer given to us by Jesus Christ himself, in response to the request of the disciples 'Lord, teach us to pray.' The Lord's Prayer appears in two versions in the 2004 *Book of Common Prayer*. Version 1 begins 'Our Father, who art in heaven', and is a slightly amended form of the version in the 1926 *Book of Common Prayer*, using 'who' instead of 'which' in line 1, and 'those who', instead of 'them that' in line 8. It is, in fact, the way the vast majority of people say the Lord's Prayer. Version 2 is the one which begins 'Our Father in heaven', which is essentially the version arrived at by the *English Language Liturgical Consultation*,[8] except for the line, 'And lead us not into temptation', which in the *ELLC* form is 'Save us from the time of trial'. In reality, this line is notoriously difficult to translate, but the General Synod of the Church of Ireland in 2004 decided that they preferred 'temptation' to 'time of trial' and, in line with the Church of England, have kept to the version in the former alternative services. The Lord's Prayer sets the scene for our other intercessions beginning with:

c) Versicles and Responses. The roots of most of these are in the Sarum Brievary[9] They are taken from the following texts: *Psalm*

---

8. Further details of the *English Language Liturgical Consultation* (ELLC) may be found in chapter 4 on the canticles.

9. In the pre-Reformation church there were several 'books' used for

85:7; 1 Samuel 10:24; Psalm 20:9; Psalm 132:9; Psalm 28:9; Psalm 51:10, 11. The themes in them corresponded to the themes of the prayers which followed in the Prayer for the King, the Prayer for the Clergy and People, the Collect for Peace and the Collect for Grace. In *Morning and Evening Prayer Two* they are not a mandatory part of the service. From time to time they are used as a framework for the whole time of prayer, with the leader praying for the different areas, and concluding each section with the versicle and response. They are a symbol of the fact that, even in our prayer, we are totally biblical.

d) The Collects. There are three in order *One*, beginning with the Collect of the Day, and at least two in order *Two*, again beginning with the Collect of the Day. The whole question of what type of prayer a collect is, and how most collects are formed, will be dealt with in chapter nine. For now, we might notice one subtle but important distinction: the difference between a 'Collect of' and a 'Collect for'.

A 'Collect *of*' relates to the particular occasion on which the collect is used. For example, you have the 'Collect *of* the Conversion of St Paul'. In other words we are not praying for St Paul to be converted. That has already happened! Or you have the 'Collect of the Second Sunday of Easter', etc. But, you have the 'Collect *for* purity ... or grace ... or aid against perils' etc., where the intention of the prayer is the subject of the title. It is worth noting at this point that many collects can simply pass us by in worship because, so often, they are praying about the kinds of things which we would forget to pray about, and indeed, so often they are saturated in the prayer-themes of scripture and especially of St Paul. We would do well to memorise some of the collects, and allow ourselves to make them our own. If we do so, we will find our prayer life deepened by them.

worship. The breviary was one of these, and was the book in which the daily offices were provided. There were also several 'uses' which varied from place to place, and the Sarum one had its roots in Salisbury (for which Sarum is the latin name), but was used much more widely. Another 'use' was that of our own Bangor.

e) Occasional Prayers. These are, as the title implies, the prayers we are using on this particular occasion. They will engage with the needs of the world, the church, people around us, and indeed, ourselves. Some possible prayers are given in the book at the end of *Morning and Evening Prayer One* and a whole variety of ways of praying are available to us at this point in the service:

– Sometimes, the worship leader will lead us in a bidding, silence, set prayer model. 'Let us pray for ...' with a time to focus and perhaps one of the prayers from pp. 145-153.

– Sometimes the Litany, to be found on p. 170 (*One*) or p. 175 (*Two*), may be used, though generally when it is some of the earlier parts of this section will be left out, as the Litany is a very full form of prayer, with responses. It was, in fact, the first service to be translated into English in 1544.

– Sometimes the congregation will be invited to join in prayers, such as the most beautiful and memorable General Thanksgiving, which can be found on p. 99. This prayer is so etched in the minds of many Anglicans that it has only been included in a traditional language version. There was a more contemporary version in the *Alternative Prayer Book,* but it never really gained popularity.

– Sometimes, when the service takes place mid-week, the *Weekday Intercessions and Thanksgivings* will be used (pp. 139-144).

– Sometimes a person or a group of people will lead the prayers in their own words. A Taizé chant, or some other prayer chant, may be used as a response.

– Sometimes, a time of open prayer will take place, where any person may lead prayer in their own words.

f) Concluding Prayers. The rubric in *Morning and Evening Prayer One* says: 'The prayers always conclude with The Prayer of St Chrysostom and The Grace.' In actual fact, the Prayer of St Chrysostom is often not used, but is a most beautiful prayer and summation of all our intercessions. It roots our praying in God's promises, depends totally on his supreme knowledge of what is best for us, and holds together both this life and the next. As with so many of these prayers, you can see exactly why this one has been remembered, and realise that we would never think up such words in extempore prayer.[10]

The rubric in order *Two* is simpler, and states: Prayers and thanksgivings, or a litany, may be said.

Going out as God's People
How to end Morning or Evening Prayer is one of the great conundrums. In the 1662 *Book of Common Prayer*, the Grace was the end of Morning and Evening Prayer. The rubric comes after it, for example, in Evening Prayer:

Here endeth the Order of Evening Prayer throughout the Year.

What has happened is that we have stuck another bit on, with the sermon being added, and have not realised that the ending should be at the real end of the whole service. So, at least in order *Two*, the Grace, if it is used, should be part of the Going Out, and should not be used as a neat ending to the prayers section of the service, only to be followed later by another 'ending' to the service. Several possible endings are given, and these may be replaced with an appropriate blessing. This means that, where there is something else put in between the prayers and the 'Going out as God's People' section, the Grace should come at the end of the service, but not at the end of the prayers.

In reality, of course, all sorts of things come in at this point: the collection, a recessional[11] hymn, a dismissal etc. Sometimes the danger is of too complex an ending. The key thing, however,

---

10. 'Extempore' prayer is prayer made up by the person praying in their own words at the time, or on the hoof!
11. Some have questioned whether the word 'recessional' does not have a rather odd ring to it, and whether the exit of the choir and clergy is actually a procession out! 'Recessional' hymns are amazingly popular, as they allow a congregation to finish on a high, and enable the choir to get out in the least intrusive way, but placing them after the Ending is not liturgically pure. Perhaps the choir and everyone other than the presiding minister should process down the aisle, then turn to the front at the end of the hymn, at which point the minister could end the service, with everyone standing.

is that we are going out to serve God in the world, so that our worship is not just going to be a 'trampling of God's courts' (Isaiah 1:12b), but, as the back of one Church notice-board put it to worshippers emerging from church: 'The worship is over; the service begins'!

Questions for reflection and discussion

1. What is special for you about the service of Morning or Evening Prayer?

2. Do you find it helpful for the worship at a particular time each Sunday to be the same service, or do you prefer a variety of styles of worship? Why?

3. Do you think Morning and Evening Prayer are effective or not in storing the memory with scripture? You may like to go through the whole of one of the services and ask: 'Which parts are directly from the bible?'

4. What adaptations could be made to these services to bring them more to life?

5. Morning and Evening Prayer were originally daily 'offices', and not intended as the main worship of a Sunday. Do they work well in that role? Are there enough differences morning and evening to encourage people to be 'twicers' on a Sunday?

CHAPTER FOUR

The Canticles

The Book of Common Prayer provides us with a range of twenty canticles, eight of which are in both contemporary and traditional forms (Please note that the order of these in the Canticles section is different from the order in the rest of the book, i.e. the contemporary version comes first, and the traditional language second). There are also eight canticles which are provided only in contemporary language:

Great and Wonderful
Saviour of the World
Bless the Lord
Glory and Honour
The Song of Christ's Glory
The Song of Isaiah
The Song of Wisdom
Ecce Nunc (Psalm 134)

And four canticles only in traditional language:

Urbs Fortitudinis
Cantate Domino (also found in more modern form as *Psalm 98*)
Deus Misereatur (also found in more modern form as *Psalm 67*)
A Song of the Light.

This is the largest selection of canticles there has been in any Church of Ireland prayer book, but it is in fact small in comparison to the new Church of England *Common Worship*, and many other prayer books in the Anglican Communion. The reason for having a focused list of canticles is, quite simply, memorability: the more canticles there are, the more difficult they are to remember. The Liturgical Advisory Committee felt it was wise to keep them to a basic minimum, while allowing for adequate variety.

In this chapter, we will look in some detail at the different canticles individuallly, and at the message conveyed by each one. We will note the source of the canticle, review the versions used in the *Book of Common Prayer*, and explore where other versions, if they are available, are to be found.

Before we begin, you may have noticed that certain canticles are ended by using the doxology which we usually call the *Gloria Patri*, while others are not. This doxology is used in *Venite*, *Jubilate*, Easter Anthems, *Benedictus*, *Benedicite* (traditional version), *Magnificat*, *Nunc Dimittis*, *Urbs Fortitudinis*, The Song of Isaiah, The Song of Wisdom, *Ecce Nunc*, *Cantate Domino*, and *Deus Misereatur*. It is not used in *Benedicite* (contemporary version), *Te Deum*, Great and Wonderful, Saviour of the World, Bless the Lord, Glory and Honour, The Song of Christ's Glory and A Song of the Light. People try to find a logic in this, which can be difficult. We can reasonably say that canticles which have been composed after the full revelation of Jesus Christ do not generally have a trinitarian doxology. This list includes those canticles which come from the epistles, the Book of *Revelation* and the life of the church since the canon of holy scripture has been completed. The only exception is *Benedicite* and Bless the Lord, which although they are from the Apocrypha, have had another trinitarian blessing added.

Canticle 1: *Venite* Frost[1] / *APB*
Canticle 2: *Venite* 1926 *BCP* version
Other versions:
CH[2] 687: Come, let us praise the Lord
CH 689: Come, sing praises to the Lord above
CH 690: Come, worship God who is worthy of honour

The *Venite* is surely one of the keynotes of Anglican morning worship. It has everything required at this point in the service, and says what needs to be said better than any other psalm. It

---

1. The version of the *Venite* here is basically the version in *APB 1984*, with one word change, which comes from the *Liturgical Psalter* (1977), David L. Frost *et al.*
2. CH in this chapter, is an abbreviation for *Church Hymnal fifth edition.*

begins by the congregation calling each other to the worship of
God, which is after all one of our chief tasks when we come together corporately. Otherwise we could do it on our own. But
here, the gathered people of God incite each other to 'man's *(sic)*
chief end'[3] – that is, to worship God and enjoy him for ever. On a
Sunday the *Venite*, when used, should be sung rather than said,
and should be sung in whatever version allows the congregation
to enter into it with gusto. The second part of the first verse sets
the mood:

'let us shout in triumph to the rock of our salvation' *One*

'let us heartily rejoice in the strength of our salvation' *Two*

Here there is no drawing back from worship, no whispering our
singing, no half-heartedness or uncertainty, but rather an entering in with everything we are and have to the praise of God.
This is continued in the thanksgiving of verse 2, with its joy and
gladness in God's presence.

The next part of the psalm (vv. 3-5) is a reminder that we
worship God because of who he is. It is not that we don't already
know all these things, but rather that we constantly need to be
reminded of them. He is the 'king above all gods'; he's got the
whole world in his hands; he made the heights, the depths, the
sea and the land. Everything is his creation, and he deserves our
praise as the only true God.

At this point, the organist often (and rightly) softens the tone
of the music:

Come let us worship and bow down:

and kneel before the Lord our maker.

In the light of the greatness of the Creator, we see our role as the
creatures, which is at the very heart of the meaning of worship:
we bow down[4] and kneel before our God. In other words, we respond with our bodies, which show physically what is in our
hearts. Perhaps that is why St Paul in *Romans 12* put it like this:

3. The famous first question and answer from the *Westminster Shorter
   Catechism.*
4. One of the key Greek words for worship in the New Testament is
   proskuneo – to bow down.

> I appeal to you ... to present your bodies as a living sacrifice
> ... which is your spiritual worship.

It is sad when the physical body and its role in worship is forgotten, and it is certainly not how God intended it to be for his creatures. We are to worship with all our being in the presence of the greatness and holiness of God. But v. 7 reminds us of something more: it is not just that we are the creatures of the Creator – it is that we are also his chosen people, and (in the warmest of terms) 'the sheep of his pasture'. He is not just 'God'. But he is our personal God, 'the Lord *our* God'.

Just as this psalm has brought us to the heights, so it also plunges us into the depths. That is part of the art of this particular composition, and it is sad to see the last verses left out on a regular basis, as happens in some churches, because they actually have the effect of turning our attention to the Word of God, which is exactly what we are about to engage with at this point in the liturgy. Verses 8 and 9 are a reminder:

a) to hear God's word and listen to what it says into our lives,

b) not to harden our hearts,

c) not to test or provoke God.

The writer to the Hebrews also sees the vital importance of this psalm, and expounds this part of it in *Hebrews 3* (Remember, so often scripture explains scripture). He is reminding the Church that they are not to sin as the children of Israel did at Meribah and Masseh (see version of *Psalm 95* on p. 702). Having quoted these last verses, he charges them:

> Take care, brothers and sisters, lest there be in any of you an evil, unbelieving heart, leading you to fall away from the living God. But exhort each other every day, as long as it is called 'today' that none of you may be hardened by the deceitfulness of sin. *Hebrews 3:12-13*

and the last two verses are, of course, a reminder of the seriousness of sin, and the judgement of God, who did not allow that generation to enjoy the fullness of his promises in the promised land. How sad it would be if any church or person failed to fully enter into what God has prepared for those who love him.

Canticle 3: *Jubilate* Frost / *APB* version
Canticle 4: *Jubilate* 1926 *BCP* version.
Other versions:
CH 683: All people that on earth do dwell
CH 701: Jubilate, everybody!

The *Jubilate, Psalm 100*, is actually most famous in its metrical version: 'All people that on earth do dwell', especially since the Coronation of Queen Elizabeth II and the specially written arrangement by Ralph Vaughan Williams. Although this psalm came before the lesson in the office of Lauds,[5] Cranmer, for some reason or other, placed it at the end of the readings. So, in *Morning Prayer One*, we find it as the climax of praise, alternative to the *Benedictus*, whereas in *Morning Prayer Two*, it stirs up our praise at the beginning. Actually, there is good reason for both positions. In the psalter, it is the climax of a series of homage-psalms. Derek Kidner says in his commentary on the psalms,[6] speaking about the Jubilate:

'A song of thankful praise brings this group of homage-psalms to an unclouded summit after their alternations of exuberance and awe.'

So the position in order *One* is the summit of praise, as the whole world joins with the people of God in worship, while the position in order *Two* uses *Psalm 100* in the same way as the *Venite*, to incite and invite all to the praise of their maker.

The essential structure of the *Jubilate* is not actually very different from the structure of the first part of the *Venite*. It begins with the same kinds of words: 'triumph', 'gladness', 'joy', but this time the whole earth is invited to join in the act of praise. This is a very common theme in the psalms, and one which we can easily forget – that the whole of creation is God's, and indeed, part of his final redemptive plan, and the whole of creation owes praise to God its maker.

The next verses are a reminder of the reality of God, 'the Lord he is God', and in the older version, of the fact that we are not

---

5. The second of the morning monastic offices, after Mattins.
6. *Psalms 73-150* (1973) Derek Kidner, IVP.

our own creators: 'it is he that hath made us and not we ourselves ...', and it again employs the image of sheep for the people of God.

Verse 3 has the people of God entering into the courts of the
Temple: the place of God's close presence, with thanksgiving
and praise on their lips. Of course, nowadays, and even then,
God does not dwell in buildings made with human hands, but
the Temple was in a very special way the place where the people
of God met with the living Lord, and knew their sins forgiven,
and we surely have reason to pray that our churches will be the
same: that they will be so filled with thanksgiving and worship
that they will be places of special meeting with the living God.

In the last verse, the psalmist again gives good reasons for
praising God:

For the Lord is good,

his loving mercy is for ever.

His faithfulness (truth) throughout all generations.

These go beyond the simple facts of the wonder of creation, into
the very nature of God. On one level, they are qualities of God
which all of us know well, but on another, they are the very basis
of a relationship of trust in him. God is good, and therefore there
is no evil in him. His will for us and for our lives is only good.
God is love *(1 John 4:8);* God is merciful, which is the very basis
on which we dare to come to him as sinners, with the prayer
'Lord, have mercy' on our lips; and God is faithful and true. This
is a God who deserves our praise because of his qualities and
character.

Canticle 5: The Easter Anthems *APB* version
Canticle 6: The Easter Anthems 1926 *BCP* version
Other versions: CH 703: Now lives the Lamb of God

The roots of the Easter Anthems, in the reformed tradition, go
back to the 1549 *Book of Common Prayer.* There, in the provisions
for Easter Day, the book prescribes a short devotion to be used
before Mattins. It consists of *Romans 6:9-11,* with two Alleluias, *1
Corinthians 15:20-22,* with one Alleluia, a versicle, a response and

a collect. In 1552, the versicle, the response and the collect were deleted, and the two anthems were to be used instead of the *Venite* on Easter Day. In 1662, *1 Corinthians 5:7-8* were added at the beginning and the *Gloria Patri* at the end.

What we have ended up with is a memorable and balanced synopsis of the truth of the resurrection from the writings of St Paul, with the following themes:

a) *The Passover.* Of course, Easter, for the Christian, is the time when we enter into Paschal mystery. It is the Passover fulfilled. It happens at the time of the Passover, and uses the story of the deliverance of the people of Israel from bondage to freedom as a 'type'[7] of the deliverance of all who are in Christ, from death to life. Many of the oldest Christian hymns make a great deal of this interplay between the resurrection and the Passover,[8] and the traditional readings used in the Easter vigil are focused on this as well. So, at the very beginning of the Easter Anthems, we are drawn into the theology of Christ as our Passover, the lamb sacrificed for our freedom and covering. The other thing about the Passover is that it was one of the main festivals, as it still is, in the life of Jewish people. The writings of Paul sometimes see the keeping of festivals as a question of taste,[9] but here, in no uncertain terms he says: 'Therefore let us keep the feast.'

b) *Opposites:* Much of the rest of the Easter Anthems set up a series of comparisions: comparisons between the life of Christ and the life of the world; between death and life; between the work of the old Adam (who brought death for all) and the new Adam, Jesus Christ (who brings life for all).

7. A 'type' in this sense is an event before the coming of Jesus and the full revelation of God's salvation, which points towards and in a sense foreshadows the reality which is later disclosed.

8. For example, *At the Lamb's high feast we sing,* CH254, and *Come ye faithful, raise the strain,* CH 262. These are wonderful hymns of theological depth, from the 7th and 8th centuries.

9. E.g. *Romans 14:5:* 'Again, some make a distinction between this day and that; others regard all days alike. Everyone must act on his own convictions.' *Revised English Bible.*

c) *Christ the Firstfruits:* In other words, the resurrection of Jesus Christ is not only the most amazing miracle in the world, it is also the guarantee that we who are in Christ will also be raised with him at the last day. Easter is not just an actual event at a particular time in history – it is the foretaste of the resurrection of all the people of God. And that begins now as we reckon ourselves to be 'dead indeed unto sin, and alive unto God through Jesus Christ our Lord'.

Canticle 7: *Benedictus ELLC* version
Canticle 8: *Benedictus* 1926 *BCP* version
Other versions:
CH 685: Blessed be the God of Israel
CH 707: O bless the God of Israel

The *Benedictus* is one of the three gospel canticles, which gives it a special place of importance as a revelation of the very core of the story of salvation. In the Western medieval brievary it was the canticle after the gospel lesson at Lauds, and it retains that essential place in both our orders for Morning Prayer. However, at the time of the Reformation, the whole question of the appropriateness of publicly using these gospel canticles, which are in Luke's gospel essentially personal songs and prayers, was a very vexed one indeed. It was the strong feelings of some of the continental reformers against such a use of these songs which led to Cranmer in the 1552 *Book of Common Prayer* offering the alternatives of the *Jubilate*, the *Cantate Domino* and the *Deus Misereatur*, all of which are psalms.

The *Benedictus* is, of course the song sung by Zechariah, the father of John the Baptist, in *Luke 1:68-79*, after the birth of John, the forerunner of the Messiah. The first six verses speak of the coming redemption of Israel as an accomplished fact, in a prophetic way. Of course, this means that these words are perfect for us to sing, who have seen God's redemption in Jesus Christ, and who stand on the other side of the cross. We can rehearse with joy the story of the freedom brought about by Christ, the saving power of the Son of David, and the salvation made available to us by the one who fulfils the covenant of God. One of the beauties of the *Benedictus* is that, although it could be considered to have particular meaning and relevance in the season of Advent – as it is a canticle written in the period when Zechariah is awaiting the revealing of the coming Messiah – nevertheless its themes are so central to the gospel that it can be sung at any time of the Christian year. In some churches, the *Benedictus* is sung each day, as the one canticle which does not change, and is sung at the end of the readings, as the climactic canticle, revealing the good news most fully.

Interestingly, the *Alternative Prayer Book*, in line with the thinking of the time, placed the *Benedictus* between the readings, with the post-biblical canticles after the New Testament reading, thus creating a more-or-less 'time ordered'[10] use of the canticles. But our new prayer book has reverted to seeing the *Benedictus* as the climax of revelation, and the normative canticle for after the gospel reading.

The second part of the canticle speaks specifically of John the Baptist, as though actually speaking to him (which is exactly what Zechariah was doing, seeing the baby before him). It speaks of John's work of preparing the way for the Saviour of the world, and for the peace which will be revealed in Christ.

Canticle 9: *Benedicite APB* version
Canticle 10: *Benedicite* 1926 *BCP* version
Other versions:
CH 682: All created things, Bless the Lord!
CH 711: *Surrexit Christus*

The *Benedicite* is one of those canticles which, in my experience, is rarely sung these days and is ripe for rediscovery. In the days of the 1926 *Book of Common Prayer*, it was often used in place of the *Te Deum* during Lent, or at times like Harvest and Rogation. And it must surely rank as one of the most popular subjects for

---

10. In other words, the ones from the Old Testament and Apocrypha come first, followed by the ones from the gospels and New Testament, followed by the ones which have been written since the completion of the canon of holy scripture.

flower festivals in churches. After all, who could not be inspired by the clarity of the themes of creation expressed by:

Bless the Lord, you sun and moon:
bless the Lord, you stars of heaven.
Bless the Lord, all rain and dew:
sing his praise and exalt him for ever.
Bless the Lord all winds that blow:
bless the Lord you fire and heat:
Bless the Lord scorching wind and bitter cold
Sing his praise and exalt him for ever.

And so it continues. Indeed, it is the very length and repetitiveness of this canticle which makes it distinct and powerful. It is in the style of *Psalm 136*, with the refrain 'for his mercy endures for ever'; and when you get a good refrain you cannot sing it enough! In this case, in former Books of Common Prayer, the refrain was repeated after every half-verse ('praise him and magnify him for ever'). In 1662, it came thirty-two times. In the traditional version here, that is reduced to three, which rather ruins it, in my view. But the modern version has a refrain ('sing his praise and exalt him for ever') twelve times, which seems a fair compromise.

This canticle takes up the theme which we saw in the *Jubilate*, of the whole of creation praising the Lord, and comes to a climax with the whole of humanity praising God, including in the traditional version: 'Ye spirits and souls of the righteous'.

But it is the reference to a book of the Apocrypha and the strange verse in the older version: 'O Ananias, Azarias and Misael, bless ye the Lord', which gives us the clue as to where the song itself comes from. It is from *The Song of the Three 35-65* which is a deuterocanonical book.[11] The revision we have as Canticle 8 without the three names was probably that which owed a good deal to Professor E. C. Ratcliff, who revised the canticle for the 1948 BBC Psalter. 'Israel' became 'People of God', the reference to Ananias, Azarias and Misael was removed, and a doxology written centuries earlier for this canticle was re-

---

11. The Apocryphal books can be found listed in *Article 6* of the Thirty-nine articles.

stored in place of the *Gloria Patri*. These three were the three thrown into the burning fiery furnace in *Daniel 1: 6, 7*, after being taken captive by Nebuchadnezzar and given the Babylonian names Shadrach, Meshach and Abed-Nego, and this song itself was inserted into the story of the Book of *Daniel* at this point in some versions. What a song of praise to be attributed to three young men as they faced death for their faith!

Canticle 11: *Te Deum ELLC* version
Canticle 12: *Te Deum* 1926 BCP version
Other versions:
CH 700: Holy God, we praise your name
CH 696: God, we praise you, God we bless you

The *Te Deum* must surely be the hymn of praise *par excellence* of all time! It is used at major services of celebration, at coronations, at victory celebrations after war, when Popes are elected, and when choirs want to sing the big one!

The song itself was composed in the fourth or fifth century, around the same time as the *Gloria in Excelsis*, which is found at the beginning or end of the Communion Service. The earliest mention of it is in the Rule of Caesarius, Bishop of Arles (470-542), and the earliest text appears in our own seventh century Bangor Antiphonary.[12] The actual hymn ended with the words 'glory everlasting' at the end of part two, and part three is a series of little verses which were probably originally antiphons, and which have come to be appended in their entirety to this hymn. The Episcopal Church in the USA has separated this last section from the canticle and uses it as versicles and responses at Morning Prayer.[13]

The *Te Deum* is a kind of Creed in praise form, and at some stages of liturgical revision the option has sometimes been given to omit the Creed where the *Te Deum* has been used. Part 2 is still

---

12. This is the same antiphonary from which we have received the wonderful communion hymn: *Draw nigh and take the body of the Lord. Church Hymnal, fifth edition,* Hymn 411.
13. See the ECUSA *Book of Common Prayer* 1979, p. 55.

used in this kind of way in *Funeral Services Two*, as an alternative to the Apostles' Creed.

Essentially, Part 1 of the *Te Deum* is a hymn of praise to the Trinity. The whole song begins in Latin with three shouts of praise, such as those which would be given to a ruler or sovereign: 'You we praise, you we acclaim, you we worship.'

The text of the *Te Deum* in the *Alternative Prayer Book* 1984 brought this out well with the translation: 'You are God, we praise you; you are the Lord and we acclaim you; you are the eternal Father, all creation worships you.' However, the 'you' style did not sound as well in English as in Latin, and the new translation, although not bringing out the idea of the three 'shouts', translates the text faithfully, not least in the words, 'we acclaim you as the Lord'.

But it is not just ourselves, or indeed the whole created order, which gives due worship to the Lord: We are also taken up into the worship of heaven, with the song of the angels and the whole company of heaven, in words also found in the *Gloria in Excelsis*, and of course based on *Isaiah 6:3*:

Holy, holy, holy Lord,

God of power and might.

Heaven and earth are full of your glory.

Here, we are brought in to the praise of cherubim and seraphim, apostles, prophets and martyrs. The Church militant and the Church triumphant come together in praise at the throne of God.

Verse 6 (verse 8 in the traditional version) is a clear Trinitarian climax of the section:

Father, of majesty unbounded,

your true and only Son,

and the Holy Spirit, advocate and guide.

Part 2 is clearly focused on God the Son: who Jesus Christ is and what he has done.

He is, first and foremost, as we see him from this side of the gospel story, 'the King of Glory'. He is 'the eternal Son of the Father'. In other words he has always been his Son, and he will always be his Son.

The person of Jesus leads to the work of Jesus. The centre of this section points to the three main aspects of the saving work of Jesus:

a) His incarnation:

> When you took our flesh to set us free,
> you humbly chose the Virgin's womb.

The incarnation of Jesus is through the womb of the Blessed Virgin Mary. It has been difficult to get the best translation of this passage of the *Te Deum* which has the right kind of ring for the ears of twenty-first-century people. The old version, which is more accurate, 'thou didst not abhor the Virgin's womb', is truer to the original text, but we rarely use 'abhor' in this kind of way nowadays.

b) His atonement:

> You overcame the sting of death
> and opened the kingdom of heaven to all believers

points to everything which Jesus has achieved in his death and resurrection, and the results of this for our salvation.

c) His parousia (second coming)

> You are seated at God's right hand in glory:
> we believe that you will come to be our judge

points to the heavenly 'session'[14] of Jesus Christ, who reigns and rules over his creation, and to the day when he will be revealed for all the world to see, and will sit in judgement over all people.

And this section ends with a prayer that all of this will be made real in the lives of the people of God: that we who are bought with the blood of Christ may also be helped by the grace of Christ and brought at the last day to his everlasting glory.

Part 3, which is really a selection of psalm verses *(Ps 28:10; Ps 145:2; Ps 123:3; Ps 56:1,3, or 33:21; Ps 31:1)* brought together, and not part of the original *Te Deum*, draws out this theme of salvation, and what it is to trust in the mercy and upholding of God on a daily basis in our lives, knowing that those who trust in the Lord will never be put to shame.

---

14. i.e 'sitting' or 'seating', in the same way as the word is used for a 'session' in the Presbyterian Church.

Canticle 13: *Magnificat ELLC* version
Canticle 14: *Magnificat 1926 BCP* version
Other versions:
CH 704: Mary sang a song, a song of love
CH 712: Tell out, my soul, the greatness of the Lord

The *Magnificat* or Song of Mary, which comes from *Luke 1:46-55*, was used in the morning offices in the East and in the Gallican churches, but has been sung at evening worship in the West since the sixth century, when St Benedict[15] is said to have assigned it for use at Vespers as the gospel canticle. This hymn, attributed to Mary at the time of her visit to her cousin Elizabeth, has roots in the Song of Hannah *(1 Samuel 2)*. It is actually a mosaic of Old Testament phrases (e.g. *1 Samuel 2:7; 2 Samuel 22:51; Psalms 89:11; 98:3; Job 5:11, 12;19; Isaiah 41:8; Micah 7:20)*. Even the listing of such a variety of bible verses is a reminder of the importance of our minds, like the mind of Mary in Luke's gospel, being stored with scriptures which we can use to pray to God from our hearts. The fact that these are words of scripture for the most part does not in any sense make them less warm and personal, and indeed it is these qualities of the Song of Mary which give it such a resonance with our own lives.

There is something very special about the *Magnificat* in the Anglican tradition. Indeed, it is often the *Magnificat* of all the canticles which modern songwriters go to for inspiration. This canticle has both weakness and strength in the one song, and holds together sentiments which at first may seem like individualistic piety:

For he hath regarded
the lowliness of his handmaiden

with ideas that have been the heart of the most politically revolutionary forms of Christianity:

he hath shewed strength with his arm:
he hath scattered the proud in the imagination of their hearts.
He hath put down the mighty from their seat:
and hath exalted the humble and meek ...

---

15. St Benedict of Nursia (c.480-c.587), founder of monasteries.

The salvation brought to birth through the womb of this humble servant girl is a salvation which will turn all worldly values upside down.

One or two thoughts on the different texts:

a) It is not possible to 'magnify' God in the normal sense of the word as we use it today. God cannot be made bigger! The contemporary version 'proclaims the greatness' is closer, and is not far from the popular metrical version by Timothy Dudley-Smith: 'Tell out, my soul, the greatness of the Lord.'[16]

b) It is clear that Mary herself saw herself as in need of the saving grace of God in the Messiah. She uses that lovely warm-hearted phrase: 'God my Saviour'. Everything done for her was done by God himself, and her own title 'Blessed' is true because God has greatly blessed her. What blessing could be greater than being the mother of the Saviour? This is how she is to be remembered for all generations.

c) As in the *Benedictus,* everything done in and through Mary is in fulfillment of the promise of God to Abraham. Here the Old and New Testaments, which are never to be seen as contrary to one another (*Article 7*, p. 779) are brought together as on a hinge.

Canticle 15: *Nunc Dimittis ELLC* version
Canticle 16: *Nunc Dimittis 1926 BCP* version
Other versions: CH 691: Faithful vigil ended

This is the Song of Simeon, recorded by St Luke in *Luke 2:29-32* as being sung by Simeon after seeing the infant Jesus in the Temple at Candlemas (the Feast of the Purification, celebrated on 2 February, forty days after Christmas). The powerful imagery of this old man holding Jesus in his arms, and seeing in the child before him the fulfillment of the whole purpose of his life, and his salvation, is one which haunts us.

This canticle has been in use in the evening worship of the church for almost sixteen centuries, from the time of the

---

16. I think it is true to say that this basic translation has its roots in the *New English Bible* version of the Song of Mary.

Apostolic Constitutions (VIII.48).[17] By the eighth century it was firmly established as a canticle in Compline. It is also used very often in the funeral offices of the Church of Ireland, as the canticle said or sung while the coffin is being removed from the church for the burial.

Some brief thoughts:

a) 'Lord' in the first line means simply 'master'. Here is a relationship between a master and a servant, made all the more amazing by the fact that the master is a tiny baby of just over a month in age.

b) The modern translation makes the meaning of line 1 clear:

'Now, Lord, you let your servant go in peace.'

It is a statement of fact, not a request, as we can imagine if using the older version.

c) 'Your word has been fulfilled.' This is the theme common to the three gospel canticles. God is faithful to his word and promises and they will always be fulfilled. What more important theme could there be for our biblical response of praise during the Ministry of the Word?

d) The most wonderful theme of this song is the fact that, right from the beginning, Jesus is seen to be the Saviour of the Gentiles as well as the Jews. This salvation is for all people – a light for the nations, but also the salvation of Israel.

Canticle 17: *Great and Wonderful* Basically *RSV* text
Other version: CH697: Great and wonderful your deeds

This canticle is a conflation of two passages from the Book of Revelation. The first three verses are from *Revelation 15:3b-4*, where those who have conquered the beast (the martyrs), with harps in their hands, sing the song of Moses (cf *Exodus 15*) and the Lamb:

Great and wonderful are your deeds, Lord God the Almighty, and the last verse puts together two verses from the shout of people of every nation, tribe and tongue:

---

17. The *Apostolic Constitutions* were eight books on church pastoral and liturgical practice, probably written in the late 4th century, and sometimes attributed to Clement of Rome.

To him who sits on the throne and to the Lamb:
be praise and honour, glory and might
for ever and ever. Amen.

This particular canticle is a reminder (as is also Canticle 21: Glory and Honour) that our worship here is always a preparation for, and in a sense a pale reflection of, the worship of heaven which goes on for all eternity. It is, therefore clearly focused on God himself and on the Lamb, rejoicing in the deeds which God has accomplished, revering the holiness of his person and name, and recognising that he puts all things to right at the end of time.

This canticle originally was known under its Latin name, *Magna et Mirabilia*. It was drafted for a revision of the Roman brieviary,[18] but became popular in these islands and beyond, after its incorporation as the canticle for Saturday morning in the 1968 Daily Office book of the Joint Liturgical Group. At that stage, it was simply the *Revelation 15* passage with the *Gloria Patri*.

The extra verse had already appeared in the 1933 Appendix to the Irish 1926 *Book of Common Prayer*, and was added to *Magna et Mirabilia* for the Series 2 services in England. Verse 4 is also the 'doxology' for Glory and Honour.

All in all, the move to use some of the songs from the Book of Revelation as canticles has been a very good one. This song is a superb paeon of praise, and also introduces worshippers to part of that book which can easily be understood – and indeed memorised.

Canticle 18: *Urbs Fortitudinis*

This canticle, from *Isaiah 26:1-4* and *7, 8* must surely be the 'National Anthem' of the Church of Ireland. One attempt was made to remove it in the course of liturgical revision, but everyone had to admit that this uniquely Church of Ireland song, introduced to the *Book of Common Prayer* in 1926, has proven to have stood the test of time, like the walls in it. The *Urbs*, as it is

---

18. A brieviary is the liturgical book in the Roman Catholic tradition which contains the material for the daily offices.

affectionately called, was probably first popular because it allowed for a shorter alternative to the *Te Deum* and the *Benedicite*, and it came to be used in one other part of the Anglican Communion, influenced by Ireland – the Anglican Church in Canada. Sadly, it does not appear in the 1985 *Book of Alternative Services* of the Anglican Church in Canada, and the Church of Ireland is probably again the only province of the Anglican Communion which uses this canticle.

It is, in my view, a superb canticle, desperately in need of some composer supplying us with a good modern singing version.

At first, the *Urbs Fortitudinis* may appear almost nationalistic. It is almost as though we are transferring God's word to his chosen people, the Jews, to our own present-day 'nation'. The words are very concrete: 'strong city', 'walls and bulwarks', 'open ye the gates'. But it soon becomes clear that this is also a deeply personal meditation:

Thou wilt keep him *(sic)* in perfect peace

whose mind is stayed on thee,

because he trusteth in thee.

This canticle holds together the theme of salvation – God's salvation for his people – with the themes of righteousness and justice and peace and trust. Surely no combination of themes can be more important in the Ireland of today. When they come together, they provide a wonderfully balanced witness to the nature of the God whom we worship, as it is seen in his people.

Canticle 19: *Saviour of the World* Original version
Other version: CH 698: Jesus, Saviour of the world

This canticle has a note appended saying, 'Suitable for use in penitential seasons'. Quite honestly, it would be my choice for Fridays, Holy Week, and Sundays in Lent, but not for Advent, where I think there are better options. This canticle may have the 'feel' of being old, but it is in fact relatively new: in truth, it is Victorian. Of course, it picks up the starting-point of the beautiful prayer:

O Saviour of the world,

who by thy Cross and precious blood hast redeemed us,

save us and help us, we humbly beseech thee, O Lord

but, in itself, is of uncertain origin, probably having been written by a Congregationalist minister, Dr Henry Allon, minister of Union Chapel, Islington in London from 1844. It first appeared in the 1860 *Congregational Hymnal,* which he edited and, as it is not attributed to anyone in that book, is thought to be by Allon himself. This canticle, therefore, is a rare kind of gift from non-conformity to the wider church, in the sense that canticles have not normally been a prominent part of nonconformist tradition.[19] It is possibly unique in being the only canticle which was to be found in most nonconformist hymnals before it was found in our offices. Its introduction, like *Great and Wonderful* came through the Joint Liturgical Group's Daily Office book, which had a warm reception in many nonconformist circles, and introduced little gems like this one.

I think it would not be an exaggeration to say that this relatively new canticle has proved popular and memorable. It develops the 'Saviour of the World' prayer around a series of bible passages, including: *Psalm 80:2; Isaiah 58:6; 63:9; Acts 21:13; 1 Peter 1:18-19 1 John 3:2* and *Revelation 21:5.* So, although it is neither 'early church' or straight from the bible, it is thoroughly scriptural in its content.

Canticle 20: *Bless the Lord*
Other versions:
CH 686: Bless the Lord
CH 688: Come, bless the Lord

This canticle is the part of the *Song of the Three* which comes in the verses just before the *Benedicite* (Canticles 9 and 10). It is in the same style as that canticle, explored earlier in this chapter on pp. 75-77. *Bless the Lord* was introduced in the Church of Ireland

---

19. Though most nonconformist denominational hymnals contain a section of canticles at the back of the book, including the Methodist *Hymns and Psalms,* and the United Reformed Church's *Rejoice and Sing.*

through the *APB*, which in turn found it in the Church of England *ASB*. It is, however, much shorter than the *Benedicite*, and provides, therefore, a much more manageable version for congregations which would not be able to cope with the length of the latter. The two versions of this canticle in *Church Hymnal fifth edition* are both by Irish composers (Donald Davison and Edward Darling). The version by Donald Davison, which was introduced first to the Church of Ireland through *Irish Church Praise*[20] popularised this canticle in some parts of the Church of Ireland.

Canticle 21: *Glory and Honour*
Other version: CH 694: Glory, honour, endless praises

This canticle, like its 'companion' canticle *Great and Wonderful* (Canticle 17), comes from the Book of Revelation, from *Revelation 4:11* and *5: 9, 10, 13b*. This is the song sung by the four living creatures, as the door of heaven is opened in the fourth chapter, after the messages to the seven churches. As it is sung, the twenty-four elders fall before the one who is seated on the throne and worship him. The second part of the canticle takes up the same theme in *Revelation 5*, and moves it on. Now the scroll is opened, and the twenty-four elders:

fell before the Lamb, each holding a harp and golden bowls
full of incense, which are the prayers of the saints,

and they sing a song of the worthiness of Jesus Christ who, by his cross and passion has ransomed us and people out of every part of the world to be given the privilege of serving God as priests with the sacrifice which is our worship.

Again, this canticle is a preparation for the worship of heaven where even members of the Church of Ireland will have to get used to incense![21]

---

20. *Irish Church Praise*, Oxford University Press (1990) was a supplement to the fourth edition of the *Church Hymnal* which prepared the ground for the fifth edition.
21. For those who do not know, incense was specifically banned in the canons of the Church of Ireland at disestablishment, out of concern that the church might be influenced by the ritualistic movement of

Canticle 22: *The Song of Christ's Glory*
Other version: CH 684: All praise to thee

The Song of Christ's Glory is of course that wonderful passage
from *Philippians 2:6-11* about the self-emptying of Jesus Christ.
This song takes us on a journey with Jesus Christ on a down-
ward spiral as he engages in his *kenosis* (self-emptying). The
canticle begins with the eternal Christ in the glory of heaven,
equal with God the Father, and sees him emptying himself, from
a servant-heart, being incarnated, obeying his Father to the end,
and dying the most excruciating and accursed death on the cross
for us. The first half of the canticle all moves in this direction:
lower and lower as he pours himself out for our salvation. But
then a change takes place: the change which makes this a wonderful canticle for Holy Week, and a wonderful canticle for
Ascension or Christ the King. The movement goes in the opposite direction after the key word 'Therefore'. God exalts Jesus,
gives him the name above all names, declares that every knee
will bow at his name, and that the time will come when every
tongue will confess his Lordship. The canticle ends with all the
glory given to God the Father, to whom, of course Jesus points.

Canticle 23: *The Song of Isaiah* NRSV Version
This canticle and the next are not included because they are considered particularly wonderful canticles, or canticles which are
likely to prove popular (though some people may consider both
of these things to be the case). They are included quite simply
because they appear in the *Revised Common Lectionary*, as an alternative to the psalm on certain Sundays. This one appears on
the Third Sunday of Advent Year C, and *The Song of Wisdom*

---

the times. This was true at the time also of crosses and candles at or
around the holy table. The other bans have been lifted, but the ban
on incense remains in Canon 40: *Use of incense forbidden.* No incense
or any substitution therefore or imitation thereof shall at any time
be used in any church or chapel or other place in which the public
services of the Church of Ireland are celebrated. An anglo-catholic
friend of mine often reminds me that there are only two smells in
eternity: sulphur and incense, and the latter is the one to get used to!

appears at Proper 19 Year B. There was obviously no point in being told that a particular canticle was appropriate on a certain occasion, and not having it available in the book!

Having said all of that, this is a good song to sing! It is a song about the salvation of God, a bit like that other canticle from *Isaiah*, the *Urbs*. R. E. Clements, in his commentary on *Isaiah 1-39*,[22] says:

These verses ... form a Song of Thanksgiving which has its closest counterpart in Psalmody,

and Alec Motyer points out[23] that this song, with its resonances of the story of the crossing of the Red Sea in *Exodus 15:1*, declares that

just as the old exodus occasioned individual and communal song, so will the coming exodus.

I have just heard a wonderful musical version of this new canticle, composed by Alison Cadden,[24] and hope and trust that it might be a song we will sing on more than that one occasion in three years when it appears in the lectionary. It is a proclamation of the wonder of God's deeds and of his involvement with his people, as God carries out his plan of salvation in his world.

Canticle 24: *The Song of Wisdom* NRSV Version

This is another of those canticles from the Apocrypha, and the material on *The Song of Wisdom* needs to be read in the light of Canticle 23. This is one of those songs about wisdom which personifies 'her', and declares the wonder of her qualities. She, for example, 'can do all things'; she 'makes all things new'; she is 'more beautiful than the sun', against her 'no evil can prevail'. Of course all her qualities are the qualities of God.

This canticle, although it in no way oversteps the mark, is a reminder to us of the issue of when we call God 'he', and

---

22. *Isaiah 1-39*, The New Bible Commentary, (1980) R. E. Clements, Eerdmans/Marshall Morgan and Scott.
23. *The Prophecy of Isaiah* (1993) Alec Motyer, IVP.
24. Alison Cadden, organist in Gilford Parish Church, has been composing a good deal of music for use with the *Book of Common Prayer*, and is hoping to publish it soon.

whether or not it is ever possible to describe God as 'she'. The 'mother hen' image has been used of Jesus in a canticle, but not one which found its way into the Church of Ireland,[25] and of course there is a passage in *Isaiah* which reminds us that God, better than an earthly mother in caring for children, will never forget us or cease to care for us.[26]

Canticle 25: *Ecce Nunc*
Other versions:
CH 718: O praise the Lord
CH 719: Praise the Lord, all you servants of the Lord

This canticle has been popularised over the past years by two things: its presence in *A Late Evening Office*, and the well-known version by the singer and composer Ian White, (Hymn 719 – the last hymn in the book) which is the only item by him in the *Church Hymnal fifth edition*. It is a psalm made memorable by its very brevity and clear obvious meaning. The *Ecce Nunc* is a kind of play on two different kinds of blessing – the blessing which we perform towards God, and the blessing which he gives to us. It is like the *Venite* and *Jubilate*, in that it is sung to each other, rather than directly to God, beginning with that incitement to praise:

Come, bless the Lord, all you servants of the Lord.

The next half verse describes who these people are: they are those who stand in the courts of the Lord at night.

The psalm continues with that beautiful way of blessing God, so usual in some cultures, and difficult for many in ours:

Lift up your hands towards the holy place.

Why is it, I so often wonder that so often, those who espouse kneeling cannot bring themselves to raise their hands in blessing to God, and *vice versa*, when both are biblical uses of our bodies in worship?

---

25. The canticle alluded to can be found in 'A Service for Mothering Sunday', *New Patterns for Worship* (2002), Church House Publishing, pp. 419-420. It is called 'A Song of St Anselm'.
26. The passage referred to is *Isaiah 49:15*.

Then this short song ends with the Lord, as it were, extending hands in blessing over us, as the Lord of heaven and earth makes himself present in the place set aside for him.

Canticle 26: *Cantate Domino* 1926 *BCP* version
Other version: Sing to God new songs of worship

The *Cantate Domino*, along with its accompanying canticle *Deus Misereatur* (Canticle 27) was well known to people who grew up on the 1926 *Book of Common Prayer*. These two were, of course, alternatives to the *Magnificat* and the *Nunc Dimittis* at Evening Prayer. The *Cantate Domino* is *Psalm 98,* and like so many other psalms, is a declaration of the marvellous things God has done for his people, and the power with which he has won the victory for us. This might and power is declared not only to those who believe, but also to the 'heathen'. God is not only the God of Israel in some domestic kind of way, but his salvation is to be seen to the ends of the world, and his judgement of the world will be righteous and true. Again, the whole of creation is brought into the praise of God:

Let the sea make a noise and all that therein is,

the round world and they that dwell therein,

let the floods clap their hands

and let the hills be joyful together before the Lord.

This canticle is a reminder that so often our God is too small, closed in to our churches, while the true God has a world vision, and indeed a vision for the whole of creation, which he is fulfilling.

The *Cantate Domino*, although it appears here only in a traditional version, can also be found in the psalter at the back of the book.

Canticle 27: *Deus Misereatur* 1926 *BCP* version
Other version: CH 695: God of mercy, God of grace

This 'twin' to Canticle 26, is actually, in many ways very like the former canticle. Why Cranmer placed these two beside each other as alternates to the main canticles in Evening Prayer, I am not sure. They are very alike in theme, though this one is sung directly to God. It is a plea for the mercy of God, for his 'saving health' to be seen in all nations, for his righteous judgement, and for his governance of the world. When all of that is in place:

> then shall the earth bring forth her increase,
> and God, even our own God shall give us his blessing.
> God shall bless us,
> And all the ends of he world shall fear him.

Canticle 28: A Song of the Light
Other versions:
CH 699: Hail, gladdening light (same as version here)
CH 702: Light of the world
CH 707: O gladsome light.

Something has been said about this canticle in Evening Prayer, where it was originally used at the lighting of the lamps, and its Latin name was the *Phos hilaron* (the latter being the root of the word 'hilarity' – not often an emotion associated with Evensong!).

The version we have here, popularised by its use in the hymnal, is a translation by John Keble, normally sung to the very fine tune *Sebaste* by John Stainer. It is s Trinitarian canticle, though focused mostly on the first two persons of the Trinity, which is theologically sound, as the Holy Spirit is there to draw us to Jesus, and does not draw attention to himself. It is a song set in a holy place, but recognising Jesus as the 'holiest of holies'. It is a song recognising this particular evening time of worship, 'the sun's hour of rest', but being pointed to the God who is worthy 'at all times to be sung'.

Other Canticles:

There are at least two other canticles which appear in the *Book of Common Prayer*, but not in this list, and for the sake of completeness, we will note the other versions of them which appear in *Church Hymnal fifth edition*. They are: *Laudate Dominum* (p. 91), which can be found in two versions: CH 708 O praise ye the Lord; and CH 709 Praise the Lord, ye heavens adore him; and *Gloria in Excelsis* (in each Communion Service), which can also be found in two versions: CH692 Glory to God in highest heav'n and CH693 Glory in the highest!

Questions for Reflection and Discussion

1. Why do you think it is important to sing the actual words of the bible? Do you think it is appropriate to use the personal songs of Mary and others as our songs of worship?

2. What do the canticles have to offer which is different from singing other hymns or songs?

3. Which of the canticles is your particular 'favourite' and why?

4. What ways have you found to sing canticles or bible songs in your church other than chanting? Which work effectively, and which do not?

5. You may individually, or with a group of others, wish to meditate on one canticle and seek to get into what it means and says into our lives today.

CHAPTER FIVE

Weekday Prayers

After the canticles, the *Book of Common Prayer* devotes almost thirty pages to other forms of prayer, and indeed offers us prayers and thanksgivings themselves, which can be used as part of the regular Christian's pattern of daily devotion. Before we explore them, it is important to point out the the Church of England is in the process of developing a fully worked-out book for daily prayer,[1] based somewhat on the popularity of *Celebrating Common Prayer*,[2] which is based in turn on the Daily Office book of the Society of St Francis.[3] The popularity of these kinds of books for the daily office in the last two decades or so has been surprising, and has pointed up the fact that many people who do use daily offices wish to have a more varied diet, based to some degree on the days of the week and the seasons of the year. There is a great deal of work needed to prepare books such as these, and it is not the intention of the Church of Ireland to repeat such work, but rather it is our hope that material such as this might be recommended for use by the bishops.

The material for daily prayer in the *Book of Common Prayer* is intended for a whole variety of uses and seeks therefore to be adaptable to different needs. In a sense the daily offices always straddle the ground between private and public prayer. When

---

1. Available at the time of writing in the form *Common Worship Daily Prayer Preliminary Edition* (2002) Church House Publishing. This is the first liturgical book I have seen which has a Questionnaire at the end, inviting readers to comment on the range of the content, the layout and anything else they wish. The book will then be revised in the light of these and other comments.
2. *Celebrating Common Prayer* (1992) Mowbray.
3. Published in 1981 for private circulation within the SSF.

they are used by individuals on their own, those individuals are nevertheless praying as part of the wider church which is also reading these readings, saying these psalms, and uttering the same core prayers on this occasion. Equally, when they are said publicly (if my experience is anything to go by), there will some-times be other people there making the event corporate, but on other occasions, the pray-er will be on their own, and may well have a sense of a priestly vocation to pray on behalf of others who cannot be present, or indeed who choose not to be present. For those unused to daily offices, there may be a sense of unreal-ity about someone saying:

O Lord, open our lips

and responding to themselves:

And our mouth will proclaim your praise.

But it becomes quite 'normal' with use and is again a reminder that this is the prayer of the church, and not just of myself indi-vidually.

Many years ago, I co-wrote a booklet called *Whose Office? Daily Prayer for the People of God* [4] in which a case was argued for doing everything in our power to restore the use of the daily of-fice to the whole body of Christians, and to rescue it from the idea that this was just for clergy or monks! And it is precisely something of that restoration which we are seeing in our time, and not least in some of the patterns suggested in the new *Book of Common Prayer*. Ordinary members of the church are crying out for something with more depth, consistency and structure than the usual 'quiet time'.

Daily Prayer: Weekdays

This section of the prayer book begins with a structure for daily prayer on weekdays, morning and evening. It simplifies the larger rites of Morning and Evening Prayer, and the following are the principles on which it is based:

a) The rites are complementary morning and evening, so that

---

4. *Whose Office? Daily Prayer for the People of God* (1982), David Cutts and Harold Miller, Grove Liturgical Study 32, Grove Books.

the penitence section is used once a day and the Apostles' Creed may be used in the mornings but is not recommended in the evening.

b) There is a different canticle for each day, morning and evening on a Monday to Saturday basis

c) There is a gospel canticle said every day, which is the traditional central canticle, i.e. *Benedictus* in the morning and *Magnificat* in the evening.

d) The Collect of the Day and Lord's Prayer, rather than starting the prayer section, conclude it. This has been my own pattern for some time, with the sense that, in the words of the introduction sometimes used to the Lord's Prayer, we are 'gathering all our prayers and praises into one', as we 'pray as our Saviour taught us'.

e) Obviously the structure is one which enables the regular systematic reading of God's word and ongoing intercession for the needs of the world.

I have to confess to being a strong advocate of the use of the daily office on a day-by-day basis. Personally I have been using it for more than thirty years, and I find it has the following advantages over less structured quiet times:

a) It gets me started. As with everything else first thing in the morning, I need a pattern, and this provides it. By the time the intercessions come, I have been warmed by the word, and usually simply intercede in my own words.

b) I remember hearing once a minister who had gone through a very traumatic time in his family life. When I asked him what had kept him going in faith during that time, he said, 'The Daily Office'. Quite honestly, at such times in our life, we do not have words of our own, and the structured prayers give words to us, and can be an anchor to our souls.

But the *Book of Common Prayer* also provides us with a 'Simple Structure' on p. 138 for 'personal or family devotions'. This structure has also been very helpfully repeated in the inside flyleaf at the beginning of the prayer book, just as the Lord's Prayer in its two versions has been placed at the back. However, we

need to know that the structure is only a skeleton, and it is unlikely that we would want to be turning to a whole range of
different pages to work it out each time. But it is a superb framework, and has been taken by Brian Mayne and worked out in a
variety of ways around the structure of the Creed in *As we believe,
so we pray*.[5] This is the kind of little book we could easily keep in
the place where we have our devotions and use as a framework. It gives fifteen little services, each with a sentence of
scripture to begin, a prayer of penitence, a song of praise, a
psalm, a bible reading, a canticle, intercessions, a collect, the
Lord's Prayer and an ending. I hope Brian Mayne and others will
produce more of these little books with worked out forms for this
simple structure.

Weekday Intercessions and Thanksgivings
A series of weekday intercessions and thanksgivings, like those
in the *Alternative Prayer Book*, is provided on pp. 139-144. These
have their roots in the work of the Joint Liturgical Group, and
have been forgotten about in most other places, but have been
quietly popular in the Church of Ireland since their use in the
APB. They can provide a structure for our prayers of introduction,
intercession, thanksgiving and concluding prayer (together). In
this pattern each day of the week has a specific focus as follows:
    Monday: Creation in Christ: Creation and Providence
    Tuesday: the Incarnate Life of Christ: Revelation and Human
    Knowledge
    Wednesday: The Cross of Christ: Reconciliation and Human
    Relationships.
    Thursday: The Resurrection of Christ: the Household of
    Faith, the Church.
    Friday: The Priestly Ministry of Christ: all that meets Human
    Need.
    Saturday: Consummation in Christ: The Fulfilment of the
    Divine Purpose.
My own experience would suggest that these intercessions are

---

5. Columba Press (2003)

useful at times, but should not be over used. However, when you come back to them, they will remind you, like a litany, of the themes you would have forgotten about.

Some Prayers and Thanksgivings

This section is subtitled: 'From earlier editions of *The Book of Common Prayer* and from *Alternative Prayer Book*. They are divided here into sections as follows: The World, Pastoral, Seasonal, the Church's Ministry, the Church, general and Concluding Prayers and Thanksgivings. Some of the most beautiful of the prayers which have been traditionally used after the third collect may be found here, and they will be a treasury for personal devotion. Generally, the 'thee', 'thou' form prayers go back to the 1926 prayer book, though a few, such as that 'for those who are to be admitted into holy orders' go right back to the 1662 prayer book. These are generally well constructed prayers, with resonant words, which, as they are used from time to time in public or private worship, provide us with memorable phrases which can inform our praying on these themes. We would not want them to be lost to future generations.

An Order for Compline

Compline was added to the *Book of Common Prayer* in the Church of Ireland in the 1933 Appendix. Work had been done on re-introducing this service (which, by the way, is still not in the official Church of England prayer books) in the ill-fated 1928 revision of the prayer book in England. Here in Ireland, the Appendix of 1933 added Compline as 'The Second Alternative form of Evening Prayer' alongside 'The First Alternative form of Evening Prayer', sometimes called Irish Vigils, which has not been retained in the 2004 book. However, in the period between the Reformation and 1933, the tradition of Compline was maintained by a succession of private manuals of devotion, beginning with Coisin's *Collection of Private Devotions* in 1627. The word Compline comes from the Latin 'completorium' or completion. This is the last office of the day. The office of Compline

is hard to describe : it is a unity in its own right, and provides an
order of service which can be used at the end of the day in small
groups, by married couples in bed, and in all sorts of circumstances. It is one of those offices which simply should be read
through, in a carefully paced manner. One of its attractions is the
kind of imagery used in it, which draws us close to themes we
do not usually think about. For example:

> Brethren, be sober, be vigilant, because your adversary the
> devil, as a roaring lion, walketh about, seeking whom he may
> devour...;

or:

> O let no evil dreams be near,
> or phantoms of the night appear;
> our ghostly enemy restrain,
> lest aught of sin our bodies stain.

And it also provides us with the most wonderful words for our
last prayers in the evening asking God to keep me as the 'apple
of his eye', to 'guard us while sleeping', to 'illuminate this night
with thy celestial brightness', and to 'let thy holy angels dwell'
in our homes.

A Late Evening Office

A Late Evening Office was the one totally new service in the
Alternative Prayer Book. It had not been given a period of trial
use, but it has proved to be very popular, not least for quiet
night-time services, and for worship in small groups. The only
other attempt to introduce such a service had been in the 1970s,
when the Liturgical Advisory Committee had suggested to
General Synod that Compline might be revised, an idea which
went down like a lead balloon.

Dean Gilbert Mayes drew up, instead, what was a new form
of service, and he based it on an order which was in use by the
ecumenical community of Taizé in France. This style of service,
along with others had been produced in English in *Praise in all
our days: Common Prayer at Taizé.* [1]

1. Published in French in 1971 and in English in 1975 by The Faith Press.

The service itself is very simple: An opening blessing of God, followed by a prayer for the work of the Holy Spirit in our lives. That is followed by the *Trisagion* [2] and *Psalm 134*,[3] or another suitable psalm. Then there is a New Testament reading, a meditation on the reading and the *Nunc Dimittis* or a hymn. That is followed by prayer, in a short litany type form with the response, **Lord, have mercy,** except after the final suffrage for the departed, where the response is **Blessed are the dead who die in the Lord**.

One of the most interesting developments in *A Late Evening Office*, which was quite a departure in the liturgies of the Church of Ireland, was a rubric which allowed for the possibility for 'open prayer' as well as silent prayer. 'Open prayer' would have been considered by some schools of thought to be quite un-Anglican, the stuff of informal prayer meetings rather than something appropriate in the context of liturgy. So this rubric is important, because it recognises that good liturgy can both have a formal structure and include informal elements. Indeed, the very structure may make the informal words all the more meaningful. The new version of the services encourages the leader to make clear whether the congregation is entering into a time of silent or open prayer, so that there will not be any confusion. This is concluded by an appropriate collect (Perhaps the Collect of the Day), the Lord's Prayer, the Common Collect (drawn from the Taizé material) and a Blessing.

One of the observations which may be made about this short service is that it does not work well when 'stretched out'. It has a natural rhythm which is broken if there are too many hymns, or if there is a long sermon in the middle. It really is for the more informal occasion. For weeknight services, *A Service of the Word* provides a better structure, and of course can be used with evening options.

---

2. The song 'Holy God, holy and strong, holy and immortal, have mercy on us.' The name is literally, in Greek, 'Thrice-holy'. This is an ancient song with its roots in the Byzantine rite.

3. You will find an exposition of this psalm under the *Ecce Nunc* in the chapter on Canticles.

Questions for Reflection and Discussion

1. How do you pray on a daily basis? Can you see ways in which a structured 'daily office' could be of help?

2. What do you find memorable about the office of Compline. Read through it and list the themes it contains. Why are these important themes for the last prayers of the day?

3. Are there certain of the 'Prayers and Thanksgivings' which you remember particularly. What is it hat makes them memorable?

4. How do you plan your regular intercessions? Have you ever used a prayer diary? What would you find helpful or unhelpful about structuring your intercessions?

CHAPTER SIX

Service of the Word

Service of the Word, as can be seen from a cursory glance, is a very different kind of service from the others in the prayer book. It is a structure, rather than a fully developed liturgy. The whole service can be put on one page, while the notes to explain it take up three pages!

This idea is not totally new within Anglicanism. For example, the present *Book of Common Prayer* of the Episcopal Church in the USA[1] has within it a 'structure' for the celebration of the eucharist, when it is celebrated in more informal contexts. Also, the book *Lent, Holy Week and Easter*[2] contained within it two pages on how to celebrate an agapé on Maundy Thursday. This gave a description of how the service might look, followed by a 'bare-bones' outline Holy Communion order, based on what was then 'Rite A' of the Church of England.

Going back into history, the concept of providing an outline service, with indications of what should happen at different stages, came particularly into focus during the period of the Commonwealth,[3] with what was called the 'Westminster Directory'. This provided, within a Presbyterian environment, a structure for worship which had a theological coherence in its order, and which allowed for different parts of the liturgy to be shaped to fit the particular needs of a particular environment.

---

1. *Book of Common Prayer 1979* of ECUSA, pp. 400-401.
2. *Lent, Holy Week, Easter: Services and Prayers* commended by the House of Bishops of the Church of England (1984), Church House Publishing/Cambridge University Press/SPCK, pp. 97-98.
3. The period from 1649-1660, when there was no king, and the episcopacy and the *Book of Common Prayer* were outlawed and replaced by Puritanism, under Cromwell.

In our generation, the 'directory' idea was pursued by two people in particular (David Silk and Trevor Lloyd) who, in June 1986 took a paper to the House of Bishops of the Church of England, with the 'directory' model as the heart of it.

They had several aims in view, including:

- To provide some indication of different ways of doing liturgy, taking into account sociological, architectural and church-manship differences.
- To provide outline structures and mandatory sections for some main services, which would provide greater freedom for those who wish either to enrich or to shorten the services (including 'Family Services' and worship in Urban Priority Areas).[4]

The Church of Ireland Liturgical Advisory Committee, working on a proposed order for family worship, independently arrived at a similar conclusion about the need for a more flexible form of service, and in 1993, the pale green booklet *A Service of the Word*[5] was authorised as an experimental service by the House of Bishops. The booklet included not only the outline structure, but also some material which could be used in the different 'slots' and four worked-out services. The material in this booklet proved to be very popular, but there was a danger that people would simply opt for the four worked-out services, rather than exploring the many possibilities which the new service made available. In the *Book of Common Prayer*, the service appears with only the structure and the attendant notes, and the outworking is for worship leaders to do for themselves.

It should be noted, at this point, that it is very unlikely that anyone will ever use this service straight from the book. It is clearly not the intention that any worship leader would say, 'Please turn to p. 165 for the Service of the Word.' This is a ser-

---

4. 'Urban Priority Areas' is a designation used in England to describe areas of particular deprivation and need. People is these areas are often not very confident with books, and therefore being presented with one or two books when at worship may well be an off-putting experience.
5. *A Service of the Word* (1994) General Synod Literature Committee.

vice which will always have to be on service sheets or Powerpoint or, for the less advanced, on OHP slides![6] The service is simply in the book to complete the provision, and because it gives worshippers an idea of the philosophy which lies behind it.

The Structure of the Service
The service itself has been compared to an *à la carte* meal. The shape of the menu is there, but you choose the particular content of the courses. Most other services, especially in their more traditional form, are more like *table d'hôte* meal, where the content is predetermined more or less the whole way through. Following through this picture with the *Service of the Word*, the meal might look something like this:

There is the starter, which in the service is called the Preparation. The whole question of what is appropriate when the people of God gather together in worship is looked at in the chapter on *Holy Communion Two*.[7] Here, the following items are suggested:

*A Liturgical Greeting
An Invitation to Worship
A Hymn *may be sung*
*Penitence *may be at this part of the service or in* Response.
*Acclamation *and/or* A Song of Praise
Metrical forms of canticles may be used, or a hymn may be sung
*The Collect

Some of the elements of the Preparation have been marked with an asterisk, conveying the fact that they are considered essential to the structure. Because this service is so flexible, it is all the more important to keep the essentials focused. There must be:

– Some greeting of the congregation. It should be a liturgical greeting. It may be 'The Lord be with you' or The Peace shared at this point, or some other greeting written for the occasion.

6. Powerpoint™ is a computer programme used very often for presenting material (both words and visuals) for worship on screens in churches. OHP is the abbreviation for overhead projector – which is now, in my view, an increasingly dated way of presenting information on screen.
7. See chapter eight.

– Penitence. This does not have to take place in the first section. Sometimes, penitence will be the perfect response to the Ministry of the Word, but it is an element which should not be ignored. The notes do not require any specific way of doing this part of the service, and our liturgies provide different possibilities: confession and absolution, penitential kyries, responsive penitential prayers. But worship leaders might also like to think of imaginative penitential 'saying sorry' actions.

– Acclamation and/or A Song of Praise. Guideline 4 explains what this means:

> 'The Acclamation is a proclamation of God's majesty and love that derives from the Greeting and Introduction. Traditional elements like the *Sursum Corda* and *Sanctus*,[8] as well as canticles such as *Gloria in Excelsis* may have a place here'.

So, very little is specified, but there should be some acclaiming of the love and glory of God, probably in responses, and/or some singing out of the praise of God. In churches where there is a 'time of praise', this is the time to do it. The services might well begin with a greeting, a quiet song, confession of sins, and then, via the Acclamation, lead to an exuberant time of praise with several songs. All of this will then be drawn together (which is the concept of 'collect') in the Collect of the Day, linking the Preparation to the Ministry of the Word.

If the Preparation is the starter, then the Ministry of the Word is, without doubt, the main course. It should feel like that. This is the meat of the service. After all, the service itself is called *Service of the Word*. Nothing should detract from the centrality of the proclamation of the Word of God in this service. The structure lists the following components for the main course:

*Readings from the Bible

*A Psalm and/or A Scripture Song may precede or follow readings

---

8. *Sursum Corda*, in Latin means 'Lift up your hearts'; *Sanctus* refers to 'Holy, holy, holy Lord …'

A Bible Responsory may follow a reading

*The Sermon

A Hymn may be sung

On one level, this all looks very traditional, so it is important to realise that, although the components are described in the normal liturgical way, that does not mean that they have to be done in a traditional manner. For example, readings from the bible could be done creatively, dramatically, with several voices, and from imaginative translations of the scriptures. What matters is that the bible comes across with real power and that the congregation engages with the meaning of the passages of scripture which have been chosen. But, readings from the bible there must be. That is a central component of all Anglican liturgy, which we are never free to omit (see Guideline 7).

Again, the asterisk before psalm or scripture song conveys that, whether this happens before or after or between readings, or in more than one of these places, it must nevertheless happen. Part of the Anglican tradition is not only to read the Word of God, but to sing the Word of God. Of course, that does not necessarily mean Anglican chant. There are more ways than could be mentioned of singing/saying the scriptures: choruses, worship songs, responsorial psalms, solos, items by a music group, anthems, recorded music, congregational shouting, saying psalms etc. We must all think laterally but not replace the scriptures with something else!

After the Guidelines, information is provided on p. 168 as to how bible responsories might be composed, and as to where some ready-made responsories might be found.

The most traditional term of all in the Ministry of the Word section is the word 'sermon'. An explanation is given in Guideline 8:

The use of the terminology, *The Sermon*, the legally recognized word in the Church of Ireland, does not rule out a variety of ways of proclaiming the Gospel; these may include drama, interviews and other techniques.

This is a very important note, because one of the main uses of

the *Service of the Word* will be in all-age worship, where a traditional sermon will not fit the bill. The kind of teaching which
will be required will be much more visual, much more interactive, and will probably use a variety of methods of learning.
What is vital, however, is that the 'sermon' slot is not used simply for entertainment, but to convey the gospel and to apply the
meaning of the scriptures. This is quite an art, and there are
many books of resources to help with this. One of the most used
is probably the Sc ripture Union all-age worship material called
Salt for many years but now re-branded as *Light*.[9] In many
churches a group of people work on such material for each service.

    After the main course, comes the dessert. In this liturgy, the
Response. The ingredients are:

*An affirmation of faith
*The Apostles' Creed, the Nicene Creed, the Affirmation of faith
from the Renewal of Baptismal Vows or a scriptural Affirmation of
Faith.*
*The Prayers
    Intercession and Thanksgiving
    Penitence *(if not used above)*
A General Collect
The whole section is concluded with The Lord's Prayer *in one of
its approved forms*
A Hymn *may be sung*

The question here is quite simple: 'How do we respond to what
God has been saying into our lives through his word?' And the
answer is implicitly given: By declaring that we believe, by
praying, by repenting, by praising God. This section may also, of
course, include elements like the Collection (another response to

---

9. The material for all-age worship is called *Light Years*, produced
    quarterly, and has resources linked to the *Common Lectionary* of the
    Church of England, which is very similar to the *Revised Common
    Lectionary*.

God in tithes[10] and offerings, and notices – what we as a church will be doing in and for the world in the week to come).

And, finally, the *Coffee*, before we go home. In some churches the Dismissal will lead literally into the coffee. The Dismissal only requires a prayer – nothing else:

*A Dismissal Prayer

The Blessing

A Salutation

But it can have a blessing and salutation added if it is desired.

What makes this service 'Anglican'?

Some have asked what it is which marks this service as being in continuity with the Anglican tradition. In his introduction to *Using Common Worship: A Service of the Word*,[11] Trevor Lloyd suggests the following marks of continuity should be safeguarded:

– A recognizable structure for worship

– An emphasis on reading the word and using psalms

– Liturgical words repeated by the congregation, some of which, like the creed, would be known by heart

– Using a collect, the Lord's Prayer and some responsive forms in prayer

– A concern for form, dignity and economy of words

Trevor Lloyd also adds:

– A recognition of the centrality of the eucharist

and I will return to that issue before the end of the chapter.

My own plea to worship leaders using the *Service of the Word* is that, in planning such services, we would be more careful than ever about the structure. In many traditions, a habit has grown up of the sermon coming at the end – *de rigeur*. So, from time to time, it is possible to come across a *Service of the Word* with the sermon tacked on at the end. This goes against the whole concept of the service, completely ruining its structure and rationale.

---

10. The giving, which goes right back to Jacob in the Old Testament, of a tenth of all we have to God.

11. *Using Common Worship: A Service of the Word – A Practical Guide,* (2002) Tim Stratford, Church House Publishing.

Uses for the Service

The first of the notes relating to the *Service of the Word* says:

> *Service of the Word* is for use on occasions when the prescribed
> services of Morning and Evening Prayer or Holy Communion
> may not meet the needs of a particular congregation.

There are many occasions when that can be the case. We have already mentioned family services or all-age services, where Morning Prayer can be too heavy or inflexible. Or it may be the case in congregations where people are simply not 'book-learners' that it is better to have a service with fewer words, and a simple structure which can be contained in a four-page leaflet. Or there may be times when a service has a particular focus, and the worship-leader wants to build a creative liturgy around that focus. Or occasions when members of other denominations are present, where the liturgy is made more accessible to non-Anglicans. Or times when services are geared to people who do not come regularly to church. The examples are endless, and the amazing thing is that this structure can be adapted to almost every need of this kind.

Another use of the *Service of the Word* is as the first part of the Communion Service. In the Church of England's *Common Worship*, the way to do this is laid out clearly, and is the reason for Trevor Lloyd noting that this service can actually be part of the recognition of the centrality of the eucharist. *The Book of Common Prayer* does not lay out in detail how this is to be done, but this does not mean that it is to be discouraged. The *Service of the Word* provides, in the context of the eucharist, the material for the Gathering, the Word, and the Prayers. What we need to ensure is that there is a recognised form of penitence and a gospel reading. Celebrating at the Table then fits in after the prayers, beginning with the Peace, and continues through to the end of *Holy Communion Two*.

Resources for the Service

The Liturgical Advisory Committee has already made some basic resources available as building blocks for this service. But a decision in principle was made to encourage worship leaders to make use of the wide range of resources available for the *Service of the Word* from the Church of England. There is no point in re-inventing the wheel. Two of the key books of resources are: *(New) Patterns for Worship*[12] and *Times and Seasons*.[13]

New Patterns of Worship is a stunning book of material for this service. To give something of its flavour, it has:

- thirty-four greetings, calls to worship and other introductions;
- ten opening prayers, some said by the leader, some corporately, some responsorial;
- thirty-two invitations to confession;
- twenty-three forms of confession, some corporate, some in kyrie form, some with responses;
- sixteen absolutions;
- thirty-four praise responses;
- twelve creeds and affirmations of faith;
- thirty-seven responsive forms of intercessions and litanies;
- thirty-six thanksgivings;
- forty-two introductory words to the Peace;
- sixty blessings.

And that is only some of the material available.[14]

Many of these options fit services of a particular type or with a particular theme or at a particular time of year. Most of the material in *New Patterns for Worship* can freely be used in the Church of Ireland. Some of it will, however, need to be looked at sensitively. For example, it moves into the area of prayers for the departed; but overall, it is useable material, in line with the

---

12. *New Patterns for Worship* (2002), Church House Publishing.
13. *Times and Seasons* is due in 2005, and will include services for different times in the Christian Year. It will draw together the areas previously covered by *Promise of his Glory, Lent, Holy Week, Easter* and *Enriching the Christian Year*, (The last of these is a compilation for parts of the year not covered by the other two by Michael Perham (1993) SPCK) and indeed will add new areas as well.
14. Brian Mayne is in the process of drawing up a whole set of worked-out services of the word, which will be published by Canterbury Press in 2004 under the title *Celebrating the Word*.

teaching of the Church of Ireland. The part of the book which cannot simply be used directly is where particular eucharistic prayers of the Church of England appear which are not authorised in the Church of Ireland. Having said that, this book will give worship leaders all they need for services of the word for many years to come. Copyright information can be found on p. 418 of *New Patterns for Worship*. Just one final note, to say that the headings in the Church of England structure are slightly different from our own, and we should carefully follow the Church of Ireland ones, not least for the sake of consistency.

Questions for Reflection or Discussion

1. What are the benefits of a service structure which allows freedom within a framework, and what are the drawbacks?

2. Which ways of presenting the 'sermon' slot might be used in an all-age worship service?

3. When might it be appropriate to confess our sins after the sermon rather than at the beginning?

4. If you are someone involved in planning or leading worship, what resources do you have at you disposal to 'fill out' the different aspects of the *Service of the Word*?

5. What other contexts can you imagine this service being used in other than all-age worship?

CHAPTER SEVEN

The Litany

What is a Litany?

A litany, as defined by E. C. Radcliff, 'is a form of prayer in which fixed responses are made by the people to short biddings or petitions'. Most litanies are intercessory in whole or in part, though there are from time to time litanies of adoration, confession or thanksgiving.

The form of the Litany

'The' Litany appears in the *Book of Common Prayer* in two forms, the form found in the 1926 *Book of Common Prayer*,[1] and the form found in the *Alternative Prayer Book* 1984. Litany style prayers have been in use in the Church for many centuries, probably dating back to early Greek forms, using the response: 'Kyrie eleison' (Lord, have mercy). The earliest form known in the west is a litany translated from the Greek by Pope Gelasius,[2] but it seems that the litany form was not really widely used in the western church until the litany of the saints[3] became popular in the seventh century. As the litany became developed in the west, it contained the following elements, as charted by Paul Bradshaw:[4]

− An introductory kyrie, followed by invocations of the Trinity, with the response, 'Lord, have mercy upon us';

1. Revised to remove anachronisms caused by the political changes after the 1926 book was published.
2. Gelasius I, Pope from 492-496.
3. The type of litany still used in the Roman Catholic Church, for example at ordinations, listing different saints with the response after each one, 'pray for us'.
4. *Companion to Common Worship,* ed Paul Bradshaw, Alcuin Club Collections 78, SPCK (2001).

- The invocation of the saints;
- The deprecations – supplications for deliverance, with the response, 'deliver us, Lord';
- The obsecrations – supplications through various events of Christ's life, with the response, 'deliver us, Lord';
- The intercessions, with the response, 'we beseech you to hear us'; and
- Concluding devotions to the cross and to Jesus Christ as the Lamb of God.

Interestingly, the Litany was the very first service to be translated into Latin by Cranmer at the Reformation (probably because Henry VIII was at war at the time and a litany in English was required as a form of prayer during the war). The new English litany came out in 1544, and had within it a famous (or infamous!) prayer for deliverance from the Bishop of Rome and his 'detestable enormities'. The order was essentially the same as in the historic litanies, charted above, except for the 'invocation of the saints', which was reduced to three in 1544 and omitted completely in 1549. Such invocation did not fit with the doctrines of the Reformation.

When we look at the contemporary language litany on p. 175ff, we can see the main headings and shape preserved in the same order today.

- *Section 1* is simple invocations to the Father, the Son and the Holy Spirit, with the response, 'have mercy on us.'
- *Section 2* is supplications for deliverance, in five different sentences, asking God to deliver us from all sorts of evil and sin which might come against us. The response here is 'save us, good Lord.'
- *Section 3* is four supplications taking us through the different aspects of the life and work of Christ by which our salvation has been won. The response to these prayers to Christ is 'save us, Lord Christ.'
- *Section 4* is the intercessions. The first part is for the church; the second is for the state and the third is for all people according to their needs. The response to these is 'hear us, good

Lord.' In the *APB* Litany, it was suggested that one of these three sections might be chosen and the other two omitted, but here, the presupposition is that all will be used.[5]

– *Section 5* is the concluding section, with the focus being on Christ as the Saviour of the World, and concluding with the words of the *Agnus Dei*.

The use of the Litany

The 1926 *Book of Common Prayer* begins the Litany with the rubric:

… to be sung or said upon Sundays, Wednesdays and Fridays, and on such other days as shall be commanded by the Ordinary.[6]

How often this was the actual case, I cannot tell. But many of us can remember the Sunday on which the Litany was said or sung once a month at Matins and once a month at Evensong. Sometimes, there was almost a perceptible groan as the Litany was announced. It seemed lengthy, sometimes tedious, and in some ways a world very different from the ordinary world we inhabited. And, of course, for a child, the whole thing was heightened by the fact that the rector said words such as 'bloody' and 'damnation'!

The new prayer book has the following instruction at the beginning of *Litany Two*:

The Litany is recommended for use on Sundays, Wednesdays and Fridays, particularly in the seasons of Advent and Lent and on Rogation Days.

In a sense, this is a form of prayer which we use when we want to take our prayers particularly seriously. It is a form of prayer

---

5. However, the use of the Litany in *Ordination Services Two* suggests that at times it is appropriate to select sections.

6. For anyone who believes that rubrics change essentially because of orders from above, an archaeological dig through the rubric at the beginning of the litany is a salutary experience. In reality, the rubric reflects what is actually happening in the church, and what is deemed possible. Just like civil laws, to some degree church legislation reflects what people actually do!

which charts out the kind of things we should be praying for, but would often forget. Granted, we do not get time to go into detail, or wait around to meditate, but we have seen the total picture, and been reminded of those things which we may have forgotten.

Some of the ways of rescuing the litany at this point in time in the church are:

a) To make it part of the daily prayer of the church. Why not use it on a Friday in our own private prayers, as a form of prayer which we do not have to put into our own words?

b) To ensure that it gets its place during the penitential seasons of Advent and Lent.

c) To allow it, on some Sundays, to replace the other prayers of the people in Morning or Evening Prayer or Holy Communion so that the Litany is the one form of prayer used on those occasions, rather than duplicating other prayers and making the time of prayer unfocused and overly long.

Questions for Reflection or Discussion

1. Do you find litany-type prayers helpful or unhelpful? Does the constant response element make you feel more or less involved?

2. What are the dangers and what are the benefits of 'general' forms of prayer, like the litany, which cover a good deal of ground?

3. Is the litany part of your regular public and private devotion? How could it become so more effectively?

CHAPTER EIGHT

Holy Communion

The Holy Communion is the central act of worship in the church.[1] Because this is the case, we will find that the Holy Communion Service gives us a window in to all that is most vital in our regular worship. The pattern which expresses this most clearly is seen in the structure of *Holy Communion Two*. This was fully developed at the *International Anglican Liturgical Consultation (IALC)* when it met in Dublin in 1995.[2] You will see the structure clearly in the chart in Appendix 5, p. 249, but the 'section' headings are:
– The Gathering of God's People
– Proclaiming and Receiving of the Word
– The Prayers of the People
– Celebrating at the Lord's Table
– Going out as God's People.
In other words, this is not, as may be implied by its title *The Holy Communion, also called The Lord's Supper or the Eucharist*, simply a service of the sacrament. It is, rather, a service of word, prayer and sacrament – as Bishop Colin Buchanan has described it, 'A bible study followed by a prayer meeting followed by a meal.' It is here in this most normative and complete act of Sunday worship, that we most fully live out the agenda of *Acts 2:42*: the apostles' teaching, the fellowship, the breaking of bread and the prayers.

When we look at the five elements of the shape of this service, it is important to note that they do not have equal weight.

---

1. See General Direction 1, *Book of Common Prayer*, p. 75.
2. The Report of the Dublin Consultation is published as *Our Thanks and Praise: The Eucharist in Anglicanism Today. Papers from the Fifth International Anglican Liturgical Consultation* (1998) ed David Holeton, Anglican Book Centre Toronto.

The central sections are the Proclaiming and Receiving of the Word and Celebrating at the Lord's Table. The middle section, The Prayers of the People, was quite intentionally given greater weight in the Dublin Statement than it has previously been given, and the first and last lead into and out of the other three. These are the points at the beginning and the end when the rest of life meets with worship.

It is important for us to look at each of these sections, and understand them, if our worship is to step out from the pages of a book and become reality in our experience.

THE GATHERING OF GOD'S PEOPLE

To say that this happens each Sunday is, on one level, obvious. People gather in a certain place at a certain time and in a certain way. This is the 'assembly' or, in the Greek, the 'ecclesia' – the people who are called out to meet together with Christ as the focus; the human bodies meeting together as the one Body of Christ in the power of the Spirit. The writer to the Hebrews, in an often-quoted verse, reminds Christians of the importance of what we call 'corporate' worship:

> ...Let us consider how to provoke one another to love and good deeds, not neglecting to meet together, as is the habit of some, but encouraging one another, and all the more as you see the Day approaching. (Hebrews 10:25)

That is a wonderful passage, with a great vision for the purpose of worship – that we might provoke others and be provoked ourselves, to worship with the whole of our lives, seven days a week. In that passage, the phrase 'one another' gently walks us into the liturgy. The liturgy is essentially what we do together ('Common' Prayer). We assemble together (the word we also translate 'church'). The Presbyterians got something right when they called their buildings 'meeting houses', and the Plymouth Brethren got something right when they called their gatherings the 'assembly'. Engaging with what this means is what we are invited to do under this heading, so that our experience is not only ritualised but also real.

Holy Communion Two

THE GATHERING OF GOD'S PEOPLE
The Greeting
(Sentence of Scripture)
(Introduction of Liturgy)
|
The Collect for Purity or Opening Prayer
|
Penitence*
(Commandments or Beatitudes or Summary of the Law)
Introduction to Confession
Silence
Confession and Absolution or Penitential Kyries
|
(Gloria in Excelsis or Hymn of Praise)
|
The Collect of the Day

PROCLAIMING AND RECEIVING THE WORD
The First Reading
The Psalm
The Second Reading
(The Gradual)
The Gospel Reading
|
The Sermon
|
(The Nicene Creed)

THE PRAYERS OF THE PEOPLE
Intercessions and Thanksgivings
The Lord's Prayer**
(Penitence*)
(The Prayer of Humble Access)
|
The Peace

continued overleaf

> **CELEBRATING AT THE LORD'S TABLE**
> (The Preparation of the Table)
> (Presentation of the Gifts of Money)
> |
> The Taking of the Bread and Wine
> The Great Thanksgiving
> The Lord's Prayer**
> The Breaking of the Bread
> The Communion
> The Great Silence
>
> **GOING OUT AS GOD'S PEOPLE**
> Hymn
> Prayer(s) after Communion
> (Blessing)
> Dismissal
>
> ** Penitence may take place at either point. ** The Lord's Prayer may be said at either point.*

One of the questions we need to ask, liturgically and in a wider way, is how we in our context best express the element of 'gathering'. In some places, we gather in almost total silence. Apart from a quick 'Good Morning' at the door and a word or two with the person who gives out the books or service sheets, we enter a building which is silent. There have been times when I have thought that there was something odd about that. After all, when we gather for a meal, or people gather for a soccer match, or meet together in a pub, total silence is the one thing you are sure will not happen. If you want to be silent, you would stay on your own. 'Gathering', in our day to day lives, means catching up with all that has been happening, sharing our stories, talking about friends, engaging with issues, and even interminable small-talk. Some churches had a narthex[3] to allow exactly that to happen when we arrived for worship. However, on the other side of the coin, it is very important to recognise that pure silence can actually have the effect of bringing people together to a common and undistracted focus. Those who have been on silent retreats will know what it is to feel that it is actually

---

3. Down Cathedral is a perfect example of a church with a narthex: a separate meeting area where you could chat and meet people before going into the nave itself.

possible to get to know other people better in silence than it is with too much talking. Noise can cover up the real meeting of persons. So, each church will need to square this circle in some way, unless, like Down Cathedral, there is a narthex![4]

It is worth observing at this point that, in any particular situation, some of the people who gather will be strangers, visitors and perhaps seekers. The art of 'welcoming' such people into the assembly should be taken very seriously indeed. Sometimes newcomers feel the need for a handshake and a warm welcome but, at other times, people want to sneak quietly in and sneak quietly out.[5] The amazing thing is that the Lord has gifted some people with the instinct to recognise different temperaments, and to welcome different visitors in different ways. These are the greeters who need to be 'on the door'!

So, the people of God gather. Note that it is the people of God. We do not essentially gather for an evangelistic meeting, nor do we gather simply as human beings. We gather as those who are in Jesus Christ, to do what he has commanded us to do when we meet as his body. In so doing, others who are not yet believers will be convinced of the reality of faith.

The gathering for worship is (and we always need to remember this), a gathering of those who are baptised into Christ and believe in him. There is no other way into this fellowship except through the waters of baptism. In Roman Catholic churches the congregating people are reminded of this by water at the door in a stoup. In Church of Ireland churches the font is often near the door as a reminder. Perhaps, rather then being empty, our fonts should always have living water in them, as a sign of our readi-

---

4. One possibility is for the notices to be given out five minutes before the beginning of the service, and from that point, the people are called to silent preparation for the worship.

5. In 'the church for the unchurched' at Willow Creek, I found it interesting to discover that they did not appear to have welcomers or greeters. They had discovered, in the context of their particular part of Chicago, that people want simply to come in and out without having to meet others. I don't think this is true in most parts of Ireland, but it is certainly true for some people, perhaps especially in cathedrals.

ness to baptise a new believer, and as a constant reminder to us that we have died to sin and are alive to Christ. So often, baptism is disconnected from the rest of the Christian life, especially for those of us who were baptised as infants.[6] Perhaps we need to restore its place as the beginning of the gathering of God's people?

But there are many other liturgical elements to gathering:

– *A Processional Hymn*, so long as it is a real procession and not a 'rump',[7] can be a very powerful experience of coming together, with the procession itself symbolising the gathering of the congregation to the place of worship. If the processional hymn is the very first item on the order of worship it is best integrated with the music leading up to it, rather than announced, because the announcement is inclined to break the 'mood' and 'build up' created by the music.

– *The Greeting*. The Greeting at the Communion Service is normally in the words used in *Ruth 2:4*, 'The Lord be with you', with its response 'and also with you'. Of course this can be varied at times (eg 'The Lord of love be with you', 'The risen Lord be with you', 'the incarnate Lord …', 'the coming Lord …'etc). But the response should always be the same, so that the congregation does not have to think about it. We do not need a book to do the greeting. It should come as naturally as our answer to the question 'How are you?' The importance of this greeting at this point in the liturgy is threefold:

– It is essentially a 'Christian' greeting. It is not the same as saying 'Good Morning'. Indeed, if a worship leader says 'The Lord be with you' with conviction and meaning, they will not need to say 'Good Morning', because they will already have said more!

– It makes clear the fact that there is always a horizontal di-

6. I do not mean theologically disconnected (though sometimes it is). I mean that we cannot remember our baptism, and therefore need intentional reminders to make it feel real and central.

7. I hope I do not offend too many choirs here. But there is nothing worse than a few people acting like a large choir (robing, processing, etc). It all declares that we are trying to be something we are not!

mension to worship. Speaking to one another about the Lord is very important.

– It establishes the presidency[8] of the person leading the service. You might say, the MC. This is the person who, on this occasion will guide the community, release the gifts of the community and oversee what happens in the service.

– *The Collect for Purity.* This is the prayer beginning, 'Almighty God, to whom all hearts are open …' It is a pre-reformation Collect, given a special place by Thomas Cranmer, which has continued in Anglicanism right through since the 1549 *Book of Common Prayer.* It gathers the people of God in preparation. The importance of this prayer to both Anglicans and Methodists cannot be overestimated. You will find more about it under 'Collects', where I break it down and use it as an example of the collect form.

– *Penitence* may also be part of the Gathering of the People. This is a tradition in Anglicanism which goes back to the 1552 Prayer Book. The tradition is that, at the beginning of worship, we clear our sins in preparation. In the Communion Service, up to now, penitence has been at a later part of the service, responsive to the Word of God and in preparation specifically for communion. And it still remains an option at that point, closely linked with the peace.[9] However, I expect that this earlier point, in preparation for the whole event – the hearing of the word, the prayer of

8. One of the questions I am asked most often is what I wish to do as the presiding minister. The general convention is that the president presides over the whole event, not just the communion, and that presidency is well expressed by conducting the following parts of the service:
- The Greeting
- The Collect of the Day
- The Absolution
- The Peace
- The Eucharistic Prayer
- The Blessing
That leaves plenty of scope for lots of others to participate.
9. There is no doubt that there is something to be said for connecting together our making peace with God in the confession and absolution, and our peace with one another in sharing the peace.

the people and the communion – will find favour with many people.

– *Gloria in Excelsis*. In *Holy Communion One* the *Gloria* is at the end of the service. Here, it is in its most usual place, at or near the beginning. The present place returns to that in the 1549 Prayer Book. It is a wonderful acclamation of the glory and presence of the Lord, and is a reminder of the power of praise in gathering the people to God.

– *The Collect of the Day*. I have written a great deal about the nature of the Collect of the Day in the chapter on Collects. Suffice it to say that it ends this gathering section and 'links'[10] us in with the next section: 'Proclaiming and Receiving of the Word'.

PROCLAIMING AND RECEIVING OF THE WORD

This heading uses the most wonderfully dynamic verbs. The word is not simply read and preached, it is 'proclaimed' and when it is proclaimed, the congregation is not there to be passive but to 'receive' the word. Both of these aspects are necessary if there is to be a dynamic engagement with the scriptures in worship, and both need to be monitored in any congregation. Sometimes congregations actually discourage preachers from proclaiming and sometimes preachers discourage congregations from receiving. The model which Jesus himself used of 'discipling' included both.

The 'normative' Sunday shape for this part of the service is

– First Reading
– Psalm
– Second Reading
– Canticle, Hymn, Anthem, 'Alleluia' etc ('Gradual')
– Gospel
– Sermon
– (Creed)

This is a shape and order recognised ecumenically in our day,

---

10. Another thing I noticed about Willow Creek was the way in which care was given to doing the 'links' well. That is what makes a service flow, and gives confidence to the congregation.

and should, in my view, only be shortened or departed from with good reason. It is a very full ministry of the word of God, and that is something to be greatly treasured. In the Church of Ireland, however, some things militate against it:

a) *The Epistle/Gospel model.* This is deeply etched in people's minds. When you celebrate Holy Communion, you have an epistle and a gospel. Simple: *de facto*. What is forgotten, of course (but can be trawled up from the recesses of the memories of older parishioners), is that Cranmer's communion service was never intended as a stand-alone service. It had been preceded by Morning Prayer which provided the Old Testament reading, psalm and canticles. The epistle/gospel model is simply inadequate as a model for reading the Word of God in a full and balanced way at the main Sunday act of worship.

b) *The idea that we have 'two' lessons'.* This has been almost the law of the Medes and Persians, and there is still the feeling that people can only cope with two lessons, or even that three will lengthen the service a great deal. Perhaps it would be worth timing how long it takes to read an average lesson! And the truth is that people can easily cope with three lessons, if the readings are well prepared, and read with meaning and clarity. Except of course in a service geared to young children.

c) *An uncertainty about how to do psalms.* We will return to this in the chapter on the psalter. Meanwhile, we need to recognise that many Anglican churches do not know how to do psalms if the congregation cannot manage Anglican chant, so they often prefer to omit them.

The lectionary used by the *Book of Common Prayer* is the *Revised Common Lectionary*, which is, of course, built around the normative pattern above. It is a three-year lectionary. Year A begins on The First Sunday of Advent 2004, 2007, 2010 etc. Year B begins on The First Sunday of Advent 2005, 2008, 2011 etc. Year C begins on the First Sunday of Advent 2006, 2009, 2012 etc.

This lectionary is the basis for regular notes in the *Church of Ireland Gazette*, the *Church Times* and the *Methodist Newsletter*. There are also an increasing number of preaching resources, children's resources and liturgical resources connected with it. You will also find that Bishop Edward Darling's *Sing to the Word* [11] is built around the lections of the particular day. And, if you want to produce a worship sheet with readings, the Collect of the Day and the Post-Communion Prayer for each Sunday, you will find the materials available on the internet at the Church of Ireland website *www.ireland.anglican.org*

One of the areas of vital importance in 'The Proclaiming and Receiving of the Word' is how it is actually done. A new liturgy is a good opportunity for churches, and particularly worship leaders, to review this. I suggest that the following areas are worth considering:

Where should the readings be read from?
The obvious answer to the ordinary worshipper is 'the lectern'. But in some places this is not obvious at all. The 1926 Communion Service began with the priest at the Lord's Table, and a tradition grew up of reading the epistle from the 'epistle' side of the sanctuary and the gospel from the 'gospel' side,[12] often up a step higher, to show that the gospel was of greater importance, as we are here closest to Jesus himself. Liturgically, this died out in most places when the new liturgies began to appear in 1967, and the Ministry of the Word was re-established at the place of the word. In some other places, of lower churchmanship, readings are often read from a microphone, or from some other little 'lectern' brought in. But, in my view, the place of the word should be the place of the word, and should both be used for reading the scriptures, and not be used for any other purpose (notices, prayers, testimonies and all the rest!). This is a sacred place, symbolising the importance of the scriptures and that should not be downgraded or confused.

Might I also make a plea for bible readings to be read from

---

11. *Sing to the Word: Suggested Hymns from the Church Hymnal Fifth edition for use with the Revised Common Lectionary and other special occasions* (2000) Edward Darling, OUP.
12. The 'epistle' side was the south side and the 'gospel' side was the north.

the bible itself in the liturgy. There has been an inclination to allow other books to take the place of the full revealed Word of God on the lectern, including lectionary books. Worse still, there has been an inclination for readers to read from photocopied sheets. All of this detracts from the symbolic importance of enthroning the scriptures on the lectern, and of opening the actual book to read from it.

As an addendum to this section, there is sometimes the tradition of reading the gospel from a different place. In some cases, the pulpit (the other place of the word[13]), which is often that little bit higher than the lectern. In other places there may be a gospel procession down to the middle of the aisle with cross, candles and the gospel book, as a symbol of the gospel going out to the world. In this case, a tradition is growing in the Church of Ireland of turning toward the gospel to hear and see it proclaimed. You may also see, in some traditions, people making the sign of a small cross on their forehead, their lips and their heart as the gospel is announced, symbolising the most wonderful gospel prayer: 'Lord, may the good news of Jesus be in my mind, on my lips and in my heart.'

The Anglican tradition has always taught that we are hearing something very 'holy' when we hear the good news of the gospel. As we come close to the Person at the heart of our faith, we begin the gospel with an ascription of praise:

'Glory to you, Lord Jesus Christ',

and at the end of the reading, never saying 'Here ends the Gospel', because the gospel never ends, we declare 'This is the Gospel of the Lord' with the response:

'Praise to you, Lord Jesus Christ.'

These new responses are direct ascriptions of praise to Christ, whereas the *APB* responses were less personal.[14]

---

13. In planning modern churches, the convention now is normally to have only one focal and integrated place of the word. In the Roman Catholic tradition this will sometimes be called an 'ambo'; whatever the name, it is a good idea!

14. Basically, the new responses before and after the gospel are speaking directly to the Lord Jesus Christ, whereas the responses in the

By whom should the readings be read?

The answer is quite simple, but strangely elusive in many churches – by those who have the gift of reading the scriptures publicly. Perhaps the following could be a simple checklist:

– People who believe
– People who can be heard clearly
– People who read the bible privately in their personal devotions
– People who understand the meaning of a passage, so that they can convey it
– People who are teachable
– People who will prepare well
– People who see it as a joyful ministry.

Churches should invest time in training such people. And when we have trained them we should use them. They should be young and old, male and female, old members and new members, and any other mix we can imagine. But they need to know:

– The 'shape' of the bible and where the particular books are to be found
– The way the lectionary works, and how to find the correct reading for a particular service.
– How to discover the correct pronunciation for difficult words.
– How to use a microphone, if one is in use, or how to project their voice.
– How to prepare prayerfully for reading the Word of God.

When these people are discovered, we should all be on our guard in case clericalism takes their ministry away from them. They are not just there to fill gaps when there aren't enough clergy. They are there to exercise their God-given ministry in the body of Christ.

The 'how' of reading Lessons

Just to complete the picture, a few small but important 'hows':

– How to get to the lectern on time

APB 1984 were about Jesus Christ: 'Glory to Christ our Saviour'; 'Praise to Christ our Lord'.

- How to wait until the congregation is settled
- How to introduce the reading (Please not the way which is popular in the Roman Catholic Church, 'A Reading from Exodus' – without chapter and verse)
- How to write or find a brief introduction when needed
- How to pace the reading
- How to end the reading
- How to wait in silence for a moment, and then turn over the bible for the next reading, of necessary.

What about the sermon?

The first marker I would wish to put down is this. Just as the sacramental bread is broken to share at every eucharist, so should the bread of the word. The word and sacrament always go together in reformed tradition, and indeed, nowadays in the Roman Catholic tradition as well. There is a major return to this in every part of the Anglican Communion. Even at small communions, there should be some breaking open and applying of the scriptures even if it is brief and informal. The instruction in *Holy Communion Two* is:

'The sermon is preached here or after the creed.'

The intention, of course, is that the sermon expounds the readings, or at least one of the readings which have preceded it.

The Nicene Creed

The creed is, in one sense, part of The Proclaiming and Receiving of the Word, but is also a link in to what follows. In some of the early liturgies, the creed was said after the catechumens left the worship, and was that which identified the believers who would share in Holy Communion. The creed is used on Sundays and Principal Holy Days and is a natural response of the people of God who have heard the word proclaimed.

The Prayers of the People

Oddly, in the Dublin *IALC* headings, this is the only section heading which is not active. There is no verb. This is a pity, because the whole intention was to 'upgrade' the place of the prayers as being a key aspect of the priestly ministry of the

whole people of God. Sometimes, in modern eucharistic liturgies, the prayers have become rather formalised and lost between the major sections of the Ministry of the Word and the
Ministry of the Sacrament, but the intention here is to give them
greater prominence.

To do this, we all need to recognise several things:

i) We won't get it all into an hour! If there is a proper proclam-
    ation of the word of God, and serious time of prayer followed
    by Holy Communion, we are probably talking about an hour
    and a quarter to an hour and twenty minutes on the Lord's
    Day (which surely is not too much) and 40 minutes at a quieter
    midweek celebration. The issue here is that, for many
    Christians, what they experience on a Sunday is their wor-
    ship for the week. So, it needs to include in a meaningful
    way, all the essential elements of worship.

ii) The Prayers of the People are by far the most open section of
    Holy Communion Two. In terms of print, they take up one
    page (p. 206), and almost all of that page is in red because it is
    almost all rubrics. What we are given is a list of areas which
    should normally be included and a hint of a shape, with dif-
    ferent versicles and responses and that is about it. To give
    prayers the prominence they deserve will require the same as
    the Ministry of the Word: the seeking out of people who have
    not only a gift of prayer, but also a gift of writing and leading
    public prayer.

iii) It should be noted that these are the Prayers of the People.
    They do not belong to the clergy! It is not only the job of the
    clergy to pray. It is the task of every person born into the
    kingdom of God.

It may be useful, at this point, to chart out different ways in
which The Prayers of the People may happen in the liturgy:

a) They may take the basic form which was almost universal in
    the use of the *Alternative Prayer Book* 1984. That is, there can
    be a shape, in four or five sections, with a variable open space
    for particular intentions, followed by a versicle and response,
    led by one or two people. Some possible words for this (re-
    vised from the *APB* second form) can be found on p. 238.

b) They may take the form of the Litany, another litany or part of a litany.[15] This may be a particularly appropriate way of praying during Advent and Lent, and indeed, of ensuring that the Litany is not lost to a generation of worshippers.

c) They may take the form of biddings, followed by silent prayer or a set prayer – a pattern often used for the Occasional Prayers at Evening Prayer.

d) They may be prayers focused on a theme or time of the year, as is found in many books of resources.[16]

e) They may be extempore prayer formulated by one or two people.

f) They may be open prayer, whether asking people to speak out particular themes or topics, or simply leaving a space for anyone to pray in their own words.

g) Whatever other ideas you may have.

The important thing is that they are not simply prayers to fill a slot, but meaningful prayer for the church and the world.

Some thoughts for worship leaders to consider:

– It is good if the prayers are led from among the people. In most churches, the old *prie dieu* position[17] is probably best. It conveys something being done with and among the people, rather than something being done to the people. Again, avoid the lectern!

– Standing is probably the best posture for real involvement, but we need to recognise that the congregation will also be standing for the peace and the eucharistic prayer. If the penitence comes after the prayers, it is an opportunity to change

---

15. An example is in the *Book of Common Prayer*, p. 237.

16. Such as those by Raymond Chapman (Canterbury Press) and Susan Sayers (Kevin Mayhew). A little-known annual resource for the North American Lutheran tradition is *Sundays and Seasons* (Fortress Press). Care often needs to be taken where there is sensitivity over how we remember the departed.

17. A *prie dieu* was a little prayer desk placed in the middle of the main aisle from which prayers were led in the midst of the congregation. The desk itself is not necessary, but the position seems to me to be by far the best place to lead prayer from in churches of an essentially Victorian model (i.e. a church with a nave, chancel and sanctuary).

posture and kneel, or in some churches people may sit for the
collection of money after the peace.

– A suggestion is made that a deacon may lead the prayers. If
there is a diaconal ministry, it is intended to relate the church
and the world, and this is a very suitable role.

– It is important to note the themes and areas covered over a
period of time. Some churches are inclined to be rather navel-
gazing in their prayer, and need to be reminded from time to
time to look outward.

In the new service, the Lord's Prayer may be used as a conclusion to the Prayers of the People, again heightening the importance of this section, in place of being used just before communion.
This is expecially appropriate when Eucharistic Prayer 3 is used.

CELEBRATING AT THE LORD'S TABLE

Before we come to the 'Lord's Table' section proper, there are
two more 'links'. One is the prayer beginning 'We do not presume', which is normally given the title, *The Prayer of Humble
Access*. This prayer, like the *Collect for Purity*, is deeply etched in
the consciousness of Anglican worshippers, and it is one of
those Anglican treasures not found regularly in any other liturgies, apart from those which come from Anglican roots. It is a
prayer written by Thomas Cranmer himself, starting from a line
which came from the priest's preparation in some pre-reformation missals. Here Cranmer is taking a prayer which was only
for the priest, and making it a prayer for every believer.[18] *The
Prayer of Humble Access* is a prayer which conveys very powerfully at this critical point in the liturgy, the doctrine of
Justification by grace alone through faith alone. This prayer has
been placed either before the communion itself (as in 1549 and in
the new English *Common Worship*) or in the present place, before
the prayer over the bread and wine, as in 1552, 1662 and here. It
is a reminder that we always come to the Table of the Lord as

18. It is worth noting, however, that, although this was not generally
    followed in recent decades, the expectation of the 1926 *Book of
    Common Prayer* was that this prayer would be said by the priest alone.

unworthy though forgiven sinners. Two lines of this prayer have from time to time been omitted, but are retained here. They are:

that our sinful bodies may be made clean by his body,
and our souls washed through his most precious blood.

The argument against these lines is that there is no biblical or theological justification for separating the body and blood of Christ in these ways, so that one cleans our bodies, and the other our souls. It is an argument worth listening to, but we could see it another way, as almost parallelism[19] since the bible itself does not make a clear distinction between soul and body ('man' is a 'living soul").

The Peace

The giving of the sign of peace is the second 'link'. When the confession and absolution have just taken place before this point, the peace completes the picture, expressed in the more traditional liturgy by the words:

Ye that do truly and earnestly repent you of your sins
and are in love and charity with your neighbours ...

Here the connection is made with the use of the words said by Jesus himself after teaching the disciples The Lord's Prayer:

If you forgive others their sins,
your heavenly Father will also forgive you;
but if you do not forgive others,
neither will your Father forgive your sins.

There are, of course, many references made to the use of *The Peace* as a sign of brotherly love in the New Testament: *Romans 16:16; 1 Corinthians 16:20; 2 Corinthians 13;12; 1 Thessalonians 5:26; 1 Peter 5.14.* There are also many early church references to the use of the kiss of peace in the eucharist. Justin[20] (in his *First Apology* 65:3) says this:

---

19. Parallelism is common in the psalms, where the two parts of a verse say almost the same thing in different words, and with a slightly different angle.
20. Justin Martyr, one of the great early Christian apologists, lived from c100-165AD.

At the conclusion of the prayers, we greet one another with a
kiss. Then bread and a chalice ... are presented to the president.

This early church position for *The Peace* is the one which has
been used in most of the modern Anglican liturgies. It is the
point at which we realise, at this most holy stage in the rite, that
our worship can never be simply vertical ('God and me'), but is
always horizontal as well. Our relationships with our fellow
worshippers do matter, if we are worthily to share in holy communion together, and our differences and divisions do need to
be resolved.

So, our new service puts it like this:

It is appropriate that the congregation share with one another
a sign of peace.

Some worshippers find this difficult and resist it, but it is something which we really must learn to do, and the more regularly
we do it, the more natural it becomes.

The Prayer of Humble Access and *The Peace* are not actually
under the section headed 'Celebrating at the Lord's Table', but
are links which move in the direction of the Table. They are, in a
sense, preparatory.

In fact the next part of the service, which does come under
the heading 'Celebrating at the Lord's Table', is preparatory as
well. Normally, two things are happening, sometimes three.
One is quite distinct from the other two: The gifts of money. This
is beautifully worded in the new service. That very worldly
word 'money' is mentioned! Our gifts of money are important.
But, at this point, important though they are, they are not the
very centre of the action. I was reading recently of a school-
teacher who asked the children what things happened in worship, and one of them immediately said 'the collection'. The reason was probably that he was involved in putting his collection
in the plate, but also, in many churches there is such a drama at
the bringing forward of the collection. This can be emphasised
when a hymn has finished, by the organ playing very dramatically and loudly, and the plate being lifted high and then placed

on the 'altar'! In the new liturgy, something simpler will do, and perhaps the credence[21] table is a better final resting place for the plate!

The other two preparatory actions are:

The table may be prepared by a deacon or lay people.

The bread and wine shall be placed on the table for communion if this has not already been done.

In other words, more can be made of the preparation of the table for the meal, and this function does not have to be carried out by clergy – it can be carried out by lay people. All of it! It would be much better to have lay people actually set the table, than to continue the practice of 'bringing up' the bread and wine with the collection. No rubric in this service suggests the tradition of an 'offertory procession', and Archbishop Michael Ramsey famously suggested that the practice could lead to a 'shallow and romantic Pelagianism'.[22]

Because the emphasis is on the Preparation of the Table, the short prayers and the first of the texts listed have this as their focus. The Liturgical Advisory Committee purposely omitted the text 'Lord, yours is the greatness', largely because it has become over-used and tired. But it can also be a confusing text at this point. Does it refer to the money or the bread and wine or both? Does it hint at a different 'direction' at this point in the service, where we come as humble sinners with nothing to offer for our justification, and yet have something? Anyway, in one of those amendments which come to General Synod, and remind us that we have a very democratic way of dealing with liturgy, 'Lord, yours is the greatness' won the day, and the text is in! The other texts were intended for after the offertory of money, but

---

21. A credence table is a small table placed to the side of the sanctuary on which the bread and wine are placed for communion, sometimes along with water cruet and other items, at the beginning of the service, and on which the remaining elements may be placed at the end of the service, to be consumed when the service is over.

22. In a lecture in the late 50s or early 60s. Pelagianism means, in simple terms, that we contribute to our own salvation, rather than its being totally by the grace of God.

now this last one leads to confusion, and will undoubtedly lead to conservative practice where it is used.

Now, we come to the nub of 'Celebrating at the Lord's Table'. The actual actions instituted by Jesus himself: These are headed as follows:

1. The Taking of the bread and wine
2. The Great Thanksgiving
3. The Breaking of the Bread
4. The Communion

This conflation of what happens at the table into a 'fourfold action' has its roots in Dom Gregory Dix' influential book *The Shape of the Liturgy*.[23] In *Holy Communion One*, we can see what was the former 'sevenfold action'.[24]

These four headings, it is important to note, are not of equal weight and importance. The first and the third are less central than are 2 and 4. In other words, the bread and wine are taken so that the Great Thanksgiving Prayer may be said over them; and the bread is broken as part of the process by which the bread and wine may be shared in communion. The next part of this chapter will look at what the different 'actions' mean, and how they might be seen in the liturgy:

The Four 'Actions':
Action 1. The Taking of the Bread and Wine
In some traditions, this happens before the service begins. Bread and wine are found, placed in suitable containers, and placed on the Lord's Table or credence table, and sometimes covered by a cloth or burse and veil.[25] Churches where this is the tradition may wish to ask whether covering the elements or vessels in this

---

23. *The Shape of the Liturgy* (1945) Dom Gregory Dix, Dacre Press/A&C Black
24. i.e. He took bread, gave thanks, broke and distributed the bread; he took the cup, gave thanks, and distributed the wine.
25. The 'burse' is the purse-like item on the Communion Table, which holds the purificators and is placed on top of the chalices; the veil is the cloth which covers the elements. Both are normally coloured with the colour of the hangings.

way is really necessary. The once-popular burse and veil has, in fact, been gradually disappearing in many parts of Anglicanism, and may well have seen its day. If the vessels are on the table, why not let people see them? After all, we don't cover the bible when we're not using it!

It may also be worth mentioning at this point that chalices and patens do not have to be silver. Of course, silver, or indeed, gold, may emphasise the great worth of the sacrament in which we are participating, but there are other options. Some use pottery vessels at times, emphasising the ordinariness of the elements, and some use glass, allowing the wine to be clearly seen.

In other parts of the church, the bread and wine, and perhaps the vessels as well, are not placed on the Table until just before the 'Taking' section. In a sense, the very placing of them on the Table is like part of the 'Taking'. They are clearly being placed here for this specific purpose of being used for Holy Communion. We have just noted the options available for the Preparation of the Table.

But the 'taking' in this instance (i.e. the first of the four actions) is not quite either of the things we have mentioned, and can at times elude even the thoughtful presiding minister. The rubric at the taking is simply this:

> The bishop or priest who presides takes the bread and wine and may say:
>
> Christ our Passover has been sacrificed for us
>
> **therefore let us celebrate the feast.**

That is the totality of the instruction given, for what is clearly an action done by the presiding minister. This action, the rubric declared, is only to be performed by the *presiding* bishop or priest. It cannot be delegated, and yet it can be hard to know what it is.

Well, the answer is relatively simple. This action is the equivalent of the priest taking the paten or chalice into his hands during the Prayer of Consecration in the traditional form. It is, in its essence, designatory. It declares: 'This is the bread and wine which we are setting apart from all common use and using for holy communion.'

That means:

a) That the presiding minister should find a way of designating all the bread and all the wine which is to be used. This could be either by lifting them in his hands or by laying a hand on them.

b) That there is no need to do what I would call a 'double-take'. That is, to insist on laying hands again on the bread and wine in the course of the Great Thanksgiving. That, in my view, confuses the separation of the actions which is the basis of the way the liturgy is designed, and also drains the taking at this point of any depth or meaning.

So, the bread and wine are designated, and the 'feast is ready to begin!' That, in fact, should be the mood at this point.

Action 2. The Great Thanksgiving

Here we are participating in the Thanksgiving of all thanksgivings. It is this word from which we get our Greek title for this celebration: the eucharist. 'He gave thanks'. *Holy Communion Two* gives us three eucharistic (thanksgiving) prayers – more than we have had previously, but nowhere close to the eight in the Church of England's *Common Worship*. There are several reasons for the Church of Ireland providing less variety than the Church of England at this point. First of all, we have, in general, fewer eucharists in our churches, and therefore need fewer prayers. But also, we have been generally reticent over the years about providing too many alternatives, in case the services become too complex, and the texts do not become familiar to congregations. We will not look in great detail at the three prayers, but need to note some points about eucharistic prayers in general:

a) A eucharistic prayer should be said in a spirit of thanksgiving. Because of our history of a very quiet consecration prayer, we can be inclined to forget the fact that we are here engaged in thanksgiving. This requires strong and firm declaration by the presiding minister, and equally strong and firm responses by the gathered people. This is especially so with the last 'Amen', which is the great 'Amen' of the whole of the liturgy, and is extended, for emphasis to a threefold 'Amen' in the third prayer.

b) A eucharistic prayer is a unity.

The Giving of Thanks is all of a piece. Although it comprises a variety of parts, it is essentially one action. That means that it is not good to break it up in any way, especially by changes of posture on the part of the congregation or presiding minister. The appropriate posture for thanksgiving is standing, which also indicates that all are involved in celebrating together. (That is why we do not talk much nowadays about a celebrant – all the people are celebrants!) The *APB* 1984 included an unfortunate rubric in it after the *Sanctus* allowing for kneeling. Gradually, that practice of changing posture during the prayer has been dying out. If it is thought appropriate to kneel in certain services at certain times of the year, then the answer is to kneel for the whole prayer. *Holy Communion Two* simply has the rubric 'Stand' to imply the normative posture.

In terms of the presiding minister, the normal posture is to be behind the table with hands in the 'orans'[26] position throughout the prayer.

It is important, at this stage, to make some comments about the structure and content of eucharistic prayers. This can be a place of controversy for Anglicans, between different strands in the church. Therefore, the words used in these prayers have been chosen very carefully indeed, and I hope my exposition of them will be as fair as the choice of words.

First of all, the structure. Prayers 1 and 2 have the same basic structure. It goes something like this:

– Opening Dialogue (including *Sursum Corda*)
– Preface (including, where required, Proper Preface)
– *Sanctus* (and *Benedictus qui venit*)
– The Narrative of Institution
– Anamnesis
– Acclamations
– Epiclesis (including prayer for fruitful reception)
– Doxology and Amen.

---

26. With arms outstretched and lifted up to the shoulders.

Different people will express it in different ways. It is important, however, that worshippers understand something of these different elements:

a) Opening Dialogue:

This is the dialogue between presiding minister and people, which affirms that they are giving thanks together. It begins with the traditional 'The Lord be with you', or the newer but popular 'The Lord is here. **His Spirit is with us**', and proceeds through the *Sursum Corda*, setting the atmosphere for thanksgiving focused on the Lord:

Lift up your hearts.
We lift them to the Lord.
Let us give thanks to the Lord our God.
It is right to give our thanks and praise.

This is not the prayer proper, but the introduction to the prayer, the lead-in to thanksgiving. The text used is the *ELLC*[27] text, which the new book has followed as closely as possible. That is the reason for the change which removes 'up' from 'We lift them to the Lord', and the change which makes it 'our thanks and praise' rather than 'him thanks and praise'. This is not a totally satisfactory change, and is probably made for a less than totally satisfactory reason.[28] The opening Dialogue leads into the Preface to the Great Thanksgiving.

b) The Preface:

The Preface begins the prayer proper with an address to the Father:

'Father, Almighty and everliving God..' (Prayer 1)
'All glory and honour, thanks and praise
be given to you at all times and in all places,
Lord, holy Father, true and living God ...' (Prayer 2)

---

27. *The English Language Liturgical Consultation* which has sought to find common liturgical translations of texts ecumenically.
28. The reason for this change is undoubtedly to ensure that the male pronoun is not used too often of God in the liturgy. Overall, the policy of the Church of Ireland has not been to remove male pronouns when they relate to God, but in this case, we are seeking to be in line with agreed texts as much as possible.

In other words, this is a prayer, not just a narrative. After the opening, there may be a Proper Preface for the particular eucharist or occasion, which in prayer two comes at a variety of points. The basic task of the prayer at this point is to thank God for the whole, or some particular parts of the story of salvation, into which, at the next stage, the centre of the salvation story in the death of Jesus will be placed.

c) The Sanctus (and Benedictus qui venit):

The *Sanctus* is a very ancient Christian hymn, which some have traced back as far as the first century, and no doubt having its roots in the seraphs in *Isaiah 6:3:*

Holy, holy, holy is the Lord of hosts;

the whole earth is full of his glory.

It is the song we sing with angels and archangels and all the company of heaven, lifting us beyond this earth into the very presence of God himself.

It is followed in Prayer 1 by what is called in Latin the *Benedictus qui venit*:

Blessed is he who comes in the name of the Lord.

Hosanna in the highest!

This anthem, of course, comes from the words attributed to the crowd on Palm Sunday in *Matthew 21:9:*

Blessed is the one who comes in the name of the Lord!

Hosanna in the highest heaven!

These words are responsive to the words of the *Sanctus*, and did not appear as early as the *Sanctus* in the eucharistic liturgy. Their effect is to bring us from the heights of heaven to focus down on the saving work of Jesus, the Son of God, which is the very centre of the prayer.

In Prayer 3, the *Sanctus* comes at the conclusion of the prayer as the climax.

d) The Narrative of Institution:

The story of the saving work of Jesus focuses very quickly on what happened on the night he was betrayed, which is the very basis for what we are doing here and now. It would, theoretically, be possible to have a eucharistic prayer without this narrative (there are examples), but it would be unusual to omit the event on which our eucharist is based. This is the Lord's Supper because of both the Last Supper and the subsequent death and resurrection of Jesus. However, at times the church has ascribed almost 'magical' qualities to the words of Jesus, 'This is my body', 'This is my blood' ('hocus pocus'[29]), making their utterance a 'moment of consecration', and framing that moment with a slow and deliberate recital of the words, genuflections, raising the paten and cup and the ringing of bells. The new service does not envisage such a 'moment' of consecration. Rather, it is the whole event, the whole action which consecrates. So, the word 'consecration' is not used of the prayer as such, but is used at the end of the prayer when the presiding minister breaks what is now 'the consecrated bread'.

e) The Anamnesis:

The meaning of the word 'anamnesis' is one of the points of disagreement among Anglicans. On one level, it is simply 'remembrance'. It is the word used when Jesus says, 'Do this in remembrance of me'. But it is not simply mental remembrance. It is remembrance in the same way as the Jewish people remember at the Passover year by year. The Passover for them is not just a past event, but is also a present reality. It is as though they are there in that defining moment. The eucharist is the same. 'Were you there when they crucified my Lord?' is answered by the affirmative 'I was there'. This historic moment was not just an event in the past, but is real for me and in my life now. What we do now is our anamnesis of what Jesus did for us on the Cross of Calvary. The anamnesis indicates the way in which we fulfil the dominical command 'Do this in remembrance of me'.

f) Acclamations:

In our three Eucharistic prayers there are three sets of Acclamations.

In Prayer 1:

---

29. The very phrase 'hocus pocus' comes from a play on the words 'This is my body' in Latin.

We remember his passion and death,
we celebrate his resurrection and ascension,
and we look for the coming of his kingdom.
In Prayer 2:

Christ has died,
Christ is risen,
Christ will come again.

and in Prayer 3:

Dying, you destroyed our death,
rising, you restored our life;
Lord Jesus, come in glory.

A question which might be asked at this point is 'Which reader can spot the odd one out?' The answer is No 2. Actually, they are all different in nature, but 1 and 3 are both to God. No 1 is addressed to the first member of the Trinity, No 3 to the second member of the Trinity, but No 2, although memorable, is simply a declaration. It is not a prayer at all, and breaks the flow of the Great Thanksgiving as a prayer.

g) The Epiclesis, including a Prayer for Fruitful Reception.

Here is another Greek word which is to do with the sending or calling down of the Holy Spirit. Up to this point, that is uncontroversial. The area of the question where there are differing views is to do with who or what we call the Holy Spirit down on. Is it an epiclesis on the people who are worshipping? Or is it on the elements of bread and wine? Or both? Or is it on the 'event'? Different liturgies in the Anglican Communion come up with different answers. In the Church of Ireland, the prayer is phrased this way:

… as we eat and drink these holy gifts
grant by the power of the life-giving Spirit
that we may… (Prayer 1)

or

Renew us by your Holy Spirit (Prayer 2)

or

Holy Spirit, giver of life,
come upon us now;

may this bread and wine be to us

the body and blood of our Saviour Jesus Christ.

So, the general prayer is upon the people who are receiving the bread and wine, and continues to ask that the fruits of the reception may be seen in our lives.

h) The Doxology and Amen:

Each of the first two prayers has a very clear doxology of praise to God, in which the congregation joins with its response, and which concludes with the Great 'Amen'. Prayer No 3 works slightly differently, and we will look at this new prayer separately.

Prayer 3:

Prayer 3 is a prayer in which the congregation is much more involved. The whole prayer has a strong responsive element, and the role of the congregation in the prayer is not simply to reflect what has been said, but is integral to the 'forward movement' of the prayer. It is a version of Prayer H in *Common Worship*, and was developed in response to a request for more interactive material in the new Church of England liturgies. It does not have any options for Proper Prefaces, and is therefore probably best not used on Feast Days. But it is relatively short, and holds together all the important elements of a eucharistic prayer in a brief form.

In the Church of Ireland version of the prayer, there are differences from what became Prayer H. First of all, the prayer is addressed to God: Father, Son and Holy Spirit, in turn. So, the first part is to the Father, the second, with the institution narrative, is to Jesus, and the third, with the epiclesis, is to the Spirit. It concludes with an address to the Trinity, and adds the words after the *Sanctus*:

Thanks be to you, our God, for your gift beyond words.

Amen. Amen. Amen.

This prayer has already proved very popular in services introducing people to the new prayer book material. But it will probably not be a prayer which we would wish to use all the time.

(The Lord's Prayer:

At this point in the service, if it has not been used in the Intercessions, the Lord's Prayer is said. At this point it is used as a climax to the Eucharistic Prayer, with special focus on 'Give us today our daily bread'. The unusual Greek word for daily is considered by some to have a eucharistic significance.)

Action 3. The Breaking of the Bread

On one level, the breaking of the bread can be seen as a purely functional exercise, in that the bread needs to be broken if it is to be shared out. But it is often given meaning beyond that. It is, to put it at its simplest, a re-enactment of what the Lord himself did when 'he broke bread'. In some churches, 'The Breaking of Bread' is the title given to communion, partly because it is sometimes used in the Acts of the Apostles in that way:

They devoted themselves to ... the breaking of bread.' *Acts 2:42*

Day by day, they broke bread from house to house. *Acts 2:46*

Others give the breaking of bread a deeper meaning still, using it as a way to reflect on the broken body of Jesus Christ on the cross. This comes partly from a wrong translation of 'This is my body which is for you' *(1 Corinthians 11:24)*. Some versions, inclining to put in the missing verb, added 'given' or 'broken', even though there was a prophetic sense in which not one of his bones would be broken.

Overall, the most biblical approach to the breaking of bread is focused on *1 Corinthians 10:16-17*:

The bread that we break, is it not a sharing in the body of Christ? Because there is one bread, we whoare many are one body, because we all partake of the one bread.

This is the basis for the words said at the breaking of the bread. Reflecting on these words and this biblical theme invites worship leaders to consider the possibility of using one actual loaf of bread for communion. The fraction (breaking) is not going to have much impact if the bread is already in tidy (and tiny) little cubes!

And a final note, if it is liturgically improper for the presiding minister to take the bread twice, it is even more liturgically improper to break it twice. No breaking during the thanksgiving prayer!

Action 4. The Communion

In some earlier forms of the liturgy, this was called 'The Giving of the Bread and Wine'. In *Common Worship* it is called 'Giving of Communion'. That is unfortunate, because it puts the emphasis on the 'giving' only, whereas it is also about 'receiving'. The Communion is probably the best title. It is, of course, what most people call the whole event. But, as we have seen, any title for this service is only one aspect of it. The word 'communion' comes, of course, from *1 Corinthians 10:16*:

> The cup of blessing that we bless is it not communion in the blood of Christ? The bread that we break, is it not communion in the body of Christ.

This is holy fellowship indeed. Holy fellowship with one another in the body of Christ. Holy fellowship with our God, through the body and blood of Jesus Christ.

The way in which communion is administered will tell a great deal about what we believe. In some churches, it appears a very private affair. This may be especially so at early morning communion, where people space themselves out pew by pew, and come quietly to the rail to kneel as individuals before their God. That is one aspect. Another is the kind of communion where people receive standing in a circle, even passing the bread and wine to one another, and with a deep recognition that we are together in this. It might be useful for many churches to reflect on how communion is distributed and received, and what this conveys about what we believe.

The words used to welcome people to the table have been added to in *Holy Communion Two,*with the alternatives: 'the gifts of God for the people of God ...' and 'Jesus Christ is the Lamb of God ...' So also have the words of distribution. The beautiful words include:

> The body of Christ given for you

and

The blood of Christ shed for you.
which will have an immediate and powerful impact on commu-
nicants.

No matter what the words, the communicant seals this as
their own with their 'Amen'.

GOING OUT AS GOD'S PEOPLE

Here, again, we have a 'link': a part of the service which both
looks back, and prepares the way for moving forward. It comes
as the last part of the section 'Celebrating at the Table', and is
called 'The Great Silence'. This is a silence different from all
other silences in the worship. It should be longer and stronger. It
is almost like the quality of silence in the hymn 'Let all mortal
flesh keep silence',[30] and God has a wonderful habit of confirming in the lives of his people in those moments, what he has been
saying to them during the service. Sitting at this point is appropriate, so that we are not hurried or uncomfortable.

After the silence, or after the post-communion prayers, is a
good place to sing a hymn. The hymn does not have to be as a recessional. It is possible for choirs to get out without a recessional
hymn, or indeed, to recess during the hymn, and then wait for
the dismissal.

Post-Communion Prayers
Two are printed: the famous David Frost composition, 'Father of
all' and the well known 'Almighty God'. But there are also the
post-communion prayers printed in the collects section. Most
post-communion prayers have a looking back and a looking forward element. Or, to put it in other words, a 'Thank you' element and a 'getting ready to serve' or 'looking towards the
heavenly banquet' element.

Dismissal
In the new service, 'Dismissal' covers the Blessing and the final
versicle and response. The Blessing is no longer mandatory. In

30. *Church Hymnal, fifth edition,* Hymn 427

truth the real blessing in a eucharist is to receive the spiritual food of Christ, and any other blessing is bound to be an anti-climax. But the Dismissal (interestingly the '-miss-' part of that word is what the title 'mass'[31] comes from) is mandatory. We are sent out from worship to serve the living God. Or, to put it another way, we are sent out from the service to worship the living God from Monday to Saturday.

Questions for Reflection and Discussion

1. How can we most effectively 'draw out' the structure of this service in our worship?

2. If this service is the central act of worship of the church, should it be the regular main Sunday morning service? What would be the benefits/drawbacks of celebrating Holy Communion weekly in this way?

3. What are the aspects of the service which should be led by lay people? How might lay people best be trained for these roles?

4. Where is the communion table best placed in your church to emphasise the fact that we gather around it? What aspects of communion are highlighted by receiving a) kneeling at a rail; b) standing in a circle; c) going up to receive the bread and wine at a 'station' (i.e. a point where the person distributing is standing)?

5. What do you like about each of the eucharistic prayers in the new service?

---

31. From the Latin 'Ite missa est' (Go, it has been sent) at the end of the Roman rite.

CHAPTER NINE

The Collects

What is a Collect?

A Collect is essentially a short prayer which focuses our thoughts on a particular day or on a particular theme. When it is the first, it is described as the collect of the particular occasion (e.g. The Collect of the First Sunday in Lent). When it is the second it is described as a collect for whatever the focus may be (e.g. For aid against all perils, p. 97). When it is described by its place in the service it is the collect at the particular service (e.g. The Second Collect at Morning Prayer).

Often, collects almost pass us by in services. If we were to do a 'freeze-frame' with most worshippers immediately after the Collect of the Day is read, and ask them: 'What have we just prayed for?' many people would be stumped. But, if the truth be told, most of our collects frame our prayers in strong biblical ways, and sometimes even in direct biblical language. They are at times a reminder to us of the paucity of our own prayers, which would probably never reach the spiritual depths of St Paul:

> I pray that the God of our Lord Jesus Christ, the Father of glory may give you a spirit of wisdom and revelation as you come to know him, so that, with the eyes of your heart enlightened, you may know what is the hope to which he has called you, what are the riches of his glorious inheritance among the saints, and what is the immeasurable greatness of his power for us who believe, according to the working of his great power. *Ephesians 1:17-20*

or:

> And this is my prayer, that your love may overflow more and more with knowledge and full insight, to help you deter-

mine what is best, so that on the day of Christ you may be pure and blameless, having produced the harvest of right-eousness that comes through Jesus Christ for the glory and praise of God. *Philippians 1:9-11*

Of course there are times in worship for prayers to be in our own words. There are times when our intercessions need to be plain and simple, even faltering and in bad English. But there are also times in liturgy for prayers which are carefully constructed, say-ing the not-so-obvious, and which need to be explored because they open to us the riches of the prayer-life of the New Testament. The collects are one such place. More than that, if collects are used properly, systematically and regularly, they provide memorable prayers. What worshipping Anglican does not know how to continue when we begin:

Lighten our darkness, we beseech thee, O Lord ...

or

O God who art the author of peace and lover of concord ...?
And some of the collects have given us phrases which we use in everyday language like 'read, mark, learn and inwardly digest'.

Storing the mind with collects will be a spiritual blessing to all who do it. If I were imprisoned for my faith or on a desert is-land, it is the psalms and the collects that I would turn to as my prayers.[1]

Almost one hundred pages of the *Book of Common Prayer* (pp. 241-337) are given over to the collects and post-communion prayers for use in the liturgy of the Church of Ireland. These col-lects and post-communion prayers were published in a little book on their own a couple of years before the publication of the new prayer book, to enable people to see how the text in the 2004 book would be set out.[2] They are, I think, generally quite popu-lar, and are more traditional than the many specially composed

1. Two books which will give a great deal of information on Anglican collects are: *The Collect in Anglican Liturgy: Texts and Sources 1549-1989* (1994) Alcuin Club Collection 72, Liturgical Press, Minnesota; and *The Collects of Thomas Cranmer* (1998), Frederick Barbee and Paul Zahl, Eerdmans.
2. *The Calendar and Collects*, Columba.

and rather obvious collects composed for the themes of the *Alternative Prayer Book* 1984.

How collects are used in the liturgies

The collects available on these pages are for use in every communion service, service of Morning or Evening Prayer or Service of the Word on the day or occasion concerned. But they are used in these three services in quite different ways.

In *Holy Communion One* and *Two* and in *A Service of the Word*, the collect acts as a kind of 'hinge' between the Gathering/ Introductory material and the Proclaiming and Receiving of the Word. This use, however, is not the same as the use in the *APB*, where the collect was written or chosen to sum up in some way the theme of the readings. Indeed, during ordinary time in the *Book of Common Prayer*, the collects and readings run on quite different tracks, and have no necessary connection with each other at all. During the seasons, of course, there will be a general thematic connection, because both readings and collect are chosen to fit the particular Sunday of the year. The role of the collect in Holy Communion is as a hinge completing the preparatory part of the service, focusing down into prayer, and preparing the congregation for the Ministry of the Word. To highlight this function, it is good for the congregation to be quiet for a moment before the collect, and for the collect to be introduced briefly in a few carefully-chosen focusing words by the presiding minister.

In *Morning and Evening Prayer*, the Collect of the Day is used as one of two or three collects after the Lord's Prayer (the pattern for all prayer) and, where used, the versicles and responses. It has the function, therefore, of beginning our prayers, which will then widen out into other more specific concerns, with the prayer of the day and a prayer or two suited to the particular service.

In *Daily Prayer: Weekdays* p. 136ff, the Collect of the Day is used in quite a different way. Instead of leading in to the intercessions, it becomes the prayer which rounds off the intercessions before the Lord's Prayer.

Whichever way they are used, the collects on these pages

have an important part to play in all the normative Anglican services.

How a Collect is constructed

Martin Dudley, in *The Collect in Anglican Liturgy*[3] offers the following as a model for the construction of a collect:

Structure of a Collect

An address to God
|
A relative or participle clause referring to some attribute of God
or to one of his saving acts
|
The petition
|
The reason for which we ask
|
The conclusion

These five sections are not absolute. Sometimes ii) and iv) are dispensed with, simplifying the form even further. The collect which we all know best, and which is a good example of the model, is the Collect for Purity at the beginning of the Holy Communion service. A breakdown of this popular collect will help us to see the structure very clearly:

i) 'Almighty God'

The address is usually to 'God', 'Father' or 'Lord', sometimes with a qualifying adjective like 'Almighty God' or elaboration like 'Father in heaven', or the vocative 'O Lord'. The normal rule is that the prayer is addressed to the first person of the Trinity in some way or other. But, as with everything, there are exceptions, such as the Collect of the Third Sunday of Advent, which begins 'O Lord Jesus Christ...', and indeed, one or two where the injunction precedes the address, such as the famous collect of the Sunday before Advent, beginning 'Stir up, we beseech thee ...'

---

3. Op. cit. p. 4.

ii) 'to whom all hearts are open,
all desires known,
and from whom no secrets are hidden;'

The basis on which we come to God in prayer is not only the fact of the existence of God, but also that, through God's revelation of himself, we can know what he is like, or how he has acted in the past. This is the basis of so many of the psalms – the declaration of the nature, attributes and actions of God, on the basis of which we can trust God now and in the future. In this case, we realise that everything we are and think and do in our innermost being is known better to God than it is to ourselves. There is no point in hiding from God, and indeed no need to hide from him.

iii) 'cleanse the thoughts of our hearts
by the inspiration of your Holy Spirit,'

This is the petition: the heart of the matter. This is what we are asking God to do. The one who is almighty and all-knowing is able to prepare us to worship him by making us clean again, as he breathes his Holy Spirit into our lives and our worship. And what a wonderful juxtaposition of ideas we have in the Collect for Purity – 'the thoughts of our hearts'. Not just the thoughts of our heads, but our very intentions and desires in our deepest being. We could meditate on that one for hours!

iv) 'that we may perfectly love you,
and worthily magnify your holy name;'

This is the reason for our asking. It is not just that we want the feeling of being clean again, wonderful though that is. What we are asking for is a human impossibility, one which was meditated on by John Wesley and written about by his brother Charles in many hymns: Christian perfection, no less.[4] The realisation that we will only bring worthy worship and glory to God's name when he does a sanctifying work of grace within our hearts.

---

4. A good example is found in *Church Hymnal, fifth edition*, Hymn 638:
    A heart in every thought renewed
    and full of love divine,
    perfect and right, and pure and good,
    a copy, Lord, of thine.

v) 'Through Christ our Lord.'

This is the archetypal Christian prayer. To the Father, in the power of the Spirit, through our only Mediator, Jesus Christ. There is no other name by which we may be saved, no other name in which we come to the Father, no other name in which we dare to pray.

Where our present Collects come from

You may well notice that many of the *Collect Twos* (i.e. the contemporary language version) are actually 'you-form' versions of *Collect One* (the 1926 Prayer Book version in traditional language). This is not always true, and a trawl through the Sundays of Advent will illustrate the point.

On the first and third Sundays of Advent, the modern-language collect is simply a mild revision of the traditional version. This is because these texts are so well known – not off-by-heart, but there is a recognition factor when we hear them again. The Collect of Advent 1 was new in 1549, and by now we know it works! The Advent 3 Collect was written fresh for the 1662 *Book of Common Prayer* by John Cosin,[5] and has also stood the test of time.

In Advent 2, when the collect had been the Bible Sunday Collect in 1926, a change is made – a collect which was originally that of the Fourth Sunday of Advent is used as the traditional Collect:

O Lord,

Raise up we pray thee thy power and come among us...

This comes, originally from the Sarum Missal.

But a new and very beautiful collect is provided in contemporary language, which comes from *Celebrating Common Prayer*[6] in 1992.

---

5. John Cosin (1594-1672) became Bishop of Durham in 1660, after the Restoration of the monarchy. His *Collection of Private Devotions* (1627) shows something of the quality of his poetic writing, and includes the version of *Veni Creator* sung at most ordinations and found in the *Church Hymnal, fifth edition,* Hymn 296.
6. *Celebrating Common Prayer: A version of the Daily Office SSF* (1992) Mowbray.

In Advent 4, the traditional collect is an old 1549 one for Advent 3, but the contemporary language one is quite different, because much of the focus of this Sunday is now on the Blessed Virgin Mary. It begins:

God our redeemer,

who prepared the blessed Virgin Mary

to be the mother of your Son ...

This comes from the Church of England book *Promise of his Glory*, published in 1990.

The page at the end of the collects gives the sources for many of the new prayers but, as you can see, collects have come from all different stages in the life and growth of the church, right through from pre-Reformation days until now.

Post-Communion Prayers

The idea of having special post-communion prayers for each occasion is relatively new, and very creative. Up to now, there has been a very limited selection, in both the older and newer communion services. However, the post-communion prayers provided in the *Alternative Prayer Book* 1984 both proved to be very memorable and popular. The first of these is the famous:

Father of all we give you thanks and praise ...

written by David Frost[7] and a good example of why prayers written by one person easily beat prayers written by a committee! It is a prayer full of powerful images and well-chosen words, and is retained as an option in the *Book of Common Prayer*. The second is the one we know off by heart:

Almighty God,

we thank you for feeding us ...

which has perhaps grown a little more worn, but is nevertheless popular.

Now we have a plethora of post-communion prayers. Some are old but most are new, and they generally have a sense of giving thanks for the eucharistic gifts we have received, and a

7.   David Frost, Emeritus Professor of English Literature, University of Newcastle, New South Wales, was also the compiler of the psalter in the *APB 1984*.

looking forward to some element of the eschatological banquet at the end of time.

One of the things which will be is most noticeable in the post-communion prayers is the rich and varied ways of addressing God. Sometimes these are determined by the time of the year; at other times, they are simply a sign of the rich range of biblical imagery about God. Examples are:

'Light eternal' (Christmas 2)

'God of glory' (Epiphany 2)

'Generous God' (Epiphany 4)

'God of tender care' (4 before Lent)

'God our creator' (2 before Lent)

'God of hope' (Lent 5)

'God of our pilgrimage' (Trinity 6)

In a sense, these new and creative post-communion prayers are a reminder that so often we have limited ourselves to one or two 'addresses' to God in most of our liturgies, such as 'Almighty God' or 'Eternal God' or 'Merciful Father'. But it does not take us to search far into the scriptures (especially the psalms) to find a whole range of images, which can enrich our understanding of God.

While most of the post-communion prayers are new, there are one or two old ones. For example, the prayer to be used on Trinity 8 is an Alcuin Club[8] version of the famous prayer from the Liturgy of Malabar, best known to us in the version associated with Percy Dearmer,[9] as:

Strengthen for service, Lord, the hands

that holy things have taken ...[10]

and the prayer used on Maundy Thursday is a prayer well known in the more catholic wing of the Church which has often

---

8. The *Alcuin Club* was founded in 1897, and has over more than a century promoted good liturgical scholarship and publications.

9. Percy Dearmer (1837-1936) is famous for the rather 'fussy' *Parson's Handbook*, (1903) Grant Richards, London, which makes fascinating, dated reading for those who would like to understand Anglo-Catholic ritual.

10. *Church Hymnal, fifth edition,* Hymn 446.

been associated with Corpus Christi.[11] Although the version here is from the *Alternative Prayer Book* 1984, the prayer itself goes back at least as far as the *Scottish Prayer Book 1929*:

Lord Jesus Christ,
In this wonderful sacrament
You have given us a memorial of your passion.
Grant us so to reverence the sacred mysteries
Of your body and blood
That we may know within ourselves
The fruits of your redemption …

These new prayers will, I believe, be one of the most enriching new aspects of our new eucharistic rite. May God use them to his glory!

Questions for Reflection and Discussion

1. What collects, if any, can you recite from memory? How have they come to be part of your devotion? What in particular do they 'say' to you?

2. You may like to write a 'collect-style' prayer about some theme or aspect of the Christian life.

3. You may wish to read through some of the new post-communion prayers. What phrases do you find striking, and what phrases do you find unusual or hard to understand?

4. Am I right in saying that the collects sometimes remind us of things prayed for in the scriptures which we may forget to pray for? What kind of things?

11. The special day, set aside in the Roman Catholic Church and parts of the Anglican Communion, on which thanksgiving is offered for the institution of the eucharist. The feast of Corpus Christi is held on the Thursday following Trinity Sunday each year, and is often associated with processions in honour of the blessed sacrament.

CHAPTER TEN

Service for Ash Wednesday

In a sense, the *Service for Ash Wednesday: the Beginning of Lent* is in a category all of its own in the *Book of Common Prayer*. It is the only service which is to be used on a specific occasion in the Christian Year. This tradition of having an Ash Wednesday service in the prayer book goes right back to the Commination service in the *BCP 1662*. The mood of that particular service was expressed by its subtitle: *Denouncing of God's anger and judgements against sinners*, and it has a powerfully strong opening section, which sounds strange to modern ears:

> Brethren, in the primitive church there was a godly discipline that, at the beginning of Lent, such persons as stood convicted of notorious sin were put to open penance, and punished in this world, that their souls might be saved in the day of the Lord, and that others, admonished by their example, might be the more afraid to offend.
>
> Instead whereof, until the said discipline may be restored again, (which is much to be wished), it is thought good that at this time (in the presence of you all) should be read the general sentences of God's cursing against impenitent sinners ...

and so it continued with a series of sentences from *Deuteronomy* 27 expressing the cursing of God on different sins. This is, by the way, still the official service for Ash Wednesday in the *Book of Common Prayer* of the Church of England.

In 1926, the Church of Ireland changed the Commination Service to the Penitential Service, still using much of the introductory material in the original, and adding new verses of scripture, this time based on the ten commandments, and reflecting

Service for Ash Wednesday
The Beginning of Lent

THE GATHERING OF GOD'S PEOPLE
Opening sentence
Introduction
|
Silence
Collect

PROCLAIMING AND RECEIVING THE WORD
The First Reading
(The Psalm)
(The Second Reading)
(Canticle or Hymn)
The Gospel
|
The Sermon

THE LITURGY OF PENITENCE
The Commandments
The Litany
Silence
Confession
Prayer or Absolution

CELEBRATING AT THE LORD'S TABLE   *When there is no Communion*
Prayer of Humble Access, etc   Prayers of Intercession
                                                                The Lord's Prayer

GOING OUT AS GOD'S PEOPLE
Concluding Prayer
Silence
(Blessing and Dismissal)

on their themes from other passages of scripture. Both the Commination Service and the Penitential Service are the same from Psalm 51 onwards.

The Ash Wednesday service in the new *Book of Common Prayer* comes from one approved by the House of Bishops in the 1990s which was never published, but was available on the Church of Ireland website. Those who had used it instead of the

Penitential Service were anxious that the new service would be included in the prayer book. One reason may have been the 'movement' of the service – through from the introduction and opening prayer, to the ministry of the word, through the recital of the commandments (with New Testament interpretations) and a series of penitential prayers to a definite act of confession at the beginning of Lent. That is followed, after the assurance of forgiveness, by communion (where desired), and may end with a time of silent reflection, a brief prayer and the congregation leaving the church in silence, as is appropriate on the first day of a season of lamentation. This new service drew on some of the material in the Church of England book *Lent, Holy Week and Easter*.[1]

One of the quirky things about this service, in the context of the wider church throughout the world, is that it is an Ash Wednesday service without ashes! That is something which seems faintly ridiculous if you are part of a church in which the imposition of ashes is a key aspect of the liturgy on this occasion. Even the Methodists in the USA, and in their new service book in these islands,[2] include a form for imposing ashes in their worship material. In the Church of Ireland, living in a context where the Roman Catholic tradition is strong, and formed as a disestablished church at a time of high ritualism, ashes are to some anathema, partly because of a reaction to these things, and partly with a biblical conviction that our fasting is not something we should flaunt before others. However, in parts of the church, over recent years, the use of ashes has proven to be a highly effective symbol both of our mortality and of our penitence, with words such as:

You are dust, and to dust you will return.

Turn from your sins and follow Christ.

The Liturgical Advisory Committee could not have agreed to provide for this ceremony in the service, but a rubric was included

1. *Lent, Holy Week, Easter* (1986), Church House Publishing.
2. *The Methodist Worship Book* (1999), Methodist Publishing House, pp. 146-147.

that allows for local customs to be observed, which could include, for example, the imposition of ashes or the reading of the introduction to the 1926 Penitential Service, which I for one, hope will not be lost.

CHAPTER ELEVEN

Christian Initiation

A series of services are gathered in the *Book of Common Prayer* under the heading 'Christian Initiation'. They begin with the traditional services, under *Christian Initiation One*, which are:
- *The Ministration of Public Baptism of Infants One*
- *The Order for Confirmation One*

These seem to be rarely used these days. It is worth charting historically that one of the earliest services in the whole Anglican Communion in which both God and people were described as 'you' was the very popular *Order for the Baptism of Children*, which was included at the back of the *APB* 1984. This dates back to 1969, became very widely used and, even in places where the *BCP 1926* was used for most other services, became very often the norm for baptisms. So, the *BCP 1926* services are here in the new book to keep faith with the promise that the traditional services would be provided, but with a very real possibility that they will rarely be used. In the case of infant baptism, the service is probably thought to be hard for ordinary people to understand; in the case of confirmation, the service is devoid of any ministry of the word or eucharistic context. However, the traditional services do have a role in establishing the doctrine of the Church of Ireland in both baptism and confirmation. Interestingly, one particular part of the *Confirmation Service* became a topic for debate in the 2003 General Synod, when Dean Michael Burrows from Cork proposed that the Synod amend what is called the post-confirmation rubric from the words in the *BCP 1926*:

> Every person ought to present himself for Confirmation (unless presented by some urgent reason) before he partakes of the Lord's Supper,

to read instead (in the original words of the *BCP 1662*):

> And there shall none be admitted to the Holy Communion, until such a time as he be confirmed, or be ready and desirous to be confirmed.

Undoubtedly, the intention of changing the rubric was to make the situation a little bit more open, not least in the case of children receiving communion before confirmation.[1] Whether it will have this effect remains to be seen. But, no matter what happens, the debate over a rubric such as this in one of the older services illustrates the importance of liturgy in establishing doctrine in the Church of Ireland.[2]

The contemporary services of initiation

The revision of the initiation services has been profoundly influenced by the work of the International Anglican Liturgical Consultation meeting in Toronto in 1991. That consultation produced a statement called *Walk in Newness of Life*, which charted out the different areas which should be considered in the liturgical revision of initiation services in different parts of the Anglican Communion. The *IALC* did the same kind of groundwork on the eucharist (Dublin 1995) and on ordination (Berkeley 2001), and these statements have proved very useful in raising the issues for revision of services in these areas. It would also be true to say that the charting out of the issues to be looked at in the revision of these services has probably meant that the revised services covering baptism, eucharist and ministry have been a little bit more radical in their changes than some of the others. The text of the basic Recommendations of the Toronto *IALC* can be found as Appendix 4 on p. 248, and we will note, as we go through the services, some of the principles which have been brought to bear on their revision.

1. I am sure Dean Michael Burrows will verify this for anyone who feels that I am misrepresenting his intentions!
2. The way in which churches hold together doctrine and liturgy is summed up by the Latin tag *Lex orandi, lex credendi* (the law of prayer, the law of belief). This is a two-way process: We learn what we believe from our prayer and worship, and our prayer and worship is also formed by our doctrine.

It should also be noted at this point that the revision of baptismal liturgies has proven, over the years, to be a frustrating task for the Liturgical Advisory Committee, largely because of the popularity of the 1969 service. This service, though advanced for its time, was considered by the LAC to need further revision in the 1980s. When an attempt was made in 1983 to revise the baptismal liturgy, it failed to reach the necessary two-thirds majority among lay members of the General Synod, and the 1969 order was included to avoid there being no baptismal rite in the *APB*. It is only now, 35 years after this order was written, that it is being replaced. It must be one of the longest lasting revised services in the Anglican Communion!

Services provided in the Book of Common Prayer
The following liturgies are gathered together in the new Prayer Book under the overall heading *Initiation Services Two*:
- Holy Baptism Two
- Holy Baptism Two in the context of Morning or Evening Prayer
- The Order of Receiving into the Congregation
- Confirmation Two
- Holy Baptism, Confirmation and Holy Communion – The Structure of the Service
- The Renewal of Baptismal Vows
- Thanksgiving after Birth or after Adoption

Where the word 'Two' appears in the *Book of Common Prayer*, it conveys the fact that there are two orders of the particular service. 'One' is the traditional order in traditional language; 'Two' is the contemporary order in modern language. Where there is no 'One' or 'Two', there is only one order available. So, in this case, there is only one order (a contemporary one) for the receiving of those privately baptised, for Holy Baptism, Confirmation and Holy Communion (all three in one service), for the Renewal of Baptismal Vows, and for Thanksgiving after Birth or after Adoption.

The concept of 'Initiation'

The language of initiation has been used in relation to baptism for some time now, and is fraught with dangers, some of which can be highlighted by looking at these services. Some questions which have been posed are: 'What is sacramental initiation?', 'When is it complete?' and 'Is it an event or a process?' It is under this heading also that questions arise as to who are suitable recipients at the Lord's Table, and whether confirmation is required as a second stage of initiation before it is appropriate for a person to receive Holy Communion.

The *International Anglican Liturgical Consultation* raised this specific issue at its very first meeting in Boston in 1985, with its statement on Children and Communion. It proposed:

i. That since baptism is the sacramental sign of full incorporation into the church, all baptized persons be admitted to communion …

vii. That each province clearly affirm that confirmation is not a rite of admission to communion, a principle affirmed by the bishops at Lambeth in 1968.

It would be inappropriate to enter too fully into this debate at this point. Some attempts have been made at the General Synod to raise the issue of children receiving communion but all (apart from the change made in the confirmation rubric) have come to nothing. So, the question of what exactly comes under the heading of 'initiation' is still up in the air. However, I think it is true to say that the heading 'Christian Initiation' here is a flag of convenience by which a series of services are gathered together, rather than implying a totally worked out doctrine of the subject. Whatever we believe, it is very difficult to say that The Renewal of Baptismal Vows is initiation, except that it calls us back to our starting-point; and it is quite impossible to say that Thanksgiving after Birth or after Adoption is initiation, not least because of the rubric which declares:

It is not in any way a substitute for the sacrament of baptism.

Holy Baptism Two

Our best way into these services is thoroughly to understand the thinking behind *Holy Baptism Two*.

a) *There should be one baptismal rite for all ages*. Whatever we believe baptism is, its essential meaning must be true for all who receive the sacrament. That was emphasised by the Boston *IALC* in 1985, which asked:

> 'That provincial baptismal rites be reviewed to the end that ... only one rite be authorized for the baptism whether of adults or infants so that no essential distinction be made between persons on basis of age.

Up to now, in most of our churches, it has been assumed that baptism is, almost by its very nature, a sacrament for children. All of that is changing rapidly. In my own diocese,[3] I discovered in analysing figures for 1965 to 1995 that, during that period of time, the number of baptisms had fallen by around 50%. In some parts of the church we no longer live in a culture where granny says, 'It's time for the child to be done.' We live in a world, especially in urban areas, where many people have never been baptised, and when they come to faith as adults, they will wish to be baptised.

The second thing I have observed in this area is that, in some churches, we continue to act as though adult baptism is a rather embarrassing aberration from the norm. I am sometimes asked to confirm adults who have been quietly baptised at dusk while no one is looking, 'so that they can be confirmed'. We really need to get out of this way of thinking, and our new baptismal rite helps us to do so.

b) *Baptism is the 'main event'*

Up to now, baptism has been a 'part' of the service, slotted in at the appropriate (or sometimes, inappropriate) point. There was a desire in the General Synod that this possibility would continue to exist, in relation to Morning and Evening Prayer and a Service of the Word. Because of this, the version of the

---

3. The Diocese of Down and Dromore.

baptismal rite on p. 371 was drawn up. But the basic philosophy of the new baptismal service is that the whole service has a baptismal focus on the day on which baptism or baptisms take place. So, the service begins with an introduction about baptism, setting the scene right from the beginning. However, the collect and readings are normally those set for the day, and it is not the intention that the 'mood' of the particular season should be lost. So, special introductions, collects with a seasonal and baptismal reference and post-communion prayers have been drawn up and can be found on p. 392ff.

c) *The baptism comes as a response to the Word of God*
This is a very important theological point indeed. The baptismal rite takes place at the point, after the Ministry of the Word, where the Prayers of the People would normally come, and leads in to the peace and Celebrating at the Lord's Table (when there is a eucharist). Even in the 'slot in' rite on pp. 371-376, the rubric at the end makes it crystal clear:

> When Holy Baptism takes place during Morning and Evening Prayer, the sermon follows the Third Canticle, and the Baptismal Rite follows the sermon. The rest of Morning or Evening Prayer is omitted.

In a Service of the Word, the baptism comes as part of The Response section, after the ministry of the word.
So, the rule is the same throughout: The word, including the exposition of the word, is followed by the baptism. It is within the context of the word that the sacrament has meaning. It is the word which calls us to repentance and faith, whether exercised by the person being baptised or, on their behalf, by sponsors.

The Baptismal Rite itself
This begins, in its normative contemporary form, on p. 360. It has the following elements:

a) The Presentation
This is described by the rubrics:

> The presiding minister invites the candidates and their sponsors to stand in view of the congregation.

Christian Initiation Two

THE GATHERING OF GOD'S PEOPLE
Greeting
Introduction
|
Penitence
|
Gloria in Excelsis or another Hymn of Praise
|
(Silence)
Collect

PROCLAIMING AND RECEIVING THE WORD
Reading
Canticle, Psalm, Hymn or Anthem
Reading
Canticle, Psalm, Hymn or Anthem
Gospel Reading
|
Sermon
|
(Silence)

The Presentation
Candidates are presented
Questions to Parents and Godparents of those unable to answer
for themselves

The Decision
(Testimony)
|
Questions to candidates or sponsors
Question to the congregation
|
The Signing with the Cross*
|
(Hymn)

continued opposite

The Baptism
Water poured into the font
The Thanksgiving Prayer over the Water
|
Question about the Christian Faith to candidate or sponsors
Interrogatory Apostles' Creed
|
The Baptism
|
Welcome
|
The Peace

CELEBRATING AT THE LORD'S TABLE *When there is no Communion*
Post-baptismal Prayers
The Lord's Prayer

GOING OUT AS GOD'S PEOPLE
(Hymn)
(The Blessing)
The Dismissal (with the Giving of a Lighted Candle)

* The Signing with the Cross may take place here or after the Baptism

The presiding minister invites the sponsors of baptismal candidates to present the candidates.

This is true, whether the candidates are adults or children, and the sponsors are given a simple form of words to use in the presentation. In a sense this is the sponsors 'vouching' for the candidate's suitability for baptism.

Where an infant or a child is being presented, there are two subsequent questions about the responsibilities of parents and godparents to bring up the child in the life of faith. These can be very useful pastorally in focusing what is required of sponsors.

b) The Decision

This section begins with the words:

At this point, testimony may be given by one or more of the candidates.

Some people may be concerned about this rubric, that it will put undue pressure on quieter people to put their faith into words, or that it may seem to make a distinction between those who feel able to give a testimony and those who do not. However, in my experience, it can be a very important part of the liturgy. I conducted a baptism and confirmation of four adults recently in which each, in just two or three sentences said something of what had brought them to this point in their lives. It was a most powerful moment, and had the effect of lifting this section to a level of deep reality, and also of witnessing to the life of faith to others who had come to see the baptism taking place. However, it needs careful preparation, and to be kept free from clichés. Some may wonder how this applies to infant baptisms, and in a sense it does not. However, I have also experienced very useful words said by a parent about their faith (sometimes newly discovered) at the time of a child's baptism.

After the testimony, there are the more formal questions. They are longer and stronger than the older questions in the *APB* 1984. However, some people argued in the General Synod for the retention of the older questions in some form, and these have been added as an alternative in the version of the rite on p. 373. The questions asked in the new form have two different and logical foci: First, 'dying to sin', with words like: 'reject', 'renounce' and 'repent'; and secondly 'rising to new life' with words like: 'turn to Christ', 'submit to Christ', 'come to Christ'. In my view, though these are not as immediately memorable as the simpler form, they are a much warmer set of questions and answers.

After the response to these questions has been heard, the congregation is asked also to support the candidate in their new calling.

This section then ends with the signing with the sign of the cross. Here, an alternative is offered. The signing with the cross may be given either at this point, or after the baptism itself. What is important, and may be one of the arguments for having the consignation here, is that the signing with the cross should not be seen as part of the baptism itself or in any way detract from or 'cap' the pouring of or immersion into the water. There is very good early church precedent for the signing to be done at this point, but we need to realise that this gives it a different significance to that which it has when given after the baptism. At this point, the consignation is saying something like this: 'Now that you have made the decision, you are to be claimed as Christ's for ever. The cross delivers you from all that is dark and sinful, and is the gate of entry to new life in Christ.' When the signing is done later (as in the position suggested on pp. 374-5) it is more of a commissioning to be in the 'army' of Christ as his disciple. What needs to be noted, and which is not altogether clear from the rubric on p. 365, is that when the signing comes later in the normative service, it does not include the paragraph beginning 'May Almighty God deliver you.' This is only suitable at the earlier point in either form of the baptismal liturgy.

It might also be noted at this point that the whole issue of signing with the sign of the cross was controversial among the Puritans, and you will see a note explaining the whole issue of the retention of this sign in the Church in the 17th century, on p. 351.

c) The Baptism

At this point, a hymn may be sung as the presiding minister, along with the candidates, goes to the place of baptism. In some churches, the congregation will turn around to face the place of baptism at this point. In others, the children or indeed the whole congregation, may gather at the place of baptism, where the water is.

The next rubric is: 'Water is poured into the font.' Whether it be a baptism by submersion or pouring, there is a real necessity at this stage of the service, to hear the sound of living water. There should be plenty of it to make a dramatic impact. The Toronto *IALC* put it like this:

4.5 The administration of water. Whenever possible, candidates should be thoroughly immersed in water, or at least have it generously poured over them, as traditional Anglican rites direct. If appropriate provision for this method of administration cannot be made in the church building, the baptism may take place in another location. The construction or

renovation of church buildings should allow for the abun-
dant use of water in baptism.

Meanwhile, we have the prayer of thanksgiving over the water.
The verbs used in each of the prayers ask:

Pour out your Holy Spirit in blessing and sanctify this water,
so that ...

and

Sanctify this water, that ...

This is, of course the word used in the traditional form:

Sanctify this water to the mystical washing away of sin.

The intention is quite clear. This is the prayer through which we
set aside this water for a holy, sacramental purpose. The setting
aside of the water is not so that it in some sense will be holy in its
own right, but always, in the prayers we use, terminates on its
use – that those who are to be baptised in it may be made one
with Christ in his death and resurrection.

The prayers over the water, one of which is responsive and
the other of which is in a more traditional mode, focus on the
uses of water in the history of our salvation and, on the basis of
the way in which God has used water in the past, pray that he
will use it here and now in his saving purposes.

After the thanksgiving over the water, we come to the credal
declaration of faith. This always happens just before the baptism
itself. Indeed, in the case of baptism by submersion, the candidate should be stood in the water to make this declaration. This
is the gateway to baptism itself: the declaration of the baptismal
creed (The Apostles' Creed). Up to now, in our liturgies, the candidate has been asked simply to say the creed on their own, or
through their sponsors, but now, the instruction to the congregation is:

Brothers and sisters, I ask you to profess, together with these
candidates the faith of the church.

After which the creed comes in its interrogative[4] form. Doing it
this way has a doubly-positive impact:

---

4. The whole question of how to design interrogative forms of the
    creed for baptismal liturgies has been answered in various different

i) It ensures that there is not the damp-squib effect at this high
    point of an inaudible declaration of faith.
ii) It conveys the idea that baptism is in and through and into a
    community of faith.

The baptism then takes place, 'in the name of the Father and
of the Son and of them Holy Spirit'.

This baptismal formula is sacrosanct. Issues have arisen over
the years as to whether other formulae would do at this point ...
the name of Jesus ... or 'Creator, Redeemer, Sustainer'. In answer to those questions, the Toronto *IALC* concluded:

> Whatever language is used in the rest of the baptismal rite,
> both the profession of faith and the baptismal formula
> should continue to name God as Father, Son and Holy Spirit.

The danger of doing otherwise is that baptisms could take place,
with some alternative formula, which would not be acceptable
in the rest of the worldwide Christian church, and this could
have very serious repercussions.

Finally, in this section, some more thoughts about the mode
of baptism. The services itself, as the traditional *BCP 1926* service, allows for two modes of baptism: 'dipping the candidates
in the water, or pouring water over them'. There are a few things
we can learn from this:

i) The actual mode of baptism in the scriptures is not clear.
    What is clear, however, is that water is involved, and in-
    volved in a big way. The Church of Ireland does not, like the
    Baptists, insist on immersion. Nor, however, does it denigrate
    immersion. This means, in my view, that a person who is to be

---

ways over the stages of liturgical revision. E.g. on some occasions,
the sponsors or candidates have been asked to say the whole creed
themselves, either *in toto* or broken into three parts. On other occasions, a summary of the creed has been devised to reduce the number of words, but this can be a problem, as the purpose of the
Apostles' Creed is exactly that – to be an agreed summary of the
Christian faith. On other occasions, the minister asked the question
in the words of the creed, and the candidates replied, 'I believe'. In
this revision, the whole congregation say the creed in three sections
along with the candidates. This is probably the most effective option.

baptised should neither be denied immersion nor forced to be baptised by immersion. Dipping and pouring are two equal options, which should be equally available to all.

ii) 'Sprinkling' is not, however, an Anglican option. Some non-conformist churches allow sprinkling, but the Church of Ireland does not include it as an option. Basically, not only is baptism by water, but the water should be clearly seen.

iii) Although it is common Christian practice to dip or pour three times, at the mention of the three persons of the Trinity, it is not required by the liturgy. One is quite adequate, though three may to some be preferable (see Note 3, p. 368).

iv) I think we need to get used to the fact that baptism will make people wet! One of our problems in sacramental liturgy is that we have inherited a mix of solemnisation and sentiment-ality. So, the wine of communion only touches our lips, the bread is broken into neat cubes, and the water of baptism is more or less invisible. On one occasion, I heard of a minister who went to the font to baptise only to discover that the water had seeped out of the font. He went ahead with the service, pretending that there was water, and no one in the congregation noticed! 'Dry cleaning!' That sort of thing should not be possible.

v) I am also concerned about the impression given when a priest gets out a towel as soon as the baptism has taken place, and dries the water off from the forehead of the baby. Let the water drip!

vi) Both these options are available for both infants and adults. The only rider is in the old rubric in the *BCP 1926*:

> And then, naming it … he shall dip it in the water discreetly and warily, if they shall desire it and he shall be certified that the Child may well endure it; otherwise it shall suffice to pour water on it …

After the baptism and the consignation, if it takes place at this point (which if it does should be clearly separate from the baptism, by doing all baptisms first and then all signings), there are the words of welcome by the congregation to the newly-baptised, followed by the peace, in which the new member is greeted by all around, as the congregation share God's peace with one another.

The service then continues, whether with Holy Communion, or with the Prayers of the People, which may be the prayers on p. 369ff. This raises one final issue, which is always around when the subject of baptism is discussed in the Church of Ireland.

Baptismal Regeneration

To say that this has been a divisive issue historically in the Church of Ireland is probably an understatement. Along with certain doctrines of eucharistic sacrifice and prayers for the departed, this has been one of the major areas of controversy over the years. Hopefully, some of the heat engendered by these arguments has gone out of them, and light may begin to enter in.

One of the famous events in the history of the Church of England, using, of course, the same liturgy as the Church of Ireland at the time, was the Gorham judgement of 1850. The judgment of the Ecclesiastical Committee of the Privy Council on the appeal of George Gorham from the Court of Arches, stated this in relation to the teaching of the Church of England on baptismal regeneration:

> We judge that Baptism is a sacrament generally[5] necessary to salvation, but that the grace of regeneration does not so necessarily accompany the act of Baptism that regeneration invariably takes place in Baptism ... in no case is regeneration in Baptism unconditional.

The reason for raising the issue here is that some people have found difficulty in the strong sacramental language used in baptism in Church of Ireland services. In the traditional form, it is expressed in these words after the baptism:

---

5. The word 'generally' in this context, as in the Catechism (p. 769) means, of course, 'universally'. In other words, if a sacrament is instituted by Christ himself, and commanded by him, it cannot be thought of as optional.

Seeing now, dearly beloved brethren, that this Child is regen-
erate … (p. 350),

and is further expressed in the prayers which may be used after
baptism in the contemporary rite, in the words:

Father, we thank you that … have now been born again of
water and the Holy Spirit …

But what is different in the new contemporary rite is that the ap-
parently absolute declaration of regeneration after baptism is
now optional in both forms of service. The General Synod had
the opportunity to make it mandatory, at least in one version of
the service, and did not do so. So, for those who feel that the
words are too strong, other prayers may be used.

However, I would wish to make a plea for the idea that baptism is the sacrament of regeneration. When we bring our children to baptism we do so asking, in Cranmer's terms, that God
would give

to this Child that thing which my nature he cannot have …

That he, coming to thy Holy Baptism, may receive remission
of his sins by spiritual regeneration.

Nothing less is good enough as our prayer. Otherwise, we make
baptism into a dedication ceremony, rather than a proclamation
of the gospel. So, throughout the new service, whether for an
adult coming to Christian faith, or to the child of believing parents, the theme of regeneration (the secret spiritual work of God
alone in bringing to new birth) is still strong and firm:

Water is also a sign of new life; we are born again by water
and the Spirit through faith in Christ.' (*Pastoral Introduction*
p. 357)

Our Lord Jesus Christ has told us

that to enter the kingdom of heaven

we must be born again of water and the Spirit,

and has given us baptism as the sign and seal of this new
birth. (*Words of Greeting* p. 358)

And now we give you thanks that you have called … to new
birth in your Church through the waters of baptism'

(*Prayer over the Water* p. 363)

Now sanctify this water that, by the power of the Holy Spirit,
they may be cleansed from sin and born again.
(*Prayer over the Water* p. 364)

There is no meaning to becoming a member of the church without spiritual re-birth. There is no other way in to Christ. There is no prayer more important for Christian parents, who know new life in Christ, to pray for their children. Baptism is about a sacramental starting-point to faith, and the only starting-point, symbolised in baptism and needed by all, is spiritual regeneration.

The end of the service

The service concludes with The Dismissal. At this point, after the blessing, if it is used, the newly baptised is sent out with these words:

God has delivered us from the dominion of darkness
and has given us a place with the saints in light.

You have received the light of Christ;
walk in this light all the days of your life.
Shine as a light in the world
To the glory of God the Father.

Obviously, this is another reminder that the whole of the service is baptismal. The service, in the notes on p. 368, also allows for the presiding minister or another person to give a lighted candle to the newly-baptised. Sometimes this is a good role for the Sunday School superintendent, or for someone who has a particular ministry among children in the church. Such a candle can be a very important symbol for a family to hold on to, through which a growing child can be reminded of their baptism. It would be possible for a church with a 'Baptismal Roll' to send one of the cards produced by the Mothers' Union, on the anniversary of the baptism each year, and to suggest that parents light the baptismal candle, speak of the baptism, say a brief prayer over the child, and use the words above.

Holy Baptism
in the context of Morning or Evening Prayer or A Service of the Word

after the Ministry of the Word:
Introduction

The Presentation
Candidates are presented
Questions to parents and sponsors
of those unable to answer for themselves

The Decision
(Testimony)
Questions to candidates or sponsors
Question to the congregation
|
(Hymn)

The Baptism
Water poured into the font
Thanksgiving Prayer over the water
|
Question about the Christian Faith to candidate or sponsors
|
Interrogatory Apostles' Creed
|
The Baptism
|
The Signing with the Cross*
The Welcome

Prayers of the People
Prayers
The Collect of the Day
The Lord's Prayer

GOING OUT AS GOD'S PEOPLE
(Blessing)
Dismissal (with the Giving of a Lighted Candle)

---

* *The Signing with the Cross may take place here or after the questions in the Decision section.*

Receiving into the Congregation those privately baptised
The very fact that such a service exists (p. 377) highlights the importance that baptism should normally be a public event. This is also affirmed in the Notes at the end of *Holy Baptism One*:

> It is desirable that members of the parish be present to support, by their faith and prayer, those who are to be baptised and received into the fellowship of the Church.

However, there may be 'emergency' situations where a baptism takes place privately, and the sense of connectedness to the local Christian community is lost. On these occasions, this service should be used as soon as is convenient in the course of public worship. You will also note that, when emergency baptism takes place (for example when a baby is in danger of death), it is:

> Sufficient to name the candidate and pour water on the person's head, saying: '… I baptize you in the name of the Father, and of the Son, and of the Holy Spirit. Amen.'

Such a baptism may be conducted by a lay person.

Conditional Baptism
There are occasions when a person who has come to faith is unsure about whether they have been baptised or not, or indeed, whether their baptism is valid or not. Generally speaking, this will happen because there is no certificate, or because of uncertainty about whether the person was 'dedicated' or baptised. On certain occasions, there may also be the uncertainty about whether a previous 'baptism' was in the name of the Trinity; or there may be uncertainties about certain sects or churches which do not hold to Trinitarian doctrine.

The answer, in most of these cases where there is uncertainty, is conditional baptism, where the following words are used:

> … If you have not already been baptised,
> I baptise you in the name of the Father, and of the Son, and of the Holy Spirit. Amen.

Confirmation
The revised confirmation service begins on p. 382, and has many of the same starting-points as the new baptismal rite. For example:

Confirmation Two

THE GATHERING OF GOD'S PEOPLE
Greeting
Introduction
|
Penitence
|
Gloria in Excelsis or other Hymn of Praise
|
(Silence)
The Collect of the Day

PROCLAIMING AND RECEIVING THE WORD
Reading
(Canticle, Psalm, Hymn or Anthem)
Reading
(Canticle, Psalm, Hymn or Anthem)
The Gospel
|
Sermon
(Silence)

The Presentation
Candidates are presented to the bishop
Preliminary questions to the Candidates
Question to those responsible for the pastoral care of the candidates
|
(Testimony)

The Decision
Questions to the candidates
Question to the Congregation

The Profession of Faith
Question about the Christian Faith to the Candidates
Interrogatory Apostles' Creed
|
(Hymn, Chant or Litany)

continued opposite

The Confirmation
Versicles and Responses
Silence
The Confirmation Prayer and the Laying on of hands
For Confirmation or Reaffirmation

The Commission
Questions of Commissioning
|
The Peace
|
(Hymn)

CELEBRATING AT THE LORD'S TABLE   *When there is no Communion*
                                        The Prayers of the People
                                        The Lord's Prayer

GOING OUT AS GOD'S PEOPLE
(The Blessing)
The Dismissal

*Where there is a service of Holy Baptism, Confirmation and Holy
Communion, the structures is as laid out on p. 397*

– The structure is essentially the eucharistic structure
– The readings are normally to be those of the day
– The special seasonal baptismal material may be used.

The introduction to the new confirmation service may be adapted by the bishop to suit the needs of the particular occasion, but the set text plays on the idea of confirmation being a two-sided coin: the candidate affirming their faith in Christ, and Christ by the Spirit confirming and strengthening them to live for him.

After Proclaiming and Receiving the Word, the confirmation proper begins. We will go through it stage by stage, though much is the same as with baptism.

a) The Presentation

The candidates are presented to the congregation by their god-parents or sponsors, where this is appropriate. Sometimes it may be by others. The question is then asked as to whether or not they have been baptised. (It may be obvious, but perhaps needs to be spelt out: You cannot confirm a promise which has not already been made!) Then the bishop asks a question of the clergy who have been responsible for the pastoral care of the candidates. (In some cases, lay people will hopefully have taken some of the responsibility also.) And testimony may follow.

b) The Decision

c) The Profession of Faith
are exactly as they were in the baptismal service, except for one question.
At this point,

> The bishop and the candidates gather at the place of confirmation.

Sometimes this will be the communion rail. Sometimes it will be the chancel step. If it is possible for the candidates to do their moving at this point, it gives them a real chance to 'settle' for the confirmation prayer. When they are moving out of and into seats, they are often more concerned about getting the logistics right than they are about the content and meaning of the prayer.

d) The Confirmation

Two responses follow – a reminder that all we do in calling down the power of the Holy Spirit is empty without the presence of God. Then silence. Total silence for as long as the congregation can reasonably pray. And the Confirmation Prayer. Everything from the rubric two-thirds of the way down p. 387 to the 'Amen' at the bottom of the next page, is the Confirmation Prayer. All of this is prayed over all the candidates. It is appropriate for the hands of the bishop to be outstretched. If there are not too many candidates, it is also appropriate for the congregation to be standing, praying over each person.

Please also note that there is also a prayer for re-affirmation of baptismal promises. This may be suitable where someone has been confirmed in another denomination, or where a person had had a recent conversion experience, but has been confirmed earlier in life.

e) The Commission

The Commission on p. 389 may be used with the candidates or with the entire congregation, so that the life to which the committed believer is called is made clear. The service then continues with the Peace and Holy Communion, or special prayers.

Holy Baptism, Confirmation and Holy Communion

This, we must admit, is a lengthy and complicated service, and needs to be prepared for very thoroughly in conjunction with the bishop. The kinds of questions which need to be answered are:

– How are the questions in the presentation and at the decision to be worded?
– How do we make the connection between what is happening at the font with the people being baptised, and what is happening with those who are being confirmed? In my view all the candidates should be at the font either to be baptised or to renew their promises, and to share in the creed.
– Who does the baptism? The bishop, who is presiding over the service or the local priest? Often, it will be delegated by the bishop to the local minister, but this raises the interesting question as to whether the bishop is primarily a minister of baptism or of confirmation, and as to which of the two actions is more important. It might also raise the issue of whether confirmation is theologically necessary at all after adult baptism, where the person has themselves made the promises.

The prayer book simply gives us a structure, but a service sheet will need to be designed for such an occasion, and designed with an eye to detail. Having said that, done well, it can be a powerful and memorable service.

The Renewal of Baptismal Vows

The penultimate service in the section *Christian Initiation Two* is *The Renewal of Baptismal Vows*. This is a very useful little service and may be used on a variety of occasions, but should not be used too often. Certain options are mentions at the beginning of the service itself: Easter, Pentecost, The Baptism of our Lord. To these might be added: Occasions when we use the Methodist Covenant Service (usually the First Sunday of the new year), or the Conclusion of or Thanksgiving for a major Mission in a parish.

The most common usage of this service in the Anglican Communion is probably Easter Eve, at the Easter Vigil Service, in preparation for the celebrations of Easter Day.

However, the service does not always have to be something used by every member of the congregation. It could also be used by people who have come to faith through an *Alpha, Emmaus* or *Christianity Explored* course to make a public witness in front of a congregation. It is vitally important that the liturgy of the Church is able to respond to and fit situations of evangelism. After all, baptism in its essence is to do with evangelism, and when people have a life-transforming experience they often need a way to share it publicly, and to receive the affirmation of the church.

The service itself is simply a short introduction, followed by two different forms of renewal, and two short prayers.

Thanksgiving after the Birth of a Child
Thanksgiving after Adoption
In a sense, this service is the replacement for the Churching of Women, in the old *Book of Common Prayer*. The service of churching did, of course, have as its first title, *The Thanksgiving of Women after Childbirth* and, although it was given a bad press in relation to the 'cleansing' of women after childbirth, it was in fact much more to do with thanksgiving for a safe delivery.

The new service fulfils this need, but does not have to happen in church. The rubric suggests that it might happen in hospital, or at home soon after the birth. The service after adoption might also happen at home.

This service, however, has also another function: it can be used for parents who do not feel able to take the promises required for baptism. In cases like this, it may well be appropriate to hold the service in the church, but it is important that it is not seen as a substitute for baptism. There are, however, many parents who simply wish to thank God for their new-born child and leave it at that. Perhaps the birth has given them a new sense of the reality of God as Creator, and they are truly thankful. This service may well be a suitable vehicle for them.

Questions for Reflection or Discussion

1. Why do you think it is important, as much as possible, for baptism to be a public event?

2. What aspects of the meaning of the sacrament are expressed by the two different methods of baptism: a) the pouring of water and b) submersion into water?

3. How do you understand the meaning of language about regeneration (being 'born again') in the baptismal services? What do you think being 'born again' means?

4. What arguments would you give for children being allowed to receive Holy Communion before being confirmed? What arguments would you give against?

5. What do you think is the essential meaning of the rite of confirmation? How do you find this drawn out in the service of confirmation? Do you think people who have been baptised as adults need to be confirmed?

CHAPTER TWELVE

Marriage Services

The marriage services in the new *Book of Common Prayer* include, as is the case with most of the services, both a traditional rite, from the *BCP 1926*, and a revised contemporary rite, *Marriage Services Two*. In the case of marriage, the contemporary rite has been only mildly revised –it was considered in general to be working well in the version published in the white booklet format in 1987 and in *Alternative Occasional Services* 1993. We will walk through this revised rite later in this chapter, but first of all we need to note some of the issues surrounding marriage which have led to changes over the past decade or so.

A Service in Church after a Civil Marriage
First of all, the *Book of Common Prayer* now includes a service called: *A Form of Prayer and Dedication after a Civil Marriage*. In the past, a form such as this one would have been used chiefly for marriages where one party was divorced, and where the marriage itself had taken place in a Registry Office. But, nowadays, although that is still one of the scenarios in which this form may well be used, there may well be other reasons for a couple being married in a state ceremony, followed by a service in church. For example, there are many countries in Europe where a couple is required by law to be married in a civil ceremony. With our strong links to the rest of Europe there will be more cases where a couple are married in one European country, and then ask for a ceremony in church where family and friends in Ireland can be present. Or there may simply be people who wish to have a civil ceremony in this country followed by prayer in church. The Church of Ireland has always recognised the total validity of

A Form of Prayer and Dedication after a Civil Marriage

The Married couple enter the church
|
Introduction
(Hymn)
|
The Collect

PROCLAIMING AND RECEIVING THE WORD
Reading(s)
(Gospel*)
|
Sermon
|
(Hymn)

The Dedication
Words to the couple
Promises by the couple
Joining of hands and prayer over the ring(s)
Promise by the congregation
|
Prayer said by the couple
Prayers for blessing of the couple
|
(Hymn)
|
Prayers
|
The Peace
(Hymn)

CELEBRATING AT THE LORD'S TABLE   *When there is no Communion*
                                           The Lord's Prayer
|
The Ending

civil marriage ceremonies, as marriage is essentially an ordering of society, and we should have no problem with this model, if people wish to follow it. The 'form' for this is found on p. 431.

There are several things we should note about this form:

a) It avoids the title 'blessing'. So should we all, in speaking
    about such a ceremony. This is not a 'blessing ceremony' as
    such, although we ask for God's blessing on the new mar-
    riage. If it is called a 'blessing' and offered, for example, to a
    couple where one has been divorced, the church can very
    easily be accused of hypocrisy. This is really a form of prayer
    and dedication.

b) It does not repeat what has happened in the marriage cere-
    mony. Although it is quite possible that a bride may arrive at
    such a ceremony in all the wedding 'gear', nevertheless, this
    is not the marriage ceremony proper, and a couple cannot be
    allowed to act in circumstances such as this, as though they
    are not already married. So, although much of the text of the
    service is reminiscent of the Marriage Service (after all, it is
    still declaring a Christian understanding of marriage), never-
    theless, it is re-calling the couple to the marriage vows which
    they have already taken, and should never be seen as the
    marriage itself, or worse, as being more important than the
    marriage ceremony. The couple is fully married in the eyes of
    God when the civil ceremony has taken place. So, the dedica-
    tion after the marriage begins with the words (p. 433):
        '… and …, you have committed yourselves to each other
        in marriage, and your marriage is recognised by law.'
    and the service continues in this vein with words such as
    'you have taken'. When it comes to the rings, the couple do
    not give and receive rings, but simply join their wedding-
    ring hands.

c) No entry should be made in any marriage register, in case
    that might cause confusion.

Service of Preparation where one of a couple is divorced

The General Synod Legislation on the Remarriage of Divorced
Persons[1] is another change which has taken place in the Church
of Ireland in this area, since the last revision of the marriage services. The legislation requires the clergyperson who is applying

1. General Synod of the Church of Ireland 1996. Embodied in Canon
    31 in the Constitution of the Church of Ireland.

to the bishop, with the possibility that they might conduct such a service, first of all to listen carefully to and consider the bishop's opinion in the matter, before making a final decision. If a decision is made to conduct such a service, the couple concerned are required to engage in a Service of Preparation (Appendix 6, p. 250). This service is not to be found in the *Book of Common Prayer*, but is one of the resources which the Liturgical Advisory Committee would hope to make easily available. After such a service has been conducted, the Marriage Service proceeds as it is in the *Book of Common Prayer*. One of the areas of confusion which some clergy have about the remarriage of divorced persons is what should be done if a particular minister is not happy on principle about conducting such services. My understanding is that such a person should make this known to the couple who are applying for marriage after divorce, and that the archdeacon then acts as the rector in that situation. Because, when the legislation was drawn up, buildings were licensed for the conduct of marriages rather than persons, this was the one occasion on which the archdeacon could require the use of a rector's church for the ceremony. However, the situation in Northern Ireland is now more confused, as from 1 January 2004 it is people rather than buildings which will be licensed for the conduct of marriages. This means that anyone other than the rector of the parish, asking to conduct a marriage in a particular church, on any occasion including the above, will be required by the church to have the permission of the incumbent.

New Legislation in Northern Ireland

As I have mentioned above, the new marriage legislation licenses certain people for the conduct of marriages, rather than certain places. This means that each bishop will return a list of those clergy within the diocese who are to be allowed to conduct marriages. Generally, this will include at least all licensed serving clergy in a diocese. It means that, according to the state, the people licensed are free to conduct marriages anywhere they wish (hotels, big dippers, mountain-tops, etc, etc). However, this new 'freedom' will be limited by regulations drawn up by the church, which may well at some point enter into canon law. This will restrict clergy of the Church of Ireland from conducting marriages elsewhere than in churches, except in very clearly specified situations. There are several reasons for doing this:

a) If a person wants a ceremony in one of these places, it can be a civil ceremony. If they want a religious ceremony, it should be in a suitable building.

b) It is very important to the church that marriage should be a public, societal event. Holding more 'private' marriages in a range of places can make the event less public.

c) The context of the ceremony should not lead in any way to marriage being treated less than seriously, and some of the well-argued options would!

Teaching about marriage in Marriage One *and* Marriage Two
As I will not be dealing in detail with the actual liturgy of Marriage One in this volume, it is worth charting out some of the similarities and some of the differences in understanding about marriage in the two services.

Similarities
One of the chief similarities is, quite simply, that holy matrimony takes place both before God and before public witnesses. Marriage is een as partly God's plan for the right ordering of society, but also as a 'holy mystery' and as a sign of 'the mystical union' of Christ and his church.

Both services also agree on the traditional Christian starting points for marriage. These are a kind of three-legged stool:

Leg 1: Marriage is to be monogamous. Only two people are involved, committing their lives to each other exclusively, 'forsaking all others'. This is further spelt out in the Constitution of the Church of Ireland, Canon 31, section 1:

> The Church of Ireland affirms, according to our Lord's teaching, that marriage is in its purpose a union … of one man and one woman, to the exclusion of all others on either side.

Leg 2: Marriage is to be lifelong. In *Marriage One* 'as long as ye both shall live', 'till death us do part'; in *Marriage Two* the same, with the exception that 'ye' becomes 'you'. In Canon 31: 'permanent and life-long'.

It is only in the light of all this that any legislation about the remarriage of divorced persons can be understood. No one should run away with the idea, *simpliciter*, that 'the Church of Ireland remarries divorced people in church.

Leg 3: Marriage is to be heterosexual. This is clear from Canon 31: 'of one man with one woman', and is partly the definition of marriage itself and the Church of Ireland's understanding of it. Both services are premised on the concept of a husband and a wife – a concept which will be increasingly challenged in years to come.

Differences

There are, however, several differences in emphasis in the two services. In *Marriage One*, the order of the 'causes for which matrimony was ordained' are: 'First, for the increase of mankind'; secondly for 'the hallowing of the union betwixt man and woman, and for the avoidance of sin'; and thirdly 'for the mutual society, help and comfort, that the one ought to have of the other'. In *Marriage Two*, the emphasis is different. First comes the comforting and help of one another, second 'that with delight and tenderness they may know each other in love, and through the joy opf their bodily union they might strengthen the union of their hearts and lives'; and, third, the blessing of children.

It would not be appropriate for me to suggest which order is better, but undoubtedly the latter reflects a change in emphasis not least in the recognition that not every couplke will be able to have children, or even choose to have children (which is a serious theological issue).

Marriage Two

The Entry
(Greeting of the Bridal or Marriage Party)
(Hymn or music)
|
Greeting

The Introduction
Introduction
|
The Collect

PROCLAIMING AND RECEIVING THE WORD
Reading(s)
|
Sermon

THE MARRIAGE
Question to the congregation
Words to the couple
|
The Consent
|
The Vows
|
Giving and receiving of a ring
|
The Declaration,
Including the joining of hands
|
The Blessing of the Couple
|
Affirmation by the People
|
The Acclamations
|
(The Registration of the Marriage)
(A Psalm or Hymn)

continued opposite

THE PRAYERS
Intercessions
(Silence)
(Prayer said by the couple)
|
The Peace
(Hymn)
|
The Lord's Prayer
|
(The Grace or The Blessing)

Marriage Two

Now to the marriage service itself. I wrote in detail on the previous version of the Marriage Service in *Making an Occasion of it*,[2] and will repeat some of that material here.

First of all, the couple needs to be thoroughly involved in designing their Marriage Service. Note 4 puts it like this:

The minister and the couple should together choose the readings, hymns and the prayers to be used in the service.

Now, this needs to be treated both seriously and carefully. The service is being conducted in a church, and is a Christian event. So, there must always be reading from the scriptures (note 2 says 'All readings in Proclaiming and Receiving the Word must be from Holy Scripture.') Although there are times when a favourite piece of secular music, or even a song, can be very powerful, the hymns or songs sung by the congregation will be Christian hymns or songs. Clergy in the Church of Ireland might well wish to equip themselves with the Guidelines from the Irish (Roman Catholic) Episcopal Conference on this matter. In the version which I have, the following is said about music at weddings:

Music plays an important role at weddings. As with any celebration, it heightens the atmosphere of festivity and joy, an atmosphere which is particularly appropriate to the rich festive celebration of the sacrament of marriage.

---

2. Op. cit. p. 17.

Unfortunately, music at weddings has tended at times to be looked upon as something merely ornamental, something added to help build up a pleasant background to the ceremony. Certain items customarily requested, such as the *Wedding March* of Mendelssohn, the *Bridal March* of Wagner, or the *Ave Maria* of Gounod or Schubert in no way reflect the richness of the sacrament in which Christ himself is present to grace the union of bride and groom.'

However, the minister conducting the service (who will normally be a priest, but may be a deacon) will need to sit down and talk through with the couple how the marriage service is to be drawn up.

Secondly, the couple need to be thoroughly prepared for their marriage. When the Church agrees to conduct a marriage, it takes on at least some of the responsibility for preparation. Note 1 makes this clear:

As much notice as possible should be given to the minister of the parish to allow sufficient time for adequate preparation before marriage.

In some churches, the pastor will do the preparation. Other larger parishes should probably have their own course, led by lay people. Others may feed people into a pre-packaged course done centrally, or even by video or DVD.

Thirdly, it is fascinating to discover the number of traditions which people coming to weddings in general, and wedding services in particular, consider to be *de rigeur*. For example:

- The family of the bride must be on one side, the family of the groom on the other.
- The groom must be seated at the front of the church at the beginning, and the bride must come up the aisle in her father's arm.
- The bride must wear a white dress.
- The bride must be 'given away' by her father (even when it doesn't come in the service, as with the contemporary version).
- The registration must be in the vestry …

And so they continue.

Now, far be it from me to be an iconoclast, because many of these traditions give stability – the sense that there is a right and proper thing to do, and all you need to do is find out and do it right! But it is worth clergy at times freeing people from some of the less meaningful traditions (Like the father giving the bride away, as a kind of chattel and the registration being done away from people's sight).

So, we walk through the service:

a. The Entry
The minister may greet the bridal party at the door, with the words:

Blessed are they who come in the name of the Lord.

We bless you from the house of the Lord.

O give thanks to the Lord for he is good,

For his steadfast love endures for ever.

This is a new device in the service, and one which has the potential to fall flat on its face, if it is not properly thought out and planned. Most brides are in the midst of a photoshoot at this stage, making sure the dress is right, and getting to the church on time, or not on time, as the case may be. They may feel too hassled to have any words said to them at this point. But these words could be sensitively used at the door to quieten things down after all the fuss, and to prepare the bridal party to enter the church for the wedding service.

b. Greeting and Introduction
As with most services, the minister greets the congregation with the words 'The Lord be with you', a sentence of scripture setting the scene and an introduction, stating clearly what we are here to do. There is a balance to be achieved here, because the whole congregation is being welcomed, but the bride and groom have a special place and should, at an early stage, be named by name. This is their occasion, and everyone is here to support them. The introductory part finishes with the gathering prayer, the collect.

c. Proclaiming and Receiving the Word

Here, the service varies from its predecessor, in that the word is given pride of place at this point. Note that in *Marriage Two* the sermon is given a normative part of the liturgy, whereas in *Marriage One* the rubric says 'If there is a sermon ...' In wedding services generally, the marriage has taken place before the word, with the bride and groom duly settled, having been declared husband and wife. But here, the preferred place is before the marriage proper. Note 2 on p. 428, however, allows for the readings later: 'These [the readings] may be used where printed in the service or after The Affirmation of the People.' What is practically important is that bride and groom (and the bridal party) be allowed to sit for the Proclaiming and Receiving of the Word (apart from the reading of the gospel, of course, in the context of Holy Communion). Another note suggests that if a bible is to be given to the bride and groom, it should be given before the readings; but I must confess that I normally give it to the couple at the end of the address, with the text used for the address written on the fly leaf. What is important about the address is that it should be a word from God, given to the couple, but relevant to the whole congregation.

d. The Marriage

Here the minister asks if anyone objects to the marriage taking place. At this point, people often wonder what would happen if there were to be an objection. The official answer is to be found on p. 429:

> ... the person alleging or declaring the impediment is required to deposit or by sureties guarantee, such a sum as would cover the cost of the wedding and of all other expenses incurred therewith ...

Then the bride and groom give their consent, the vows are made (now totally without 'obey' on the bride's part – you have to go to the older form of service for that one!), the ring or rings are given, and the priest declares them to be husband and wife, joins their hands and pronounces:

> What God has joined together let no one put asunder.

This is followed by a nuptial blessing on the couple, with the congregation standing, as it were gathered around them in prayer. As their response, a new prayer has been added – a prayer of thanksgiving which the couple may choose to say publically, in gratitude to God for bringing their lives together. This is followed by the Affirmation of the People (another new addition), and the Acclamations.

e. The Registration

We will deal with the registration of the marriage at this point, because, although traditional in many places, it does not really need to take place in some hidden-away room as a kind of anti-climax to the service, while a soloist fills the time required. A small table, placed at the chancel steps, is adequate for a signing in public which will take a much shorter period of time. This really does work, and integrates the registration into the service proper, and perhaps a photograph can be allowed at this juncture?

f. The Prayers

The couple traditionally kneel at the Lord's Table, where they would remain until communion. In my view, it is best if the prayers at this point are led by friends gathered around the bride and groom. The prayers given at this point are revised versions of the prayers in the 1987 service, which needed some small changes. The new revision is cleaner, clearer and better, and a few new prayers have been added, including another prayer which may be said by the couple (p. 427) and a prayer thanking God for the gift of 'sexual love' (p. 426).

g. Holy Communion

If Holy Communion is to be celebrated, then the note on p. 428 should be observed:

> If Holy Communion is celebrated at the marriage, its reception should not be restricted to the bridal party.

Such a note was not part of the 1993 service, and amazingly, sometimes people still ask to have the sacrament for just the bride and groom. But communion, by its very nature and the meaning of the word, is for the whole body of Christ. What a wonderful way to end a wedding service: to be at the table of the Lord with your sisters and brothers in Christ!

Questions for Reflection or Discussion
1. You may wish to reflect on the reasons given for marriage in *Marriage One* and *Marriage Two*. What differences are there, and why?
2. What do you think is the difference between a marriage in church and the dedication after a civil ceremony? How would you feel if, as in some parts of Europe, all marriages were civil ceremonies, and these were followed by Christians by a dedication in church?
3. Which of the traditional ceremonies surrounding marriage in church are, in your view, expressing an important point, and which might be reconsidered?
4. What message does celebrating Holy Communion during a marriage in church send out?

CHAPTER THIRTEEN

Ministry to those who are Sick

Material provided

The 'material' provided for Ministry to those who are Sick comes on pages 440-464. Some of it is what we would traditionally describe as 'services', but much, in fact, is material for personal devotional use, which is particularly helpful when people are unwell. This is a reminder that, within the Anglican tradition, a *Book of Common Prayer* has never been simply a book for using in church, but has also been a devotional and teaching aid. People, at times of weakness, will hopefully turn to these pages and find there the comfort and strength they need in times of sickness.

It is perhaps worth charting the material which is actually provided:

– Preparation for Communion, *for private personal use before the service*;
– Holy Communion One;
– Holy Communion Two *with shorter adapted form*;
– Penitence and Reconciliation *for those who feel their conscience troubled*;
– The Laying on of Hands;
– Anointing with oil;
– Prayers and Readings *particularly suitable for personal use*;
– Preparation for death;
– A Celebration of Wholeness and Healing – *A form for a healing service.*

Even reading through what is contained in this section of the book is a reminder of several things: First of all, that there is a real richness of material here, which has not been found in quite the same way in former Church of Ireland prayer books. Second,

---

**Ministry to those who are Sick
and to others requiring particular pastoral care**

The components of this section of the Prayer Book are as follows:

Preparation for Communion
For private personal use before the service

A Shorter Form of Holy Communion for those who are sick

Material for Penitence and Reconciliation

Material for the Laying on of Hands

Material for Anointing with Oil

Prayers

Readings suitable for those who are sick

Preparation for Death

A Celebration of Wholeness and Healing
*The Structure for this is laid out on p. 457,
and material for the service on pp. 458-464*

---

that this *Book of Common Prayer* is not just a Sunday service book, but a book which provides for us at many different stages of our lives. And, third, that healing, difficult though we may find the issues at times, is central to the gospel of Jesus Christ, and should be part of the ministry of every local church. The *Church's Ministry of Healing* has been a constant reminder of this over many years, as has *Divine Healing Ministries*, but this ministry will be part of the pastoral care of every minister, and of the people in every parish. While we are healthy and well, we may wonder about providing twenty-five pages of material here, but the time may come in our lives when we will benefit greatly from it.

Holy Communion and Healing

The provision begins with Holy Communion, which must surely be the right place to start. It is, as is conveyed in Note 1 on page 440, one of the chief 'means of grace' in times of sickness. When someone is ill, they are often isolated from the community of faith, and unable to be at the Lord's Table in their local parish church. Note 2 reminds them:

> Christians unable to receive Holy Communion in their local church because of illness or disability are encouraged to ask for the sacrament.

Pastors will be more than glad to bring Holy Communion to those who are ill at home or in hospital.

One of my personal sadnesses with the provision for Ministry to those who are Sick is that it has not been able to include, officially, a provision for extended communion, as is, for example, provided by the Church of England in their services, on p. 74 of *Common Worship: Pastoral Services*. Some feared that this might be construed as 'reservation' of the sacrament. The idea of extended communion is simply that those who are unable to be in the fellowship of God's people at the Lord's Table on a Sunday might be remembered during the service in prayer, and that Holy Communion might be brought to them from the communion service in church immediately after the service. This would, of course, require the permission of the Ordinary.[1] Extended communion can make the sick person feel very much part of the community of faith, and does not need to be done by a priest: it is possible for agreed 'lay ministers' to bring the consecrated bread and wine from the main service. The words they

---

1. The 'Ordinary' in most cases will be the diocesan bishop. There is no provision for extended communion in the *BCP 2004*, but this does not mean that it is not allowed. Indeed, some dioceses have made provision for it in certain circumstances. The *General Directions for Public Worship* on p. 77 simply say: 'Any of the consecrated bread and wine remaining after the administration of the communion is to be reverently consumed', which would seem to me to preclude reservation but not the immediate distribution to others who are ill.

use in the Church of England service, when they come with the
bread and wine to the recipient, are:

> The Church of God, of which we are members, has taken
> bread and wine and given thanks over them according to our
> Lord's command. These holy gifts are now offered to us that,
> with faith and thanksgiving, we may share in the commu-
> nion of the body and blood of Christ.

This is followed by a simple liturgy of penitence, the collect,
scripture readings, etc. On such an occasion, it is wonderful if
the person ministering can tell the person a little bit about the
service in church, and even what the preacher said about the
gospel in the sermon. But, not too long!

Meanwhile, back to the communion services and material
provided in the *Book of Common Prayer*. First of all, there is material for preparation. Much of this could well be used by people
who are well. It is a way in which the sick person can get ready
for receiving Holy Communion. It is important that those caring
for the sick person prepare for this ministry. A small table with a
simple white cloth will do, but it is very helpful for a minister to
sense that the service is not taking place in a context of fuss and
bustle, but rather, in a context of quietness and preparation.
Those caring for a sick person might well wish to read some of
p. 441 to them before the minister arrives.

Holy Communion One
The *BCP 1926* sets out the guidelines for the use of the traditional
order. (By the way, you will note that only contemporary versions of the material in this area are provided, apart from the use
of the traditional form of Holy Communion.) The guidelines are:

– Most of the service will normally be used when a person is
   well enough, with the collect, epistle and gospel of the day or
   a special (short) collect, epistle and gospel for the sick. The
   service then moves from the gospel to 'Ye that do truly ...'
– When a person is very weak, it will suffice to use the confession, absolution, prayer of consecration, form of Delivery of
   the Sacrament, Lord's Prayer and Blessing.
– The sick person should receive last (clearly with the concern

that any disease should not be passed on to others). It is also assumed that others will gather around the sick person and receive communion with them.

Holy Communion Two

This service is in a form very similar to the material found in *Alternative Occasional Services* 1993. It is basically this:

– A collect (A specially suitable one is provided);
– Scripture reading;
– Penitence;
– Prayer (anointing or laying on of hands may take place here or after communion);
– The Great Thanksgiving (in an abbreviated form for this purpose);
– The breaking of the bread;
– Communion;
– Post-communion prayer;
– Blessing.

In my own ministry, I have found it vitally important to have this service on a sheet or card, ready and available for those who will not have the book. Also, it will be important to have available some in large print, for those whose sight is poor. But any pastor will know that this is one service in which a great deal of flexibility is required, and we need to be careful when people are weak only to use responses which they know well and versions of prayer (for example the Lord's Prayer), which are stored in the person's memory.

There are some other reminders in the material for the Ministry to the Sick, about Holy Communion at a time like this. For example, there may be occasions when it is not possible for a person to hold the cup, and we may wish to intinct[2] or simply to give communion in one kind.[3] There may also be times when it

---

2. Intinction is the dipping of the bread into the wine.
3. There may well be, for example, sick people who may only be able to receive the smallest amount of wine, but not solid food, and they may need to be assured that they are thereby receiving the fullness of the sacrament.

is not possible for the person to receive the elements at all, and
they need to be re-assured at a time like this, in the words of
Note 2:

> … that, although not receiving the elements in the mouth,
> they are by faith partakers of the body and blood of Christ
> and of the benefits he conveys to us by them.

Penitence and Reconciliation

The Church of Ireland has never taught the necessity of auricu-
lar[4] confession, but has always taught its availability.

In the *BCP 1926* order, the section entitled 'Exhortation to
Repentance' includes these words:

> The minister shall examine the sick person whether he repent
> him truly of his sins … Here, if the sick person feel his con-
> science troubled with any weighty matter, he shall be moved
> to open his grief.

In the 1662 *Book of Common Prayer*, following the 1549 and 1552
versions, the priest, having heard the confession of the person
concerned, uttered the words:

> I absolve thee from all thy sins.

This was changed in the Church of Ireland in 1878, to a simple
absolution, without the personal pronoun, to make it clear that
the priest was pronouncing absolution, rather than personally
giving it. But what we must note at this point is the need, especially after a very serious and personal confession of sins, conveying contrition, for the absolution to be clear and powerful,
addressed to the person, and not generalised with 'we'. The new
service puts it like this:

> Those who feel their conscience troubled in any way should
> be encouraged to open their heart on the matter.

And the confession (as is the use of *Psalm 51* in the *BCP 1926*) is

---

4. That is when we confess our sins to another person, usually a priest.
    This is not considered absolutely necessary in the Church of Ireland,
    but is available where it would be spiritually helpful. We can, of
    course, have immediate access to the Father through Christ, and
    complete forgiveness, but there is sometimes great value in confess-
    ing our sins to another, and in being reassured of God's mercy and
    grace.

in 'I' form – first person singular. Clergy may be inclined to change this to 'we', either because of an awareness that they too are sinners, or to save the embarrassment of the person, but this would be unwise, and could even be spiritually damaging.

The Laying on of Hands

In *A Dictionary of Liturgy and Worship*,[5] Gilbert Cope, in his articles on Gestures, writes about the laying on of hands:

> The gesture of laying hands upon (or over) a person or thing has the multiple significance of blessing, setting apart, consecrating, commissioning, absolving, healing, confirming, declaring, ordaining, and other associated ideas. Underlying the liturgical act is the notion of the transmission of power, mana, authority, spiritual grace, etc. Such channeling of unseen 'charisma' is thought of as being achieved through the physical action of touching with the hands.

Of course, there are numerous biblical examples of the laying on of hands in healing, and the Church down through the ages has used this sign as a means of blessing to those who are ill. The Church of England's *Common Worship: Pastoral Services* puts some flesh on to these bare bones, in its theological introduction to the 'Wholeness and Healing' section:

> Healing, reconciliation and restoration are integral to the good news of Jesus Christ. For this reason prayer for individuals, focused through laying on of hands or anointing with oil, has a proper place within the public prayer of the Church. God's gracious activity of healing is to be seen both as part of the proclaiming of the good news and as an outworking of the presence of the Spirit in the life of the Church.

The ministry of the laying on of hands is one of the places where liturgy moves from being perceived as something being done *to* the people of God to what it really is: the actual property of the people of God. Here, it is no longer possible simply to sit back and objectify: here the prayer is focused in a sacramental kind of way, on individuals.

---

5. *A Dictionary of Liturgy and Worship*, ed J G Davies (1972), SCM Press.

It is important to note also that the laying on of hands, in the context of healing, is not simply the preserve of clergy. Charismatic renewal had the effect of restoring in a major way the sense that this is a ministry which believers can offer to one another. The 'pattern' suggested for prayer with the Laying on of Hands on p. 447 allows for a framework, with specific prayers being added.

One or two reminders about the laying on of hands may be appropriate here:

a) In the world in which we live it is generally best to exercise this ministry in public, or at least with another person present. Hands should generally be laid on a person's head, and anything that may be considered inappropriate touching must be avoided.

b) Be careful not to be drawn in to the idea that the laying on of hands has to be lengthy. While it should not be rushed, it is not made more effective by being elongated.

c) When someone is sick, the 'minister' must be careful not to put undue weight on their head. We should also be careful not to expect a person to kneel or stand if they are unable to do so. Being seated is just as effective.

We must also be careful not to tell people they are healed before we have real evidence that this is so. Also, we must never imply that, if healing does not come, it is because the individual person does not have adequate faith. Also, we should not imply that their sickness is because of sin.[6]

Anointing with Oil

One of the questions which may reasonably be asked is 'What is the difference between prayer with the laying on of hands, and prayer with anointing?' Some believe that one is, by its very nature more informal, the other more formal. In other words, we have our hands with us all the time, but we need to prepare for anointing with oil, by having the oil available. Others would feel that anointing is more appropriately done by a priest, and that is certainly the presupposition in the form on p. 448, which says

---

6. We are reminded of this in the story of the man born blind in *John* 9:2.

(about the consecration of oil): 'If oil is to be consecrated, the priest or the bishop says:' and at the anointing itself: 'the priest, having dipped his thumb in the oil, anoints the person on the forehead, saying …'. The same is true in the form on p. 462, which begins: 'Oil for anointing may be brought to the priest', and continues: 'Anointing may be administered. The priest says … 'Still others would, perhaps with both the former distinctions in mind, feel that anointing was to be used as a particularly focal ministry when someone is seriously ill, or about to undergo a serious operation.

One of the other questions we need to answer is: 'Does oil for anointing need to be consecrated, and if so, by whom and when?' The new prayer book does not give an absolute answer, but acts as though oil for healing should be specifically set aside for that purpose. Normally the oil will be pure olive oil. In some places, it may have been consecrated for the whole diocese by the bishop at a special event (e.g. A Maundy Thursday eucharist for the clergy). But there is something to be said for the thanksgiving prayer being used at each service of anointing: it focuses the minds of the congregation on the depth of meaning in what is happening.

Prayers and Readings

Suffice it to say that pp. 450-453 provides, as did the old 'Visitation of the Sick', a selection of prayers and readings for personal use by those who are sick. This is a very beautiful and appropriate selection and might, as much of the rest of this section, have wider use, as is the case with much of the material for Ministry to the Sick.

Preparation for Death

This service is rather simplified, in comparison to what it used to be. In the *AOS 1993* version, it continued to include a litany, based in part on the Visitation of the Sick material in the *BCP 1926*. But, in reality, when a family are gathered around a bedside, it is probably not the time to be giving out a book so that they can follow responses. So, the litany has been removed. What we have now is simply five sentences of scripture, some readings which are very well known, a prayer of commendation, which may be accompanied by the signing of the cross on the person's forehead (I have to say that I believe this tactile sign can be very powerful indeed as a person comes close to death), the *Nunc Dimittis*, The Lord's Prayer and The Blessing.

One of the problems with this service is to know when to use it. It can be very difficult to discern when a person is actually dying, and one of the dangers is that we never find the right moment. If we use it too early on and the person recovers, we might feel that we have put the family or the individual through unnecessary trauma. No doubt the decision will largely be made in conjunction with the family involved and the medical staff. But the recognition of the closeness of death can at times be a very healing thing for all, and can even sometimes almost give the person 'permission' to die.

A Celebration of Wholeness and Healing[7]

Previously, the Church of Ireland has not had an official 'healing' service. We have depended on the individual initiative of clergy, guided by organisations like the *Church's Ministry of Healing*. But now, for the first time, an official form with the approval of the General Synod, is available. The structure is laid out on p. 457. It is essentially the same structure as the eucharistic rite (Do you notice how often that is the case with the new services?), with the section between Proclaiming and Receiving the Word and Celebrating at the Lord's Table being used for prayers of penitence and healing, with the laying on of hands (and anointing). It does not have to be a communion service, but that would be the norm, in my view, for a full liturgy of healing. This has the effect of retaining the Holy Communion as the climax of all healing offered in the service. Much of the material in this service is new and is drawn from the Church of England rite which is imaginatively written. So, there are new prayers, a new

---

7. This wonderful title, which sums up so much of the biblical meaning of 'salvation' comes from the *Common Worship: Pastoral Services* (2000), Church House Publishing.

and appropriate form of absolution, a beautifully-composed thanksgiving over the oil, and a most appropriate set of materials for the 'sending out' section, which in this service may conclude with the Peace.

How we view sickness

Finally, it is worth noting that the whole tenor of these services is very different from the tenor in the old Visitation of the Sick. In those earlier services, the mood was much more geared towards enabling people to live with sickness, learning through the experience of suffering:

> There is great honour in suffering, if our pain be borne in the spirit of Jesus Christ; for in the bearing of pain God manifested his will to redeem the world,

or in the epistle set for Holy Communion in *BCP 1926*:

> My son, despise not the chastening of the Lord ... for whom the Lord loveth he chasteneth.

In the present age, that is not the focus we would wish to have, but the fourth note at the beginning of these services is a reminder that there is something important to be remembered in that particular angle. It says:

> The experience of illness can bring a fuller realisation of dependence on God. The courage, endurance and comfort which God gives can lead to a more mature Christian life.

Questions for Reflection and Discussion

1. If you have ever been ill, what have you found particularly helpful in terms of ministry?

2. What are the pros and cons of bring Holy Communion to a sick person from the celebration in church? If you were ill, would you find this link into the Christian community helpful or not?

3. How would you distinguish between the appropriate use of anointing with oil, and the appropriate use of the laying-on-of-hands?

4. Are set prayers more or less suitable at a time of weaknesss? Does this vary from person to person?

5. How should the church prepare people for their death?

CHAPTER FOURTEEN

Funeral Services

Funeral services are of great importance. They come at a time of sensitivity and openness, and must both express care and love for those who are grieving, and sum up all that has been memorable in the life of the person who has died. A Christian funeral service, however, must as its primary purpose do much more: it is to be a proclamation of the good news of the risen Jesus Christ, who has defeated death and opened the gate to everlasting life.

The range of 'funeral' liturgies

One of the things which clergy will be well aware of is that every funeral service is different. At some, the family are weighed down by a sense of great loss; at others, there is a recognition that the person's time has come, and that they have had a good and fulfilled life; at yet more, a child has died suddenly and there is the sense that the timing is all wrong: a life full of potential has been stolen by death. Each occasion is quite different, and those who pastor people in situations of loss know only too well how dangerous it is to assume that we understand what people's feelings will be.

The complexity is compounded by the fact that the church will be asked to conduct funeral services for people who may have been at any stage of faith, or indeed, so far as we could see, none. We cannot presume that those who will be buried at a ceremony conducted by a Church of Ireland minister will necessarily have had any connection with a church. Some, in the case of Northern Ireland, will assume that the funeral service itself will take place at home, some will want it to be in the chapel of the funeral director, and some will expect it to be conducted in the crematorium chapel. Only a small percentage, certainly around the city of Belfast, will expect a funeral service to take place in church.

The experience of those who minister in the Republic of Ireland is quite different. When I was a parish priest in Cork, I discovered that people could not get enough of funeral services! The way in which death was dealt with involved, generally speaking, large numbers of people from all over the community, surrounding the family at their time of grief. There was an expectation too that the local rector would be involved in a whole series of stages during which that grief was expressed. Some of the liturgical questions which a pastor had to face included:

- What were appropriate prayers to use in hospital or at home when you arrived to discover that the person had just died?
- What liturgy was there for use in the mortuary, as the journey of the deceased was beginning?
- Did we not need to have a liturgy which was specific to a 'Removal'.[1] Otherwise, we ended up having two funeral services.
- Were there particular prayers suitable for the burial of ashes after a cremation?

There are other areas which could be added to this list, and indeed some have been answered in the *Common Worship: Pastoral Services* material, which takes up more than 150 pages.[2] These include, for example:

-Material which might be given to people who hold a vigil with the deceased?

- A form of prayer for the close relatives and friends on the morning of a funeral – and when a family goes home after a funeral.

---

1. A 'removal' is the name given in many parts of Ireland, to the service which takes place on the night before a funeral service, when the remains are brought to the church. In many cases this is almost as well attended as the funeral itself, so that what in some places is a very private event for the family becomes a major act of public worship and memorial of the deceased.
2. Op. cit, pp. 214-401.

- An outline order for a memorial service (something which is becoming increasingly common).

Because of the plethora of different needs, and indeed, of different ways of conducting funerals, the *Book of Common Prayer* has provided us with the widest ever range of authorised Church of Ireland services, under *Funeral Services Two*. These are:

- The Funeral Service, p. 487
- When the body of brought to church on the eve of a funeral, p. 498
- A Form for use at the burial of ashes after cremation, p. 501
- The Funeral Service for a Child, p. 504
- A Form for use in the Home, Funeral Home or Mortuary prior to the service in Church, p. 514

There is also a prayer provided for use following a miscarriage or stillbirth[3] on p. 512, and there may well be other forms of service provided as resources for the church in the future. For example, the new prayer book itself does not contain details of what to do when the body of the departed is not present (see *AOS 1993* p. 95) or, apart from the one prayer, after the delivery of a stillborn child or the death of a newly-born child (*AOS 1993* p. 96).

The Funeral Service itself
The actual structure of the funeral service itself is very simple, and marked by the following sections:

    Gathering in God's Name
    Proclaiming and Receiving the Word
    The Prayers
    The Farewell in Christ
    The Committal
    The Dismissal

The *Gathering* section will be done very differently from place to place, according to the context. If the coffin is not already in the church (if that is where the service is taking place), then words

---

3. For helpful thinking and material see *Miscarriage and Stillbirth: The Changing Response*, Bruce Pierce (2003), Veritas.

Funeral Services Two

GATHERING IN GOD'S NAME
Receiving the coffin at the door
Sentences of Scripture
Greeting
Introduction
Prayer ·
(Hymn)
|
Penitential Kyries
(Absolution)
|
Silence
The Collect

PROCLAIMING AND RECEIVING GOD'S WORD
(Old or New Testament Reading)
Psalm
New Testament or Gospel Reading*
|
The Sermon
|
The Apostles' Creed** or Te Deum Part 2

The Prayers
THE FAREWELL IN CHRIST
Silence by the Coffin
Easter Anthems
'Leaving' Prayer

THE COMMITTAL
Sentences of Scripture
The Committal
Sentence of Scripture
|
The Lord's Prayer
|
The Ending

At Holy Communion a gospel reading is always used.
**At Holy Communion the Nicene Creed is used.*

are provided for the minister to receive the remains at the door, and a prayer which may suitably be said. Then, the sentences of scripture are read. Three are given in the service itself, but a further selection is provided on p. 490, and the minister may in fact use any sentences which are suitable to the particular occasion. If the remains are being brought into the church at this point, the reading of these sentences as the coffin moves to the front of the church can be very powerful, and in my view is to be commended, but if the coffin is already there, they may be best read from the front of the church. The new service allows the minister to add 'Alleluia!' to any of these sentences, which in a gentle way is a reminder that any truly Christian funeral will walk a fine line between the celebration of the resurrection and the grieving of loss. There may well be a whole gamut of emotions expressed at different stages in the service, and that can be a very important thing in coming to terms with death.

After the sentences, there is the greeting, which comes essentially from the new English rite, and establishes in simplicity what we are doing:

We meet in the name of Christ

who died and was raised

by the glory of God the Father.

Grace and mercy be with you all.

This is followed by an introduction which explains what we will be doing: remembering the departed; giving thanks for their life; leaving them in God's keeping; committing the body to be buried/cremated and comforting one another in the hope of Christ. There is then a simple prayer, penitential kyries (if desired), and the collect of the service.

One of the items which is new here is the idea of penitence. This too, came from the English revision, and has not previously been part of funeral services in our tradition. That is a pity, because there can often be, among mourners, and especially among close family, a sense of unresolved business, or of not having cared for the departed person as well as they might. Penitence, sensitively expressed at this point, can allow them to leave some of these things behind, resolved by the forgiveness of Christ.

Proclaiming and Receiving the Word is intended to be exactly what it says. There must be one reading, but two are suggested, and a psalm (which almost everyone wants at a funeral service). Here, if the family is able, it is good that they should have some say in choosing readings, psalms, and indeed hymns and music. These are the things which often express something of what was at the heart of the life of the person who has died, and also something of what has meaning at this time for the family. However, we will often need to help people at this point. The numbness of grief can make it difficult for people to think clearly about such things, and there will be times for the pastor or others to take the burden of choices off their shoulders.

I am also aware of the importance, when it is known that someone is dying, of enabling them, if they feel able to do so, to begin thinking about their own funeral service. In my own experience, this can be a way in for clergy to speak about the things of eternity, and to prepare a dying person to meet God. Of course, some people will not be able to cope with this, and we must be sensitive.

The key thing about the Proclaiming and Receiving of the Word is that it should be exactly what it claims to be. A eulogy at a funeral is not the Word of God. Proclaiming the word means bringing the good news of the gospel to people at their time of need, expounding the scriptures and the sure hope they hold out for those who will trust in Christ. That does not mean ignoring the person who has died, but it does means that the message proclaimed will be centred on Christ. There is nothing worse than the pulpit being used for an obituary, often with the implication that justification is by works, and 'didn't he do well'.

The proclamation of the word may be concluded with the Apostles' Creed or *Te Deum* Part 2, but when Holy Communion is celebrated the Nicene Creed is used.

Clergy need to be well prepared if they wish to use service sheets for funerals, which are the norm today. If a service sheet is being used, and there are any responses, creed, canticles etc, these need to be conveyed to the printer. Otherwise, the service leader may be saying the *Te Deum* alone! And, realistically, in most cases a large prayer book is not the best thing to give out at a funeral service, even if the members of the congregation are regular churchgoers.

The Prayers. A structure for the prayers is suggested on p. 486:
Thanksgiving for the life of the departed.
Prayer for those who mourn.
Prayer for readiness to live in the light of eternity.
A whole range of very useful and beautiful prayers are on offer in the new prayer book. These can be found beginning on p. 491, and include some responsive prayers. It should be remembered that the clergyperson does not have to lead these prayers. Especially in a case where the family is surrounded by believing people, the prayers might be led by some friends. It is also good to remember that for some people too many words are not helpful. There need to be breathing-spaces in a funeral service, where the members of the congregation can remember experiences of the person who has died, and pray for the family by name. And sometimes, this is the service above all services which benefits from the depth of set prayers carefully phrased and memorable which are known by or have resonances with the mourners. Prayers are probably best led from near to the coffin, rather than from the lectern.

The Farewell in Christ. The Liturgical Advisory Committee wanted to find here a phrase which would be universally acceptable, across any churchmanship divide. The word 'commendation' was not acceptable to all, so the new phrase 'farewell in Christ' was used. It is a very attractive phrase, and seems to sum up what we are doing at this point. We are saying our earthly 'goodbye', in the recognition and realisation that God is merciful and the God of eternity. This is the point when the family might gather around the coffin with the minister. In an odd way, in Church of Ireland funeral services, it has been possible to act almost as though the remains of the dead person were not actually there. We need to find ways of recognising that we are here, in one sense, because the coffin is there! I suggested in *Making an Occasion of it* that the lighting of the paschal candle beside the coffin might be an appropriate sign of the resurrection, and this certainly would make sense with the suggested saying of the Easter Anthems as part of the farewell.

At this point the service simply changes venue. There is no blessing, no ending, because the service will continue at the graveyard or the crematorium, with the committal.

The Committal takes the usual form at the graveside or in the crematorium, with the sprinkling of soil on the coffin in the grave, and the concluding with the Lord's Prayer. The small piece of creativity in this part of the service is in the dismissal, which suggests 'God be in my head' as a suitable prayer, with its last two lines:

God be at mine end

and at my departing.

And the three endings, including one which I have always found particularly focusing at the end of a funeral service, from *Psalm 16*:

Lord, you will show us the path of life:

in your presence is the fullness of joy,

and from your right hand flow delights for evermore.

Other liturgical issues:

There are some other issues surrounding funeral service which it is important to think through:

a) Eulogies

Very often at funerals, the close family is keen that someone be allowed to speak about the life of their loved one who is deceased. Indeed, in some cases, a member of the family wishes to do so. It is important that we recognise the need which is being met here. It is often the need for a person who has been particularly close to the one who has died to say a few words. For a minister, this can give the freedom for the sermon to truly be a sermon, and can rescue a rector from attempting to speak about a person whom he or she has not known particularly well. As with most things there are opportunities and dangers inherent. When it goes well, it can be one of the most powerful parts of the funeral liturgy: something people will remember for many years. This is especially the case where a person giving the eulogy manages to walk the fine line of being honest, loving and even gently humorous all at the same time. Especially where the person who has died has had a clear Christian faith, the eulogy can fit seamlessly with the rest of the worship. But the problem arises where things which are inappropriate, hurtful, overly-sentimental or sometimes even untrue are said, or when the truth about the person's life is that they were not a person of faith or Christian living, and that is trumpeted as acceptable. There are some ways of resolving this issue, but most clergy will have to weigh up whether the risk is worth taking or not:

i) A close relative can be invited to write down what they wish to say, and the minister read it to make sure it is all right.

ii) It is possible, rather than saying something in front of the congregation, to write down a tribute, which can be printed out, distributed with the service sheets, and read before the service or at home afterwards.

My own personal judgement (and I respect that fact that others will differ) has been to take the risk at times. I don't think it is possible or right for clergy to totally 'control' worship and if, after proper preparation, there is a glitch or two, well, that's life! But we should help those writing eulogies not to say things which are contrary to Christian faith, to stick to the facts, and to make an appropriate tribute to the person's life.

If a tribute or a eulogy is being given it should, in my view, not be part of the Proclaiming and Receiving the Word. It would best be given either before that section, but or before the farewell in Christ. The earlier point has one benefit: it allows the preacher mildly to correct any wrong emphasis.[4]

---

4. Note 3, p. 480 says: 'An appropriate place for any tribute is before the Penitential Kyries.'

b) Poems and Songs

From time to time, people also wish to read particular poems and songs which either they have heard at other funeral services, or which have been particularly close to the person who has died. Again, caution should be exercised. We have probably all heard inappropriate or slushy material in these. The important thing is to talk things through with the people, make it clear that the minister has the final decision, and try to find some compromise. Another possibility is to have a written policy which is made clear to all who are asking for funerals, so that no one feels they are being treated unfairly or differently.

c) Prayers for the Departed

This is one of those 'hot' issues in the Church of Ireland, not least when liturgy is being revised. In some parts of the church, prayers for the departed may be added (*de facto*, if not legally), in others they would be avoided at all costs. What needs to be remembered here is that a great deal of thought has gone into our liturgies in areas such as this, drawing a careful line which will hold people together, while allowing reasonable freedom. So, for example, some prayers can be interpreted in two ways, such as (p. 486):

> We pray for the coming of your kingdom,
>
> that in the last day,
>
> when you bring together all things in Christ,
>
> we, with all who have died in him,
>
> may enjoy the fulfillment of your promises …,

while others allow a certain kind of prayer for the departed which is clearly in line with God's will for the end of time:

> May God in his infinite love and mercy
>
> bring the whole Church
>
> living and departed in the Lord Jesus,
>
> to a joyful resurrection … (also p. 486)

This is clearly a prayer in line with God's eternal purposes (and is not all prayer an aligning of ourselves with the will of God?), about an event in the future (the general resurrection), and should in my view, not be considered offensive.

The first and second prayers under the heading *The Communion of Saints* on p. 494 may also be thought of as having a *double entendre*.

However, the prayers used in a funeral service are not limited to the ones printed in the book, but sensitivity should be exercised as to where lines are drawn about this issue. It can be very hurtful to those who do not believe in prayer for the departed to have it thrust upon them at a sensitive point in their lives.

The interment of ashes and their dispersal at sea

On p. 501 a form is provided for the burial of ashes after cremation. In some parts of the country this is a very common thing, and clergy can at times be asked to deal with ashes in a veriety of ways. The church considers the interment and dispersal of ashes to be an important act which should be acrried out in a dignified and reverent way. Because of this, as is noted in the *Book of Common Prayer* p. 503, the House of Bishops issue guidlines with regard to ashes. The current set of guidelines can be found as Appendix 7, p. 254.

Questions for Reflection and Discussion

1. Are there times when it is appropriate for a pastor to invite a person to think about the readings, hymns, etc they would like at their own funeral service? You may like to ask that question of yourself.

2. When are tributes appropriate and when are they inappropriate at funeral services? What has your response been to the particular eulogies you may have heard?

3. What, in your view (if any) would be an appropriate and biblical way to remember the departed in prayer, and what would be inappropriate?

4. Should the Church enable us to remember the Communion of Saints more meaningfully, for example, around All Saintstide? In what ways?

5. What message would the celebration of Holy Communion at a funeral convey?

CHAPTER FIFTEEN

Ordination Services

The *BCP 2004* contains two full sets of ordination services, labelled *One* and *Two*, and introduces them, in the case of the first set, by The Preface (which goes back to the 1550 ordinal), and in the case of the second by a set of notes. These two introductory pages set the scene for ordination in the Church of Ireland.

Threefold Order

First of all, the preface declares:

> It is evident unto all persons diligently reading holy Scripture and ancient Authors, that from the Apostles' time there have been these orders of Ministers in Christ's Church: Bishops, Priests and Deacons.

One of the issues at the time of the Reformation, of course, was whether the church of its day should or should not retain this threefold pattern of ministry. The Reformed churches in some parts of Europe dispensed with this tradition, while in other places, bishops were allowed but not required. The Church of England at the time, however, retained bishops, priests and deacons, and has continued with this historic threefold order ever since. This is emphasised also in the set of notes prefacing *Ordination Services Two*:

> 1. The threefold ministry
> The Church of Ireland maintains the historic threefold ministry of bishops, priests (as in the past, but also called presbyters) and deacons.

This is re-iterated, not just as being the position of the Church of Ireland in the past, but also as its intention for the future, in the introductory words read now by the bishop at each ordination, which say:

We are maintaining the historic threefold ministry of bishops, priests or presbyters, and deacons in the Church which it has received.

So, the ordination services we are looking at are based around the ministry of bishops, priests or presbyters and deacons.

Several issues follow from this:

1) The fact that the Church of Ireland retains a threefold order of ministry does not mean that it denigrates other forms of ministry, or believes them to be invalid. Certainly, in relation to churches which do not have this threefold order, we recognise the efficacy of their ministries.[1] However, that does not mean that we would not wish to convince such churches of the value and importance of the threefold ministry which we have inherited.

2) The threefold pattern, which many would describe as being of the *bene esse*[2] of the Church, means that every church in some way needs ministry which is

- Episcopal (overseeing the wider church, exercises pastoral care and discipline, and passes the faith on to future generations faithfully);
- Presbyteral (caring for the needs of the local church, exercising eldership, and ministering the word and sacrament) and
- Diaconal (looking after practical needs, serving the community, and linking the church and the world).

3) To say that bishops, priests and deacons are three orders, does not mean that there is the same kind of distinctiveness between each order. For the 'person in the pew' there will some-

---

1. The Church of Ireland position, and indeed, the agreed position of the Methodist Church in Ireland and the Presbyterian Church in Ireland, is made clear in a resolution of the General Synod in 1974, which states: 'We recognise the ordained ministries of our three churches as real and efficacious ministries of the word and sacraments through which God's love is proclaimed, his grace mediated and his fatherly care exercised. We also recognise that our (three) churches have different forms of Church order and that each of us continued to cherish the forms we have inherited ...'

2. That is, the threefold order is for the well-being of the Church, which is often placed in counter-distinction to the *esse*, which would mean that it is of the very essence of the Church.

times be difficulty in telling the difference between deacons and priests, because they are both 'up there leading the service'; but, theologically, as is well expounded by Bishop Lightfoot in his classic commentary on the Epistle to the Philippians,[3] the orders which lie closest together are bishop and priest, because they both come from what was essentially one order (*episcopoi* simply being the Greek version of the Hebrew *presbuteroi*[4]). The issue at stake here is not so much whether these two were originally one, but whether the development into two orders, like the development of the doctrine of the Trinity, is a good and valuable development true to both the leading of the Holy Spirit and the authority of the Word of God.

4) It may be best to point out at this stage that the retention of the word 'priest' by the Church of Ireland is clearly done on the basis that a priest is simply a presbyter and not a sacerdotal priest. Indeed, the word 'priest' itself is etymologically a development of the word 'presbyter'. This is made clear not only in the texts we have before us, where on several occasions the connection is made in case there might be any misunderstanding, but also in the *Preamble and Declaration* on pp. 776-777, which declared in 1870:

2. The Church of Ireland ... will maintain inviolate the three orders of bishops, priests or presbyters and deacons in the sacred ministry.

This point is not really a controversial one. The Episcopal Church in Scotland uses the word 'presbyter' in its liturgy as the norm (in a 'Presbyterian' environment); and Roman Catholic priests quite regularly live in a 'presbytery'! What it tells us is that the words 'priest' or 'presbyter' are equally good. In fact, they are the same thing!

3. J. B. Lightfoot, *St Paul's Epistle to the Philippians*, (1897) republished in the Crossway Classic Commentaries series, (1994) Crossway Books.

4. The word *episcopos* is, of course, the word from which 'episcopal', meaning relating to a bishop, comes, and the word *presbuteros* is the word from which the word 'presbyter' comes, and also etymologically the word from which 'priest', which is a contraction of 'presbyter'.

The last shall be first!

Another major factor we should note about the new services in general is that they are the second revision of the ordination services in the Church of Ireland in just over ten years. I noted the following in *Making an Occasion of it*:[5]

> Between 1990 and 1992, the Church of Ireland was, with regard to ordination, at one and the same time one of the most 'forward-looking' churches in the Anglican Communion and one of the most 'backward-looking'. We had, in other words, begun to ordain women to the priesthood, but we were ordaining them according to an Ordinal which had not been essentially changed since 1550! Going to an ordination felt, to those who were using the alternative services regularly, like stepping back into another world.

What I did not confess at that time was that the reason for this was that the Liturgical Advisory Committee had produced material for a new ordinal, based on the material in the Church of England's *ASB 1980*, but could not get agreement to move ahead from the House of Bishops. On one level, the nervousness of the bishops at that time was understandable, because they rightly discerned some major changes of emphasis had taken place in the new ordinal. This was especially focused, as can be seen by looking at *Ordination Services One* and comparing them with *Ordination Services Two*, on two things (or at least I so imagine):

a) That the ordination in the new services was simply by the laying-on-of-hands with prayer, whereas it had previously been through an 'imperative formula' :

> Receive the Holy Ghost for the office and work of a Priest in the Church of God, now committed to thee by the imposition of our hands.
>
> Whose sins thou dost forgive, they are forgiven;
>
> And whose sins thou dost retain, they are retained …

And later:

> Take thou authority …

---

5. Op. cit. p. 39.

Of course, theological thinking about ordination had developed, especially since the Church of South India Ordinal of 1958,[6] and the essential element of ordination biblically was seen to be prayer with the laying-on-of-hands.

b) The second area which I imagine was problematical was the whole question of the assent of or election by the people. It would not be an exaggeration to say that the more traditional ordinal was highly clericalised, and the people did not get much of a look in, except for the possibility that someone might declare an impediment. However, modern thinking had recognised the important place given in some early ordinals (going right back to Hippolytus[7]) to the election and approval by the people before an ordination takes place. Although this is practically implemented in the process of selection for ordination, it is also liturgically implemented in the service itself. So, in the end, the *AOS 1993* ordinal adds the question to the people:

Will you uphold these persons in their ministry?

Having charted something of the history, we are now in the reverse position. In 2001, the *IALC* meeting in Berkeley, California, produced a document on revising Anglican ordination rites, called *To Equip the Saints*.[8] As it happened, the Church of Ireland was just finalising the material for the *Book of Common Prayer*, and was able to revise its ordination services in the light of the Berkeley Statement, being on this occasion the first church in the Anglican Communion to do so, rather than the last tram!

---

6. This ordinal (from a relatively new united church) became the starting point for much of the imaginative thinking which has taken place about ordination in the second half of the twentieth century on ordinaltion rites.

7. Hippolytus (d.c.236) has had a profound influence on the development of our new eucharistic rites, but he also lets us in on some of the earliest thinking on holy orders, in his *Apostolic Tradition* c. 215. See *Early Sources of the Liturgy*, Lucien Deiss (1967), Geoffrey Chapman, p. 34.

8. Published by Grove Books, Worship series 168.

Principles in To Equip the Saints

To Equip the Saints was the result of a six-year period of work and study on behalf of the International Anglican Liturgical Consultation, which took place at three meetings of the Consultation. I had the pleasure of being present at the meetings in Kottayam in the state of Kerala, India, which was banned by the Indian Government, and therefore we could not meet formally to do the work we had hoped to do. I was also present at Berkeley when the statement was drawn up. Canon Brian Mayne, editor of the new prayer book, was present at all three.

Before looking at our new ordination services in detail, it is worth noting some of the issues and principles charted by the *IALC* – both those which have influenced the new ordinal, and those which remain up in the air, being perhaps too radical at the present, but which the church may well return to at a later stage:

1. *The Ministry of the Whole People of God*

   Through the Holy Spirit, God baptizes us into the life and ministry of Christ and forms us into the *laos*, the people of God ... This is the *ecclesia*, the Church, the new community called into being by God.

In other words, baptism is the starting point of ministry. Or, to put it in a different way, every person who is in Christ has a ministry, and it is within the context of this wider ministry of the whole Church that the specific ministries of bishop, priest and deacon find their place. The report continues:

   understanding baptism as the foundation of the life and ministry of the Church ... leads us to see ordained ministers as integral members of the body of Christ, called by God and discerned by the body to be signs and animators of Christ's self-giving life and ministry to which all people are called by God and for which we are empowered by the Spirit.

2. *The distinctive ministries of deacon, presbyter and bishop*

To Equip the Saints recommends that each of these ministries is allowed to develop and be renewed, and that each ordination service is only to one order. (That is why we have no service for both priests and deacons together – it confuses the distinctiveness of their ministries.) We are seeing something of a renewed understanding of bishops in the present day. The report puts it like this:

> In the Anglican Communion today, a renewed model of episcopal leadership is emerging, one that more fully reflects the servant-ministry of Jesus and the baptismal calling of the whole people of God. In this style of episcopal leadership, the ministries of all the baptized are nurtured in ways which are personal, collegial and communal.

The report goes on to say how this might influence particular liturgies for bishops:

> … the ordination of a bishop should affirm and celebrate the ministry of the bishop in and among the members of the Spirit-filled community in which the bishop has been called to exercise oversight. In a similar fashion, the seating of the bishop should be a sign of the bishop's role as chief pastor and teacher of the community, rather than an enthronement reminiscent of the imperial model.

With regard to deacons, there is a great deal of discussion about whether the diaconate should be restored as a separate order in its own right, and several parts of the Anglican Communion have moved in this direction. The report says:

> In this renewed understanding the ministry of the deacon is primarily directed towards the servant-mission of the church in the world, and has as one of its principal aims 'to interpret to the church the needs, concerns and hopes of the world'. The liturgical role of the deacon expresses this interface between the world and the baptismal community.

The report goes on to question whether the idea of the diaconate as a 'servant-ministry' basis for all ministry is a right one:

> Although it is sometimes asserted today that the diaconate is the basis for the servant character of all three orders, it is baptism into the life of Christ which is the basis for the servant character of all the Church's ministries. The distinctive nature of the diaconate is not servant ministry in itself, but the call-

ing of deacons to be signs and animators of the Christ-like service of the whole people of God in the world.

3. The question of direct ordination

Now, this may seem radical, because we have all grown up with the idea of what we might call 'sequential' ordination, which has been the practice of the Church of Ireland. What the Berkeley Statement is doing here is inviting the different provinces of the Anglican Communion to re-examine this particular area. The paragraph on direct ordination sets out the issue in a clear and succinct fashion:

> Because the three orders are viewed as distinct ministries, direct ordination to the presbyterate, and even direct ordination to the episcopate, are being advocated by some in the Anglican Communion. There is historical precedent for both sequential and direct ordination. In the pre-Nicene church, direct ordination was commonly practised, and sequential ordination did not become universal until the eleventh century. Provinces may therefore wish to consider the possibility of direct ordination to the presbyterate and the episcopate.

Ordination Services Two

We will now take time to examine the newly revised services. As each has essentially the same basic structure, we will examine the shape that is common to all three, and in the process note the distinctives for different orders.

The Gathering of God's People

The heading is, of course, exactly the same as in Holy Communion or other services, but the point is that the people of God are gathered on this particular occasion with a specific purpose in view. It is worth noting right at the beginning, however, that the context in which ordination always takes place, whatever the order, is the context of the Holy Communion. Ordination happens as the people are gathered together to do what the people of God do – to meet around the word and the sacrament. That may seem obvious, but some of us can remember the time when only those being ordained and their close families received communion on an occasion such as this. The rationale, no doubt, was that the numbers would be too large to communicate, or that some people may not wish to receive; but, thankfully, such things are no longer, and the ordination takes place in the context of a fully-communicating eucharist.

Under the 'Gathering' section of this service several things happen:

a) The bishop, as the presiding minister (or the archbishop at a consecration of a bishop) greets the people. The reason is that this person is the presiding minister at this service.

b) After the greeting a short dialogue takes place, followed by an introduction, setting the ordained ministry within the context of the ministry of the whole people of God. The same happens again in the collect used in these services, where we pray:

Hear our prayer for your faithful people
that in their vocation and ministry
they may be instruments of your love,
and give to these your servants now to be ordained
the needful gifts of grace.

c) The initial presentation of the candidates is done. Up to now, this had taken place later in the service and was done by the archdeacon alone. Now, it happens right at the beginning of the service, to convey that the whole service is to do with ordination; and it is done initially by 'sponsors'. The question of who these sponsors may be is not specifically answered, and needs to be thought through very carefully. In some parts of the communion, and particularly in the ordination of presbyters, they may well be representatives of the parish which the person is serving. In relation to the ordination of deacons, they may well be people who have been particularly influential in bringing the ordinand to this point in their life. The second and perhaps more formal part of the presentation at this point is by the archdeacon, who assures the congregation that those being presented for ordination have been properly selected and trained.

Ordination Services Two

THE GATHERING OF GOD'S PEOPLE
Entry (Hymn, canticle or psalm)
Greeting
Introduction
|
Presentation of Candidates
Question to each candidate about their call
|
Silence
Collect

PROCLAIMING AND RECEIVING THE WORD
First Reading
Psalm
Second Reading
(Canticle, Hymn or Anthem)
Gospel
|
Sermon
|
Nicene Creed

THE RITE OF ORDINATION
(*Bishops:* The Presentation)
The Charge
The Declarations
The Affirmation of the People
|
Call to Prayer
An Ordination Litany
Silence
Hymn of Invocation to the Holy Spirit*
The Ordination Prayer with the Laying on of hands
|
(Vesting**)
The Giving of the Bible
The Welcome
|
The Peace

* Veni Creator *in Priests and Bishops, an appropriate hymn of invocation in Deacons.*
** *May take place before the service.*

continued opposite

CELEBRATING AT THE LORD'S TABLE
as in Holy Communion Two

GOING OUT AS GOD'S PEOPLE
The Great Silence
(Hymn)
Post-Communion Prayers
Blessing
(*Bishops:* The Giving of the Pastoral Staff)
Dismissal
The newly-ordained depart for ministry

---

d) The question to the candidates, who have now been presented, about their vocation: '… do you believe that God has called you to the office and work of a deacon in his Church?', and the reply: 'I believe that God has called me.' From time to time, I have been asked if those being ordained might give a word of testimony about the calling of God in their lives, and have suggested, on one occasion where six or seven were bring ordained, that each person might like to tell their story in a brief number of words, and we would then give each of the congregation a leaflet with these stories of vocation. It was much appreciated. In the Methodist Church , when ordinations take place, the telling out of the candidates' stories of vocation is the norm. Sometimes it works well, other times it can become over-long and tedious. However, if it is to happen on any occasion, this is clearly the point in the service where it should take place, and I could imagine it being very powerful where one or two people were being ordained.

Proclaiming and Receiving the Word
In an ordination service, the readings may be either the readings set for the particular service (The references are printed in the order) or the readings of the day. The same is true, on principal holy days or festivals, of the collect.

In my own opinion, bishops should give consideration to

using the readings of the day, especially if the day is a saint's day or holy day. To take my own ordinations as an example, I was ordained deacon on the Birth of St John the Baptist, priest on St Peter's Day and bishop on St Mark's Day. These saints are godly (though thankfully often flawed) examples for all of us in our ministry, and it sometimes seems a pity that ordinations on their particular days can forget about them altogether.

Another thought about the ministry of the word on occasions like this: it seems very important to me that readings on occasions like this are not all done by clergy. Sometimes there is an inclination, when we robe clergy up, to try to give them all something to do. If clergy read all the readings, it implies the exact opposite of what the introduction to the service has laid out as central. The worst example of this is found in the actual rubrics in *Ordination Services One: Bishops*. The rubric before the epistle says:

And another bishop shall read …
and the same is true before the gospel. And, in my view, what is worse is that the scriptures can tend on these occasions to be read according to seniority, so that the lowly deacon is airbrushed out from reading the gospel, which is done instead by the most senior bishop. No such rubrics appear in the new service, which will undoubtedly the one most commonly used in the future, and it is important that this tradition is not carried over.

Proclaiming and Receiving the Word concludes with the recital of the Nicene Creed, introduced by the sentence: 'Mindful of our baptism we proclaim the faith of the universal Church:' In the text of the service the creed is not fully printed out. The reason is quite simply that the congregation at almost every ordination has a service booklet, and so it will be a very unusual occasion when anyone is actually following this service from the book.

The Rite of Ordination

This has the following structure in all three services:

- [(Bishops only) The reading of the authority for the ordination and the Declaration of Canonical Obedience]
- Exhortation about the particular order
- The Declarations
- The assent of the people
- Prayers (using a litany)
- Silent prayer
- Hymn of invocation to the Holy Spirit (*Veni Creator* in the case of priests and bishops)
- The ordination prayer with the laying on of hands
- The vesting (if this has not already been done)
- The giving of a bible
- The welcome of the newly-ordained.

Leaving aside the part in square brackets, which takes place only at the consecration of a bishop, we will look at the other aspects of this liturgy.

a) Exhortation about the particular order

As this exhortation is being read, the candidate or candidates are standing before the bishop, while the people are seated. In a sense this is a focal reminder of what this particular ministry is about, read to the people just about to be ordained, but very much in the hearing of the congregation. Please note that in the first printing of the *Book of Common Prayer* a small section of the exhortation said to priests was inadvertently omitted. Each book where this is the case has been supplied with an Errata slip correcting the omission.

b) The Declarations

No major changes have been made in these declarations from the service in *AOS 1993*. They vary slightly between the different orders, but most of them are about the very basics of faith and ministry, and this section of the service is a very solemn commitment by those who are being ordained to follow in the way of Christ, to serve his people, and to fashion their own lives in holiness.

c) *The Assent of the People*

This has been moved to follow the declarations, and been strengthened greatly. In the 1993 service it was largely negative ('If any of you knows any sufficient cause why any of these persons should not be ordained deacon ...' etc); followed by: 'Will you uphold these persons in their ministry?', but in the new service, it is firmer. Having heard the declarations from their own lips, the question is now asked (in all three orders):

Is it therefore your will that they should be ordained?

to which the congregation replies (hopefully thunderously):

It is,

and this is followed by the question about the upholding of them in their ministry.

d) *Prayers (using a Litany)*

What must be remembered at this point is that ordination in the New Testament is always in the context of prayer with the laying on of hands. So, a very powerful context of prayer is now created. This is the section which is called The Prayers of the People in the context of a normal Sunday eucharist, and it is never more truly the prayers of the people than it is at an ordination.

The new service gives two litany forms, where the 1993 service gave only one. Both place the ordination within the context of wider prayers for the church and the world. These litany forms are found on p. 585ff. The first is exactly as it was in the 1993 service: an abbreviated form of the litany in the *APB 1984*; the second is a litany specially composed for ordination services, and about half the length of the first. Whichever litany is used, and whether it is sung or said, the important thing is that it is genuinely an expression of the prayers of God's people gathered for the ordination.

e) *Silent Prayer*

The order in which these different types of prayer come is changed in the new service. In 1993, it was: Silent Prayer, Hymn to the Holy Spirit, followed by the Litany. This never 'felt' quite right. The new order is litany, followed by silent prayer, followed by hymn of invocation, focusing down on the ordination from the wider context. A great deal of attention needs to be given to creating the space for total silence here, often with a very large congregation.

f) Hymn of Invocation to the Holy Spirit

In the ordination of priests and the consecration of bishops, this is always the *Veni Creator*. A very powerful hymn, with wonderful words. This was, however the point at which Thomas Cranmer in his ordination services of 1550 almost fell flat on his face! He attempted to write a version of the *Veni Creator* which could only, at its kindest, be described as doggerel.[9] Even Cranmer could not do everything, and this one attempt at hymn-writing proved that it was not for him! But, still today, with John Cosin's beautiful version of the hymn in our liturgy, there is a danger here that, at the very point of focus, congregations will not be able to manage to sing the *Veni Creator* well. If that is so, it may be better to have it sung by a choir or as a solo, which can have an equally focusing effect.

g) The Ordination Prayer with the Laying on of hands

The new service gives us two different types of ordination prayer. The first is in the traditional form, except that it is now introduced by two versicles and responses. The bishop says the first part of the prayer, then in the middle of the prayer each person is ordained, and the prayer is completed. But it is all the Ordination Prayer and, as with confirmation, it is best to avoid too much to-ing and fro-ing during it.

The second, new form, is not terribly different in its wording, but is from an idea of Paul Bradshaw,[10] where the prayer is

---

9. A small portion gives the 'mood':
    Come, holy ghost eternall God procedinge from above
    Both from the father and the sonne, the God of peace and love:
    Vysyte our minds and into us, thy heavenlie grace inspire;
    That in all trueth and godlunesse, we may have true desire.
    It did not quite come up to the poetry of Coisin's version!
10. Paul Bradshaw is Professor of Liturgy and Director of Undergraduate Studies in London for the University of Notre Dame. He is

punctuated with responses from the congregation, just as some eucharistic prayers are punctuated with responses. In the first half of the prayer, the response is **'Glory to you, Lord'**, and in the second, it is **'Pour out your Spirit, Lord'**. It remains to be seen how much the new form will be used, but it could be a very powerful statement that ordination is not simply the territory of the bishop, but something in which the whole people of God are involved.

It should also be noted that the posture for ordination is: The bishop stands. The congregation stands. What matters at this point is not that everybody sees something being done to someone else but, rather, that everybody is involved in the action.

Where presbyters gather around the bishop for the ordination of presbyters, they should be there for the whole ordination prayer; and the same is true for the consecration of bishops, when other bishops gather around the three consecrating bishops.[11]

h) The Vesting (if this has not already been done)
There was a desire on the part of the IALC in the Berkeley Statement, not to confuse the ordination itself with other ceremonies, and not to allow other customs to detract from the centrality of the laying on of hands. One of the issues discussed under this heading was the issue of vesting, and the following advice was agreed:

> Vesting is not part of the act of ordination, but discloses the new standing of the ordained person. Care should therefore be taken that vesting does not in any sense distract attention from the laying on of hands. The following places might be acceptable:
> – candidates are vested before the service, entering already dressed for the ministry to which they have been called by the church, a practice adopted in the ancient Roman tradition.

undoubtedly one of the leading liturgists and most prolific writers on liturgy in the Anglican Communion.
11. It is required that at least three bishops be present and lay on hands at the consecration of a bishop, and this is increasingly symbolised by seating the two other 'key' bishops to either side of the archbishop.

 – the newly ordained are vested after the conclusion of the prayer of ordination and the welcome – not during or immediately after the prayer, where it would disrupt the integrity of the rite. The vesting need not be done in a place that is highly visible.

i) The giving of the bible

Here, there is a change. The bible is given to each order, rather than giving a New Testament to a deacon. This is based on the view expressed by the IALC:

> ... because the word of God provides the basis for all ministry, a copy of the whole bible should be presented to deacons, presbyters, and bishops alike, and for the same reason its presentation should be the action of the presider rather than another minister.

Another rubric has been added at the end of the service, saying:

> The newly ordained depart, each carrying the bible ...

Would that they would all continue to carry that bible as a sign of the authority by which they preach and teach!

j) The Welcome

On one level, this is new to the service, on another, it happens in some places already. There comes a point in a service, especially one which has been quite lengthy and intense, and sometimes full of emotion, where the congregation simply needs to let their hair down. The candidates have now been ordained to their new order, everything is in place, and the time has come for the congregation to have them presented to them, and hopefully to applaud with a great sense of celebration. Some may feel that this is less than solemn, but in fact liturgy, when at its best, will allow a congregation to enter into the whole gamut of human emotion, sometimes even within the parameters of one service. The welcome is, quite naturally (now that we have relaxed) followed by the peace, and a good strong song or hymn of celebration, leading into the eucharistic feast.

Celebrating at the Lord's Table

This is fully covered in the commentary on the eucharistic rite.

Going out as God's People

Here, there is a new departure, literally. After the post communion prayers and hymn, two of the ordination services have a
short final commissioning to the newly ordained. In the service
for the ordination of presbyters, immediately the newly-ordained stand before the bishop, who used the words (from earlier
editions of the ordinal, but there at a different point in the service):

Remember always with thanksgiving

That the treasure now entrusted to you is Christ's own flock

After this commissioning and the dismissal, the newly-ordained
depart, carrying the bibles they have been given as their 'tools of
the trade', and going out accompanied by representatives of the
parish and the diocese.

In the case of a bishop, this is the point at which he is given
the pastoral staff, accompanied by the words:

Keep watch over the flock of which the Holy Spirit has appointed you shepherd …

And the new bishop departs, carrying the bible and the pastoral
staff, accompanied by the diocesan representatives.

Now all of this, as the part at the beginning of the service, requires thinking about choreography. Otherwise the symbolism
will be lost. Perhaps we should forget about all our presupposi-
tions with regard to the order of processions and, as soon as the
dismissal has been said, the bishop should go out first, as an
apostolic leader of mission, with the newly-ordained following
immediately, accompanied by others. Then the other clergy may
leave. Otherwise, there will be a hiatus, and the dramatic point
will be lost. At an episcopal ordination, the new bishop of the
diocese should probably leave first.

All in all, the new liturgy for ordinations is one which should
bring to life some of the teaching of the church of our day about
ministry, if we allow the rite to speak. And, better still, it should
re-open for us some radical biblical teaching.

Questions for Reflection and Discussion

1. Is it helpful, as the new Ordinal does, to root all Christian ministry, lay and ordained, essentially in our baptismal calling? In what ways?

2. What do you think are the differences between diaconal, presbyteral and episcopal forms of ministry? Are they absolutely necessary for the church, or are they simply for the good of the church?

3. Who actually ordains in the new ordinal? Is it a) the bishop (along with other bishops and/or priests); b) the whole people of God, represented by the bishop and others or c) God?

4. What do you think the laying-on-of-hands with prayer symbolises in ordination? Is it different from the laying-on-of-hands in confirmation and the ministry of healing?

5. Why do you think it is that the newly-ordained in the new rites, are always presented with a bible?

CHAPTER SIXTEEN

The Psalter

David Stancliffe, Bishop of Salisbury and chair of the Church of England Liturgical Commission, introduced *The Psalter 1998: A Draft text for Common Worship*[1] with the following words:

'The Church with psalms must shout, no door can keep them out' wrote the poet and Anglican priest George Herbert in the early seventeenth century,[2] and in doing so he gave magnificent expression to the desire to praise and lament which lies at the heart of all Christian worship. Whether said or sung, the psalms have featured at the core of the Church's worship from its earliest days ... the vividness of the imagery evoked by the psalms and their range of expression and content continue to ensure their place at the heart of Christian worship.

In the *BCP 1926*, the psalms were laid out in the same way as they had been in the 1662 prayer book, according to the day of the month, and morning or evening. So the idea was, quite simply, that the set of psalms appointed for each day, twice daily, would be said or sung, just as they still are in many cathedrals in these islands.

Two Psalters or One?

When the new prayer book was being planned, the General Synod expected that there would be two psalters included in it, one being the tradition Irish revision of the Coverdale Psalter, and the other being a modern psalter in contradistinction to it.

---

1. *The Psalter 1998: A Draft text for Common Worship* (1999), Church House Publishing.
2. *Church Hymnal fifth edition*, Hymn 360.

The Liturgical Advisory Committee looked at several psalters, including:

- The new ICEL Psalter,[3] which had a very imaginative and fresh style, but had proven not to be acceptable to the Roman Catholic Church, perhaps because it was considered too radical and inaccurate in detail. Rather than being a word for word translation, it sought to grasp the tenor and mood of the psalms. It is well worth reading and using in personal devotions, and I hope and trust that it will not get lost in the mist of time.

- The 'David Frost' psalter in the *APB 1984*, which had been rather reluctantly revised for inclusive language purposes, in *The Liturgical Psalter: An Inclusive Language Version* published by HarperCollins in 1995. However, it was sensed that, overall this psalter had not proved particularly memorable in the *APB*, and that there was not adequate affection for it after two decades of use.

- The ECUSA Psalter, in the 1979 American prayer book. This had been made popular in a mildly revised version in these islands in *Celebrating Common Prayer*, which had been used by some members of the Liturgical Advisory Committee over a period of time, and proved quite popular.

The Committee was moving towards a point where it would have recommended the two psalters in the new prayer book to be: Coverdale revised (as in *BCP 1926*) and the ECUSA Psalter, when it became aware, largely because of the controversy about the weight and size of the *Church Hymnal fifth edition*, that there was some concern among Church members, and especially members of the General Synod, that the new prayer book should not prove to be over-bulky. The LAC then went to the synod for its advice about whether the church wanted to have two psalters or one (a second psalter, as it has emerged, would have added

---

3. *The Psalter: A faithful and inclusive rendering from the Hebrew into contemporary English poetry, intended primarily for communal song and recitation* (1994), Liturgy Training Publications. The rather lengthy title goes on to say: *This translation is offered for study and for comment by the International Commission on English in the Liturgy.*

another 170 pages to the book). The synod was given the option of Coverdale and ECUSA *or* the *Common Worship* Psalter, which had been adapted from ECUSA, but retained many of the resonances in Coverdale. The decision was to have one psalter in the book, but to allow the continued use of the psalter from the 1926 Book.

The Common Worship Psalter

The *Common Worship* psalter of the Church of England was specifically prepared to complement the *Common Worship* services. Work began on it in 1994, and in 1997, fifty versions of psalms were brought before the Church of England General Synod. The full psalter was ready in draft form for 1998, and four principal criteria were identified as being important for a psalter for liturgical use in the Church of England. These were:

– The accuracy of the translation of the psalter from the Hebrew text in a way which is sympathetic to liturgical use in the Church of England;
– The quality of the language on the tongue of those who sing and say the psalms;
– The memorability of the translation and its resonance with known psalter traditions in the Church of England;
– The accessibility of the language of the psalms to a wide range of worshippers.

(*The Psalter 1998: A draft text for Common Worship*, p.ix)

So, it is the *Common Worship* psalter which we find in the *Book of Common Prayer*. This psalter is in 'you' form. There was a time when it was believe that 'you' and 'thee-thou' forms did not mix well in worship, but we have discovered, simply by practice over the past years, that congregations, and not least young people,[4] are able quite easily to go from one to the other, without

---

4. Evidence for this can be found at the youth festival, *Summer Madness*, every year. Not only can young people go straight from the most up-to-date song to an old hymn, but they don't even appear to notice 'sexist' language, and would never think of revising 'Be thou my vision'!

any necessary 'grating'. So, it is hoped that this version will be quite useable with the traditional language services.

It is also, as far as is possible, an inclusive language psalter. So, where the psalm is speaking of both men and women, it does not use exclusive language. Jane Sinclair, in the *Companion to Common Worship*[5] details the different and creative ways in which this has been achieved. The truth is that most of us will not notice, because it has been done seamlessly.

Another issue which we should note is that this psalter has decided not to use the convention of bracketed verses, as the *APB 1984* did, for the imprecatory verses,[6] which were considered to be unsuitable for public worship. The starting point here is that the lectionary selects psalm verses for Sunday and daily worship, but that the psalter itself should be complete, and have its full integrity.

Singing and Saying the Psalms in public worship

In *Common Worship*, the psalter is unencumbered by pointing.[7] However, in the *Book of Common Prayer*, it was decided to include the pointing for Anglican Chant, which was drawn up by the Royal School of Church Music.[8] This means that materials from that source may well be available, or at least adapted, to the needs of the Church of Ireland. It may well also be the case that the *Common Worship* psalter may be available in a version with responses when the final edition of *Common Worship: Daily Prayer* is made available. There are also other simplified ways of

5. Op. cit. pp. 236ff.
6. The verses which call down the judgement of God on his enemies, often in very colourful terms!
7. The method of marking which allows congregations to sing psalms, using methods of chanting, the classic one being Anglican chant. To leave the psalter unpointed makes the page clean and clear, but makes it difficult to know where to change notes in chant.
8. This can also be found in the *Common Worship Psalter with Chants* (2002), RSCM. This could be used, if desired, for the psalms, but the user would need to be very careful with canticles, where some of our versions, and indeed some of our canticles are different in wording from those in *Common Worship*.

singing psalms, and *Church Hymnal fifth edition* includes many
hymn- and song-type psalms.

At the time of writing, the Liturgical Advisory Committee is
in the process of drawing together a group of people to advise
on different ways of singing the psalms. I am also aware of some
original music which has been composed both for the psalms
and canticles in the versions used in the *Book of Common Prayer*
by Alison Cadden.[9] Hopefully some fresh ways of singing the
psalms will be available to us.

It may also be useful at this point to chart out the different
ways of saying psalms in church, so that there is an awareness of
the different methods, and a vocabulary which can be agreed:

A psalm can be said:
– together;
– by minister and people in alternate verses;
– by minister and people in alternate half-verses (using the red
  square as the dividing point);
– antiphonally by verses or half verses (i.e. starting on one side
  of the church and alternating with the other);
– alternating men and women by verses or half verses.

Normally, psalms are said seated, in a meditative fashion. But, it
is also possible to shout out certain psalms standing. In fact
some of the psalms are designed to be used in procession.

It is also possible to choose out a verse as a response, teach it
to the congregation at the beginning of the psalm, and use it
after every two or three verses, but the response should be carefully chosen.

When the *Gloria Patri* is used (and it does not always have to
be used), it should be the version which fits the particular service, traditional or modern. It does not need to be used at the
end of each psalm. Sometimes a space is adequate. Nor does it
need to be used at the end of each part of *Psalm 119*.

The psalter is now the last word in the prayer book, before
the theological and doctrinal material, which begins with the
Catechism on p. 766. And there can surely be no more fitting

---

9. See footnote 24, p. 88.

finale to the Book of Common Prayer than the ecstatic and all-embracing praise of Psalm 150, coming to a climax in the words:

let everything that has breath
praise the Lord. Alleluia.

Questions for Reflection and Discussion

1. Is there still a value today in using the whole psalter for our daily devotions? Are some of the psalms unsuitable for public prayer?

2. You may like to choose one or two favourite psalms in the version appointed in the new psalter. What changes do you notice? Do they make the meaning more or less clear?

3. Do you find chanting the most appropriate way to sing the psalms? What other ways have you experienced? Is one way suitable for all, or do different psalms require different treatment?

4. What 'moods' do you find in the psalter? You may like to reflect on a time when a particular psalm came to mean a great deal to you in your life. What was it about that psalm which engaged with you?

5. Can hymns ever replace psalms? What is different about the two?

APPENDIX 1:

Versions of the Bible authorised for use by the House of Bishops

Authorised Version (1611)
Revised Version
American Standard Revised Version
Revised Standard Version
New Revised Standard Version
New English Bible
Revised English Bible
Jerusalem Bible
New Jerusalem Bible
New International Version
New International Version (inclusive language edition)
Today's English Version

APPENDIX 2:

Copyright regulations
issued by the Standing Committee of the Church of Ireland

PRAYER BOOK

Copyright in *The Book of Common Prayer* is held by the Representative Church Body.

Permission to reproduce the text of any service or prayer is required and requests should be made to the Copyright Secretary, Church of Ireland House, Rathmines, Dublin. 6.

Single occasion use of extracts

The need for written permission is waived for the use of material from The *Book of Common Prayer* on a particular occasion provided:

1. No charge is made for the publicationb.

2. The date and location or name of church are clearly stated.

3. The following copyright acknowledgement is made: 'Material in this service from *The Book of Common Prayer* copyright © RCB 2004'.

4. Not more than 500 copies are made.

Local orders of service

Where it is desired to produce local oredrs of service for use on more than one occasion from *The Book of Common Prayer* (with the exception of Service of the Word) drafts of such proposed orders of service must be submitted in advance to the Copyright Secretary, Church of Ireland House, for approval.

A numbered licence may then be issued.

The following copyright acknowledged must be included: 'Material in this service reproduced from *The Book of Common Prayer* under licence number 000, copyright © RCB 2004'.

CHURCH HYMNAL

Hymns in the public domain may be freely reporduced. The absence of any copyright notice in *Church Hymnal, Fifth Edition*, indicates such hymns.

The premission of copyright hol,ders should be obtained for any reproduction of a hymn covered by copyright. This applies even to reproduction for a single occasion, defined above.

Annual licences covering the reporduction of the majority of modern hymns may be obtained from CCLE in Eastbourne, England. This licence does not cover all copyright hymns in Church Hymnal, e.g. those by Timothy Dudley-Smith. The majority of the authors of these make only a minimal charge. Where a considerable fee is asked for, the advice is not to use the item.

BIBLE VERSIONS

Lectionary portions in a dated Sunday leaflet are freely permitted by the copyright holders of most versions in common use. The initials of the version should be indicated in brackets at the end of the printed portions, e.g. (NIV), (NRSV). If one version is used a note may be appended to the leaflet saying: 'Bible portions in this leaflet are from ...'

January 2004

APPENDIX 3:

Additional verses of Saints' Days Hymn

St Joseph of Nazareth, March 31
We praise you, Christ, for Joseph, a carpenter by fame,
who, as your earthly father, enriched your holy name.
He taught you faith and wisdom, and nurtured you in mind,
till you became his Master, the Saviour of mankind. *E. F. D.*

St Philip the Deacon, October 11
Lord, as your Church grew stronger and did become well known,
new ministers were needed for loving care alone;
so Philip was commissioned, a deacon kind and true,
who witnessed to your gospel, in loving service too. *E. F. D.*

St James, the brother of our Lord, October 23
Lord, James your earthly brother, became a bishop too,
when knowing you had risen, he placed new faith in you.
Presiding at the Council that set the Gentlies free,
he welcomed them as kindred on equal terms to be.

Horatio Nelson (1823-1913), altd.

APPENDIX 4:

Principles of Christian Initiation
from *Walk in Newness of Life: The findings of the International Anglican Liturgical Consultation Toronto 1991.*

a. The renewal of baptismal practice is an integral part of mission and evangelism. Liturgical texts must point beyond the life of the church to God's mission in the world.
b. Baptism is for people of all ages, both adults and infants. Baptism is administered after preparation and instruction of the candidates, or where they are unable to answer for themselves, of their parent(s) or guardian(s).
c. Baptism is complete sacramental initiation and leads to participation in the eucharist. Confirmation and other rites of affirmation have a continuing pastoral role in the renewal of faith among the baptized but are in no way to be seen as a completion of baptism or as necessary for admission to communion.
d. The catechumenate is a model for preparation and formation for baptism. We recognize that its constituent liturgical rites may vary in different cultural contexts.
e. Whatever language is used in the rest of the baptismal rite, both the profession of faith and the baptismal formula should continue to name God as Father, Son and Holy Spirit.
f. Baptism once received is unrepeatable and any rites of renewal must avoid being misconstrued as rebaptism.
g. The pastoral rite of confirmation may be delegated by the bishop to a presbyter.

APPENDIX 5:

The Structure of the Eucharist
from *Our Thanks and Praise: Papers from the fifth International Anglican Liturgical Consultation: Dublin 1995*

The material in this service structure is graded as follows:

1 = indispensable

2 = integral, but not indispensable

3 = would not be omitted in principle, may be limited or varied according to liturgical seasons or special occasions

4 = not necessary but may be desirable at times

The Gathering of God's People
Greeting	1
*Penitential Rite	3
Song / Act of Praise	1
Opening Prayer (collect)	1

Proclaiming and Receiving the Word
First Reading	1
Psalm	2
Second Reading	2
Gospel	1
Sermon	1
Creed	3
*Silence, songs and other responses	2

Prayers of the People
Prayers	1
*Lord's Prayer	1
*Penitential Rite	3
Peace	1

Celebrating at the Lord's Table
Preparing the Table	1
Prayer over the gifts	4
Eucharistic Prayer	1
*Lord's Prayer	1
Silence	1
Breaking of the Bread	1
Invitation	2
Communion	1

Going out as God's People
Silence	1
Hymn	4
Prayer after Communion	2
Blessing	4
Dismissal	1

APPENDIX 6:

Service of Preparation for Remarriage in Church
To be held in a church prior to the marriage

INTRODUCTION

1.

The priest says

Jesus says, As the Father has loved me, so have I loved you. *John 15.9*

The Lord be with you

And also with you

2.

The priest says

xxx and *yyy* you come together to seek God's Blessing on your intended marriage. Do you affirm your desire to live as followers of Christ, strengthened through the prayers of the Church?

We do

Acknowledging the breakdown of a former covenant of marriage, will you together pray for God's strength to fulfil in love and faithfulness the vows you are about to take?

We will

THE COLLECT

3.

The priest says

Let us pray:

Almighty God, giver of life and love:

Strengthen and guide your servants *xxx* and *yyy*

as they seek your blessing in marriage.

Help us to acknowledge all that is past,

and to turn to you in faith and hope,

trusting in the new life that lies ahead,

through Jesus Christ our Lord. **Amen**

THE MINISTRY OF THE WORD

4.

Te Deum, part iii

Save your people Lord and bless your inheritance:

govern them and uphold them for ever.

Day by day we bless you:

we praise your name for ever

Today Lord keep us from all sin:

have mercy on us, Lord have mercy

In you Lord is our hope:

may we never be confounded.

5.

Ephesians 3.14 – end

For this reason I bow my knees before the Father, from whom every family in heaven and on earth takes its name. I pray that, according to the riches of his glory, he may grant that you may be strengthened in your inner being with power through his Spirit, and that Christ may dwell in your hearts through faith, as you are being rooted and grounded in love. I pray that you may have the power to comprehend, with all the saints, what is the breadth and length and height and depth, and to know the love of Christ that surpasses knowledge, so that you may be filled with all the fullness of God. Now to him who by the power at work within us is able to accomplish abundantly far more than all we can ask or imagine, to him be glory in the church and in Christ Jesus to all generations, forever and ever. Amen.

PENITENCE

6.

The priest says

If we say we have no sin we deceive ourselves,
and the truth is not in us.
If we confess our sins,
God is faithful and just
and will forgive our sins
and cleanse us from all unrighteousness. *1 John 1.8, 2*

Let us confess our sins in penitence and faith,
firmly resolved to keep God's commandments,
and to live in love and peace with all people.

After a short pause for self examination, all say

Almighty God, our heavenly Father, we have sinned in thought and word and deed, and in what we have left undone.
We are truly sorry, and we humbly repent. For the sake of your Son, Jesus Christ, have mercy on us and forgive us, that we may walk in newness of life to the glory of your name. Amen.

The priest pronounces the absolution:

Almighty God
who forgives all who truly repent,
have mercy on you,
pardon and deliver you from all your sins,
confirm and strengthen you in all goodness,
and keep you in eternal life;
through Jesus Christ our Lord. **Amen**

PRAYERS

7.

Almighty and merciful Father,
the strength of all who put their trust in you:
We pray that you will enrich *xxx* and *yyy* by your grace
that they may truly and faithfully keep those vows
which they will make to one another in your sight;
through Jesus Christ our Lord. **Amen**

Most blessed Father
from whom all pure love comes,
bless your children *xxx* and *yyy*.
Grant that the hopes and prayers in their hearts
may be fulfilled through your mercy.
Draw them closer to each other and to you;
give them grace to bear one another's burdens
and to share one another's joys;
and grant that they may live together in your love
unto their lives' end;
through Jesus Christ our Lord. Amen
Direct us, Lord, in all our doings,
with your most gracious favour,
and further us with your continual help;
that in all our works
begun, continued and ended in you,
we may glorify your holy name
and finally, by your mercy
attain everlasting life;
through Jesus Christ our Lord. **Amen**

O Lord,
forgive what we have been,
sanctify what we are,
and direct what we shall be,
through Jesus Christ our Lord. **Amen**

8.

As our Saviour Christ has taught us, so we pray:
Our Father in heaven,
hallowed be your name,
your kingdom come
your will be done,
on earth as in heaven.
Give us today our daily bread.
Forgive us our sins
as we forgive those who sin against us.
Lead us not into temptation
and deliver us from evil.

For the kingdom, the power, and the glory are yours
now and for ever. Amen

THE GRACE:
The grace of our Lord Jesus Christ,
and the love of God,
and the fellowship of the Holy Spirit,
be with us all evermore. Amen

APPENDIX 7:

Guidelines for the interment of ashes and their dispersal at sea
issued by the House of Bishops, 16th October 2003

1. The duty of burial of the dead enjoined on a minister in Canon 32 shall be taken to include the burial of ashes following cremation. In the context of Canon 32, 'remains' shall be understood as including ashes after cremation.

2. The act of cremation is symbolically incomplete without interment.

3. The ashes of a cremated body, therefore, should be reverently buried in consecrated ground or in some place set aside for that purpose. They should be placed directly in the soil or buried in a container made of biodegradable material.

4. No ground may be consecrated (even as a Garden of Remembrance only for the interment of ashes) without the appropriate faculty from the Bishop of the Diocese, and without the appropriate poermission of the civil authorities, including planning permission.

5. Such interment of ashes should be recorded in the Burial Register in like manner to other burials.

6. Ashes, once interred in consecrated ground or placed in a consecrated area (such as a columbarium) should not be moved or exhumed other than in exceptional circumstances, and then only under the supervision of the Incumbent, to be placed in another consecrated place. Such exhumation or approval would require a faculty from the Bishop.

7. When ashes are to be strewn at sea care should be taken to ensure that this happens in a seemly, practicable manner, taking into account the prevailing wind, and doing so at an adequate distance from the shore.

8. The Bishops are advised, and therefore suggest, that it is inappropriate to dispose of urns of ashes at sea, particularly because of the risk of these being washed ashore at some point in the future.

9. These guidelines pertain in all cases involving the rites and ministry of the Church of Ireland.

List of Charts